# 2045
# GLOBAL PROJECTS AT WAR

TECTONIC PROCESSES OF GLOBAL TRANSFORMATION

DANIEL ESTULIN

Published by:
Trine Day LLC
PO Box 577
Walterville, OR 97489
1-800-556-2012
www.TrineDay.com
trineday@icloud.com

Library of Congress Control Number: 2020947083

Estulin, Daniel
Global Projects at War: Tectonic Processes of Global Transformation– 1st ed.
p. cm.
Epub (ISBN-13) 978-1-63424-321-6
Kindle (ISBN-13) 978-1-63424-322-3
Print (ISBN-13) 978-1-63424-320-9
1.Internationalism. 2. Cosmopolitanism. 3. Globalization. 4. Economic devel-
opment. 5. International Cooperation. 6. Public Policy . I. Title

Cover design by: Oswaldo Sagástegui

FIRST EDITION
10 9 8 7 6 5 4 3

Printed in the USA
Distribution to the Trade by:
Independent Publishers Group (IPG)
814 North Franklin Street
Chicago, Illinois 60610
312.337.0747
www.ipgbook.com

*Make thy two eyes, like stars, start from their spheres,*
*Thy knotted and combinèd locks to part*
*And each particular hair to stand on end,*
*Like quills upon the fearful porpentine.*
*But this eternal blazon must not be*
*To ears of flesh and blood. List, list, O, list!*
*If thou didst ever thy dear father love—*
                    –William Shakespeare

# Contents

# Prologue

# ONWARD?

To quote Jane Wilde Hawkins, "When we wrestle fate, only the universal questions – life, survival, and death – are of any importance." The question we must urgently answer is whether the human species, when faced with its own self-destruction, is wise enough to change its destiny, from the currently ruinous paradigm of countries/corporations trying to consolidate a world empire and the resolution of geopolitical conflicts through war, or substitute that paradigm with a moral example that simultaneously inspires both the imagination and the hope of Humanity.

The moral example of great visionaries like Cardinal Nicholas of Cusa, Leonardo da Vinci, Johannes Kepler, Gottfried Wilhelm Leibniz, Simón Bolivar "el Libertador," President Benito Juárez García, Gandhi, who inspire the population through their legacy and example of this immortal quality of achievement attained beyond the death of the individual person. If the leadership is moral, then the population will immediately develop the type of consciousness sufficient to reject evil and seek perfection and self-perfection.

It will not be easy to achieve this change. It is not easy, but if it were easy, everyone would do it. It is our world! We must not allow the current state of global affairs to depress us, collective humanity. We must not let this destroy us. Let us make a solemn promise: Let us be better prepared to confront our destiny with dignity, unwavering resolve, and fortitude, amid global cataclysms.

We have to make a declaration of principles. *This is who we are! This is what we represent!* We will defend to the end our present and our future, our planetary Homeland, the future of our children and our grandchildren. We will defend to the end the right to live in peace. To be able to feel protected in our homes, in our streets, in our cities and our countries. To be able to educate our children and base this education on examples of heroes and not pedophiles, murderers, drug traffickers, degenerates, and sadists. We need to believe in something. Long for something better. Work with freedom and inspiration to improve everyone's life per square kilometer of space against nature. If we do not act with wisdom, if we have no ideology, if we lack scientific and technical knowledge, we cannot build a better world.

We have to restore the sense of belonging, as humanity, to the vast universe around us, restore the human mission towards a better and more fraternal existence, which assumes its responsibility for the rest of the species. We have to work unfailingly and unwaveringly in building the future of humanity, even if we each die long before we can fulfill our mission.

Human nature is synonymous with the pursuit of excellence. We want to leave something for the next generation, or the one after that, to show them that we existed, to show them what we did with our time on Planet Earth. This is the impulse behind the cathedrals, the pyramids, the Great Wall of China, and so many other things we, as collective humanity, have created over the course of our existence.

When we do things for the Truest of Reasons, reasons that benefit humanity, we produce our most significant achievements. The real reason we chose to go to the Moon, as JFK said, was not because it was easy, but because it was hard.

Finally, I would like to say that we are the future. Knowing that we are unique through our divine spark of reason. The oligarchy can sequester trillions of dollars of wealth, but it will never be immortal, for they act against the interests of humanity. We, on the other hand, can achieve immortality by doing something great: thinking and working in the name of the common good, the commonweal.

They say that no man is better than his conversation, that no politician can overcome his speech, but we come to a time when incongruity endangers the destiny of humanity. The idea, the word, and the action are the indispensable units of forward-thinking societies and we must not destroy it if we want to overcome our fleeting individual existence and think of "the collective land of the word: ours," as Enrique Gonzales Rojo wrote.

Although dark, heavy clouds are gathering all around us, I look to the future and see reasons for hope. "Close proximity to a majestic mountain is a mixed blessing," noted Edward Said, "One is at once graced by the magnanimity of its pastures and the bounty of its slopes," and yet one can never see where one is sitting, under the shadow of what greatness, or the embracing comfort of what assurance. Yes, there is hope.

# Part I

# Global Projects

# Chapter 1

# CAPITALISM AS A SYSTEMIC CONSPIRACY

One of the main weaknesses of conspiracy studies is that, even when we consider staggering amounts of information, often empirical material that turns one's understanding about many historical events upside-down, its authors are not able to adequately conceptualize it, turning it into a special discipline and/or rebuilding from a certain angle existing disciplines. To do this, it was necessary to incorporate conspiracies into the problems of historical and theoretical analyses of capitalism as a system, since closed ("secret") supranational structures of global agreements and control and the possibility of small groups being able to manage the course of history or, at least, try to do it, logically flows from the social nature of capitalism, due to its specificity.

Moreover, it is the capitalist system (and only it on such a scale) that gives rise to the closed supranational structures of world government and coordination existing in the area of "conspiracy"; in fact, its existence is impossible without them. They are a feature of the capitalist system, as cycles of capital accumulation or cycles of a struggle for world hegemony and world wars. Moreover, the development of capitalism is closely connected with the economic and political cycles of the capitalist system; it can be used to judge the entire system since they embody the integral (space) and long-term (time) aspects of the side of its functioning.

At the end of his life, Karl Marx noted that if he had written "Capital" again, he would have started with the state and the international system of States. Today, as historian Andrei Fursov adds: if *we* were to write "Capital" again, then we must begin with what is called the "invisible" hand; that is, with closed supranational coordination structures and management, the very fact of their existence removes one of the most important, basic contradictions of capitalism. Without this invisible element and the personifying structures of this element, the functioning of capitalism is impossible. Conspirology as a process and reality ("as a will and representation") is a necessary condition for the existence of capitalism and the process of this existence at the same time. In economic terms, capitalism is a whole-world, supranational system; the world market knows no boundaries; its *locus standi* and field of employment is the world market. But on the political plane, the capitalist system (capsystem) is not a whole, but the totality, the mosaic of states, their international organization; that is, the organization of national states. This is one of the most serious contradictions of capitalism – the contradiction between capital and the state, global and domestic.

By the middle of the 19th century, paraphrasing historian Andrei Fursov, as capitalism became integral into a system-for-itself, that is, with the acquisition of an adequate material base for it – industrial productive forces – capitalism acquired a strong manufacturing foundation. But industrial productive forces are regional, being most highly concentrated in the North Atlantic area. In contrast, industrial relations are global in nature, conflicting with state-political forms and often trying to break them.

So the contradiction between the integral world character of the economy and the total mosaic national character of the state-political organization takes on yet another dimension: world production relations (and their personifiers) are opposed to regional productive forces and not to world forces, but to national state-political structures and their personifiers.

As a result, firstly, the interests of states turn out to be, as a rule, closely related to those of industrialists, but the real, "physical" capital of the economy, and the interests of financiers objectively oppose both of them. Of course, the reality is more complicated, and it is sometimes characterized by various twists and combinations, a cunning interweaving of probability lines, caused by the conjuncture of circumstances – both historical and family-personal. Nevertheless, the fundamental contradiction mentioned above and the ways (forms) of its removal remain, determining the whole evolution, all the motility of capitalism. But I am getting ahead of myself.

In whatever country it lives (especially if it is a large country), the financial segment of the big bourgeoisie always has interests that go beyond national borders – its own and those of others. And these interests can be realized only by violating the laws of one's state, or another's, and more often one's own country and others at the same time. Moreover, this is not a one-time violation, but a constant and systematic process; which, therefore, must somehow be framed. After all, it is one thing when Capital is opposed by weak, or even not-so-weak, policies in Asia, not to mention Africa. There is enough of a forceful version of "gunboat diplomacy" to put it in its place. However, what about the world of equal or relatively equal nations: Great Britain, France, Russia, Austria; and since the second half of the 19th century, Germany, USA, Japan? And now, China has arrived in a big way. This is an entirely different matter. It's not as easy here; you need, not a firearm, but an organizational weapon that would formalize the interests of the Capitalist elites of various states, remove their contradictions with the state and become an expression of their integral (extra/supranational) and long-term interests.

Thus, since commodity chains on the world market constantly violate state-political borders, often coming into conflict with the interests of "affected" states, for the top of the capitalist class, firstly, omni-national, supranational structures/organizations are needed; secondly, these organizations should be, if not completely secret, then closed to the general public, and thirdly, these organizations/structures should be able to influence states, influence their leaders – those leaders being simultaneously above the state, and over capital.

What these structures are engaged in cannot be called anything other than a permanent and institutionalized conspiracy. And, therefore, we should talk about the "conspiracy system." Capitalist systems include all types of closed, supranational structures, most often (although not always) within the bounds of capitalism, i.e., Masonic lodges, gentlemen's clubs, secret societies, etc. Conspiracy systems in no case are exhausted by Freemasonry and quasi-masonry. However, in the 18th and in a significant part of the 19th centuries, they were the dominant organizational form of the capitalist system. However, since the end of the 19th and especially in the 20th century, new, more modern forms of the conspiracy systems arise, which do not abolish the old ones, are often associated with them, but much more directly related to politics, economics, and intelligence.

The conspiracy system is the third "corner" of capitalism as a system, and in fact, it occupies the tip of the triangle, above the capital and the state, located on the same plane. When the story of the capitalist era is written and told as the history of only nation-states and capital, it is an incomplete and false account, because it presents a two-dimensional world, when in fact, we are dealing with a three-dimensional system. Without the conspiracy system, the history of the capitalist era is incomprehensible – and impossible to explain. What's more, the history of the capitalist system should be inscribed in the history of capital weath (its cycles of accumulation) and the State (the struggle for hegemony), and their relations should be analyzed as a subject and system. Only in this way, will we get a holistic, integral history of the era, and not a scheme that simply satisfies the profane spirit.

"The conspiracy system removes not only the underlying political and economic contradiction that was discussed, but also others: between various forms of capital and, accordingly, fractions of the capitalist class, between nations. Representing both capital and the state, linking them organizationally in such an area that is outside the state and outside capital, elite conspiracy systems are above the State and capital, expressing the holistic and long-term interests of the capsystem and thus acting as a personifier of holistic and long-term interests of the capitalist class as its backbone element. Here it is necessary to give the working definition of capitalism which I will use: as Descartes would say, "*Il faut définir le sens des mots*" – "Determine the meaning of words."

"If capital, in the strict systemic sense of the word, is materialized labor, realizing itself as a self-increasing value in the process of exchange for living labor, then capitalism is the social system based on this process. But this is not a good enough definition. Capitalism is not only 'capital': capital existed before capitalism and, most likely, will exist after it. Capitalism is a complex social system that institutionally (state, politics, civil society, mass education) manipulates capital in its long-term and holistic interests (and thus extends its life) and provides expansion (space) for it.

"Expansion is necessary because capitalism is an extensively growth-oriented system: as soon as the world rate of profit declined, capitalism tore this or that part out of the non-capitalist zone and turned it into the capitalist periphery – a source of cheap labor and cheap raw materials. The exhaustion of non-capitalist zones (1991) means asphyxiation and relatively quick death, or rather, the dismantling of capitalism."[1] In this regard, globalization is the terminator not only of the Soviet Union, systemic anti-capitalism, but also of capitalism as a system. And very symptomatic - dialectics: globalization is, to a large extent, a product of the activities of the "conspiracy system."

Finally, there is another essential contradiction of bourgeois society, which the conspiracy system is called upon to remove. In bourgeoise society, official power is not sacred; secrecy is not its inherent characteristic. In the "pre-capitalist" cultures of Asia, Africa, and pre-Columbian America, this secret was an inherent characteristic of power, but this secret was in plain sight. People knew about secret power, and the secret of power, power itself was perceived in many ways as something mysterious and sacred.

The situation is entirely different in a capitalist system. Since in a capitalist society production relations are economic and exploitation is carried out as an obvious exchange of labor for materialized labor, the social process is almost transparent: the market, the dominance of commodi-

---

1    Andrei Fursov, https://www.nakanune.ru/articles/111527/

ty-money relations, the institutional separation of power from property, the economy from morality, religion from politics, politics from the economy (economic management is separated from the administrative-political process), economics from the social sphere. All this exposes the social and power relations of bourgeois society. The rationalization of economic, social, and political areas and relations maximally opens up the processes taking place in these spheres, makes them fundamentally readable, and turns it into an object of study of specialized "disciplines" – economics, sociology, political science.

The creation of the supranational structures of world governance and reconciliation is an imperative for the top of the capitalist class, including world market operators, who have become capitalists against their will. However, the bourgeoisie and the capitalizing aristocracy of the 18$^{th}$ century, when this need and task were already fully recognized, were not and could not be ready-to-use, "natural" capitalist organizations on a supranational level. It was good for the Jews, who lived "in the pores" of the modern world; like the Phoenicians, "in the pores of the ancient world." They were an international people, battered and bled by many generations of European Christians, but allowed one vital right, a great tool of survival: money lending and finance. Through this ancient network and the kinship, family system as a supranational structure, they could solve the problem of organization at the supranational level – as the Rothschilds did at the turn of the 19$^{th}$ century.

"Hence, the close connection between Jewry and capitalism, noted by many scholars, beginning with Karl Marx and Werner Sombart, and the synchronism of their rise from the beginning of the 16$^{th}$ century, which accelerated sharply in the 19$^{th}$ century. Therefore, naturally, the bourgeoisie and the capitalist-oriented aristocracy used, first of all, those organizations that were available, for example, Masonic. The latter began to perform new functions, clarifying dynastic relations in the new conditions – the world struggle for markets, and also serving as a means of fighting the state (already anti-feudal, not yet bourgeoise, but "old-order"), and not only for the bourgeoise, but also for other groups.

"The conspiracy system removes the fundamental contradiction of capitalism, and this is their function. But it is also said that the capitalist class did not have ready-made structures for fulfilling this function, and they adapted the existing ones, in particular, the Masonic structures, which served the interests not so much of the bourgeoise, as other groups, albeit related to the functional world market. Thus, old structures acquired new content that

9

modified them: old keys began to unlock new locks. However, at the same time, this content was also heavily influenced by the past, especially since the groups that organized these structures were largely included in the new capitalist class – mainly, though not only, the British.

"The New European, or rather New England, whose historical "merger" began in the 1530s-1540s, is constructed of five elements – the proto-English pentagram of the 16th century. It was represented by the English nobility, English capital (the City), English pirates, Jewish money, and the Venetians. Moreover, it was the quantitatively insignificant Venetian element that played a decisive role in this historical mutation; namely, the role of a catalyst and a fixative at the same time. The Venetians gave an impetus to the assembly process, despite the dissimilarity with England and the British, and perhaps thanks to it. Venice and England in the 16th century were completely different types of organizations that developed in entirely different directions, but at times intersected with each other when moving toward their own goals. And indeed, the Venetian-English synthesis led to a fantastic result that changed the course of development of Eurasia and the world that stretches into the future. Supporters of the East India Company in the British Parliament in the 1780s called themselves the "Venetian Party."

"Very indicative of popularity among the British upper classes of the late 18th century, is Venetian artist Antonio Canaletto (1697-1768). His paintings were bought by the Duke of Richmond, the Earl of Carlisle, and many others; the Duke of Bedford had 24 Canaletto paintings. What is the reason for this popularity? Canaletto created the famous series of views of Venice, in which the city is depicted not as it was in the second half of the 18th century, but as it was in the 15th and 16th centuries; successful, self-confident, framed by monuments, in all its splendor. Europe's only Republic. Canaletto found a treasure of images from that era. For the representatives of the British elite, Venice was such a symbol of success: they believed that it was the Venetians' foreign trade in that glorious time, from whom they took the baton, that was the motor of power and wealth, and that is why they collectively adored the paintings of the Venetian master."[2]

A century and a half later, in 1930, Hjalmar Schacht, urging European bankers to support Nazism, argued that Hitler would finally break the nation-states in Europe, and the bankers would receive, "Venice the size of Europe."

It is medieval Venice, numbering in the 16th century some 200,000 people, managed by 40 key families, rather than ancient Athens and

---

2    https://cyberleninka.ru/article/n/issledovaniya-sovremennogo-miroporyadka/viewer

Rome, which in many respects formed the modern West. The role of Venice in the history of Europe is confirmed, among other things, by its genetic and genealogical contribution. "The Venetian aristocracy gave 17 papal families, including Borgia and Orsini; related to Venice were/are: the Medici, Sforza, the Bourbons of France and Parma, the House of Savoy, the Bavarian Wittelsbachs and six or seven ducal and Margrave houses; immigrants from Venice are the Jewish families of Morpurgo (funded Napoleon), Warburgs (funded both Napoleon and Hitler), American Cabots (the Jewish Caboti family from Lombardy, who moved to Venice in the 10th century) and many others. On the female side, financiers and industrialists of non-aristocratic origin are associated with the Venetian aristocracy; for example, the owners of the Fiat Agnelli, members of the Venetian Black Nobility.

"Venice has become a catalyst for the formation of a predatory historical subject of the New European West, which turned out to be "alien" in relation not only to non-European civilizations but also to the European one itself. But the Venetian influence on England was especially strong. However, in England, only a certain process was grounded, which is due to the fundamental difference between capitalism and all other social systems. It is this difference that makes closed supranational structures of world reconciliation and governance, as a form of organization of the Western elites, a historical necessity."[3]

Perhaps the main metaphysical, meta-historical difference of capitalism from all the systems preceding it – its main secret – is that the history of this system from a certain, and rather early time, approximately from the middle of the 18th century, acquires nomogenetic character. It can not be said that until the 1700s, no one, no groups or forces have ever attempted to direct the course of history on a large scale in one way or another. However, these attempts, with rare exceptions, failed; firstly, because they were local in nature; secondly, they were short-term and, as a rule, until the middle of the 18th century, and more precisely, until the time frame of the 1750-1850s, there was no serious production base for such attempts.

In the "long 16th century"[4] (1453–1648), what is called the European (North Atlantic) world system, history takes on a global character. There appear necessary and sufficient conditions for historical design by those

3        Andrei    Fursov,    *Secret    History    of    Venice*,    https://www.pinterest.ru/pin/75294625000491294/
4        Immanuel Wallerstein, (2004), "World-systems Analysis." In World System History, ed. George Modelski, in Encyclopedia of Life Support Systems (EOLSS), Developed under the Auspices of the UNESCO, Eolss Publishers, Oxford, UK.

groups that, having pushed off from the era of the "long 16th century," within a century after its completion turned into operators of the world market, and therefore – in potentiality – into operators of world history.

An organization capable of directing the course of history in a certain way was English Freemasonry, which relied on the financial power of the City (London), the power of global market operators (bourgeoisie), aristocratic clubs, and, of course, the state of Great Britain. "At the end of the 18th century, the Masons were "joined" by the Illuminati, "created" by the Jesuits to fight Freemasonry, but who got out of their control, and the Masons themselves received the operational base they had worked out – an artificially created, polygon-historical US nation-state, to where the Illuminati transported themselves, and to this day, still reap the benefits from the US system via (Yale: "Skull & Bones" whose members Bush and Kerry represented the Republican and Democratic Parties during the 2004 Presidential elections), not to mention other groups and structures that felt "uncomfortable" in Europe.

"In the middle of the 18th century, surprisingly, at the same time, an adequate object of manipulation arose – masses ("object"), and a robust financial base (money – "energy"), and new information flows ("information").

"The middle of the 18th century is the beginning of financial growth; if in the second half of the 17th century, "high finance" reaps a harvest of the "long 16th century," then in the middle of the 18th century, the foundation of a modern financial system was being formed. Of course, in the pre-capitalist era, and at the dawn of capitalism in the 15th-16th centuries, bankers were able to have a significant impact on the course of history: the Venetians financed the Third Crusade (i.e., the destruction of Constantinople) and, in part, the Reformation; Venetian Bardi and Peruzzi in the 14th century funded the English kings, and the Fuggers in the 16th century funded Charles V; the union of bankers and moneylenders of Lombardy, closely connected by Jewish religious-kinship ties with the bankers of England and the Czech Republic (Prague), was so strong that it played a role in the sudden destruction of competitors – the Knights Templar."[5]

However, none of these forces had the capabilities that arose in the 17-18th centuries with the onset of the capitalist era. Firstly, in the 17th century, there was a financial revolution that began in the 1613-1617 period, the creation of the Baruch family of the Standard Chartered Bank and the fixation of goodwill in 1617 and culminating in the creation of the Central Bank of England in 1694 and the invention of public debt – *Perfide*

---

5     https://cyberleninka.ru/article/n/issledovaniya-sovremennogo-miroporyadka/viewer

Albion's most powerful financial weapon in the struggle for supremacy in Europe and the world.

The explosion in the development of banking capital in question, which made it omnipotent, was caused by three factors that stimulated the growth of "high finance": the British-French struggle for world domination; the colonial expansion of the European powers and the outbreak of the industrial revolution. All this required cash and improving the financial organization. Do we even need to say it out loud that bankers were active participants in the conspiracy system?

Thus, in the middle to second half of the 18th century, for the first time in history, on an unprecedented scale and form, a combination of those who came to the forefront in the logic of the development of capitalism as a system of "big finances" (money, gold), information flows and large masses of the atomized population took place. There was a merger at one point of the Object (mass), Energy (money), and Information (information flows of the idea) and their concentration in the same controlling hands. The point of connection and, at the same time, the subject of the latter, connector/controller, were, first of all, closed supranational structures of coordination and management; in this particular historical case, the Masonic conspiracy system.

This happened in accordance with the laws of the development of capitalism and its logic. Moreover, "to actively use them in their interests in confronting the monarchy and the church, the conspiracy system paid close attention to these laws, quickly identifying and ideologically fixing the contradictions between the two institutions with the development of capitalism. In connection with the development of the ideological and information sphere and the tasks of analyzing social reality, a need arises for structures of rational knowledge and, accordingly, for select branches of this knowledge that analyze mass processes, mass behavior, and historical laws."[6] To use mass processes, influencing them informationally and energetically in the right direction, that is, to saddle them, you need to study them. Still, the study itself must be closed – according to Plato – who said that even if we find out the name of the creator of this world "It" should not be shared with everyone.

It was the conspiracy system that secured the model of dual-circuit social science in the West: external – for general use, for the profane; and internal – for a limited circle of those who make history and move the needle, for its subjects.

6        Balkiliç, Özgür (27 September 2018). "Historicisizing World System Theory: Labor, Sugar, and Coffee in Caribbean and in Chiapas." Gaziantep University Journal of Social Sciences. 17 (4): 1298–1310. doi:10.21547/jss.380759.

Capitalism, despite all the supposedly spontaneous markets, significantly exaggerated and mythologized (even the so-called "mid-Victorian market" of the 1850-1870s is nothing more than a regulated social institution, just that this "regulated" system was well camouflaged), is a project. A project that is far from always being successfully implemented by a relatively small number of regular relationships of individuals, groups, and structures acting in an organized manner, per long-term plans, not at all out in the open, but usually secretly.

Similarly, the organizations of this project – its "design bureaus" – are operating behind closed doors. A secret (closed) project – what is it if not a conspiracy in the broadest sense of the word? Thus, the "conspiracy" is the essence of the normal functioning of capitalism, real capitalism, and not of the ideological scheme that is far from being scientific, which is presented by both its apologists and many of its critics from professional professorship. Without an understanding of the great socio-evolutionary change that occurred in the middle of the 18th century, we will not understand capitalism, either the past, or the present, when the dismantling of capitalism is on the agenda. We don't understand and, as a result, lose the Great Historical Game, the prize for which is a decent life and a place under the sun in the post-capitalist world.

According to Fursov, the beginning of the design phase in the history of Europe and the world coincided with the rise of the Anglo-Saxons, Great Britain, and – more broadly – the supranational North Atlantic subject with all its ethnic mosaics and its conspiracy system. This is by design: the original Masonic organizations as the first image of the conspiracy system of the capitalist era were closely linked to the political and financial interests of the English (from 1707, the British) state. For the financial and aristocratic union of world market operators and European/world politics that took shape in the century between the English Revolution and the Seven Years War, i.e., in a period filled with the final victory of the British oligarchy over the Stuarts, that is, eliminating the threat of their restoration to the throne and with two victories over France, over Louis XIV and Louis XV, Great Britain was something more than a state and an empire.

For them, it was a cluster of trading houses and Masonic organizations, a certain Matrix, in which new interests were realized and at the same time, early interests continued to develop. It is significant that it was in the middle of the 18th century, during the war for the Austrian inheritance (1740-1748), when Great Britain, started the wars absolutely dominated by commercial interests and which were conducted solely for the trade balance, not the balance of power.

Significantly, in the middle of the 18th century, the three-hundred-year-old confrontation between Austria (Habsburgs) and France finally ended, which was one of the main geopolitical axes of the 1450-1750s, that is, the era when feudalism had already ended and capitalism in a strict systemic ("formation") sense, had not yet begun – the era of the Old Order. This is another feature of what happened during the historical turning point in the middle of the 18th century.

"In other words, Great Britain, from the middle of the 1600's to the middle of the 1700's, took shape as something unprecedented until then – a new, compromise form of interaction between the old world, rooted in the English and Venetian Middle Ages, in Gnostic antiquity and the Middle-Eastern winged lion of Babylonian and Jewish antiquity; forces that became, along with new forces, operators of the world market on a supranational level. At the same time, both the market and its operators in the form of the bourgeoise and the new aristocracy seemed to breathe life, the energy of a new era, into old forms – an energy-information exchange took place."[7] At the same time, by the middle of the 18th century, a contradiction emerged that became more acute two centuries later in the USA – between the USA as a state and the USA as a cluster of multinational companies, One World Company Ltd., as described by Bilderberg attendees at their 1968 annual meeting in Mont Tremblant, Quebec, Canada.

Great Britain of the 18th century, was a contradiction between Great Britain as a state and Great Britain as a cluster, a web of trade and financial structures, aristocratic clubs, and Masonic lodges. Areas of disagreement between the interests of the state and the lodges were questions of the further fate of the East India Company and events in the North American colonies; the zone of coincidence is the expansion of lodges in Europe ("on the continent") and the destruction of France as a competitor. The Second British Empire (1780–1840s) became the process and structure, field and means of eliminating these discrepancies/contradictions. However, this was preceded by a period of active work in three "conspiracy theological directions," in which the interests of the state and the lodges partly coincided, partly conflicted:

1) the creation of a network of Masonic continental lodges managed from London;

---

7      Andrei Fursov, https://www.nakanune.ru/articles/111527/

2) the creation of a Masonic state (The United States of America), free from traditional state restrictions and, in this sense, artificial, experimental, and therefore territorially removed from Europe;

3) the undermining of France in the international arena and from within, by creating severe internal problems and unrest with the active use of Freemasonry, Masonic lodges as a powerful organizational weapon. This was the main content of the first stage of the development of the conspiracy structures/system.

These stages as a whole coincide with the main stages of the development of the capitalist system, the cycles of capital accumulation, and the struggle for hegemony. The first stage is the 1710s-1770s; the second stage starts with the emergence of the Illuminati and the French Revolution of 1789-1794, which opened a half-century period of Masonic revolutions, and culminates in the formation of the Second Reich and the unification of German Masonic lodges into a single "Secret Germany" (the early 1870s).

In the 1880s, the third stage of the development of conspiracy structures as an intrinsic form of organization of the top elite of the West began. It coincides with the beginning of the decline of Great Britain as the hegemon of the world capitalist system, and it is not surprising that it was the British elite who responded to it by creating closed, elitist structures of a new type: the "Group" ("We") of Cecil Rhodes, the "Society" ("Kindergarten") of Milner. Later, we see the emergence of continental structures – German, as well as French "Circle" ("Cercle") and "Century" ("Siècle"). The Bilderberg Group, created in 1954 to reconcile two main segments of the Western elite: the Anglo-American and the German-North Italian associated with the Vatican, crowns this series. The crisis, which the capitalist system entered at the turn of the 1960-1970s, required new structures, and they arose: The Club of Rome (1968) and the Trilateral Commission (1973). It was a foregone conclusion that the aggravation of the systemic crisis of capitalism that is taking place today required either a modification of the already existing closed structures of the Western elite or the emergence of new ones. They emerged in the form of global projects.

# Chapter 2

# GLOBAL PROJECTS – INTRODUCTION

Before explaining the significance of the global projects and the role they play in the post-industrial Westphalian world of networking, I would like to describe their history from the point of view of the analysis of the change in the prevailing value system within both capitalist and socialist blocks. This will help us understand the transition from Global 1.0 (nation-states/Westphalian world) to Global 2.0 (One World Company Ltd/corporations with more power than sovereign governments) to Global 3.0 (post-industrial/world of networking).

*****

It is no secret that the "Western" project and the "Red" communist project had quite different systems of values. It doesn't mean that the Western system of values was better than the alternative system of values in the Soviet Union, which influenced almost half of the world's population. You can, of course, call it "totalitarianism," but the Western system itself forbade the supporters of the Communist Party or even socialist ideas from engaging in certain professions at one time (as in Germany in the 70s, the famous prohibitions on the profession, as in the USA 1950s through the activities of commissions banning "un-American" activities). And it is possible that this ban in the USSR acted precisely because those who created the country (first and foremost Lenin and Stalin) knew what would happen to the Soviet economy and Soviet lifestyle if "Western values" were allowed to permeate the thinking processes of the Soviet citizens. All these examples are aimed, in general, to show that the system of meanings, which are sometimes embedded in the same words, can vary significantly.

"Beginning in the mid 1980s, something fundamentally changed in the Soviet Union. The system of meanings (or, less accurately, but more understandably, the system of values), under the influence of Western propaganda, drifted towards the West. And the corresponding mechanisms for protecting the domestic value system, on the contrary, had significantly weakened. Levis jeans, bubble gum, high heels, western fashion and music became the bar against which Russians measured success. But such a drift did not happen by chance – people felt that since the late 1970s, the old, domestic value system did not respond to their needs and wants. And the country first began to discuss publicly, and then directly act in terms of changing the system of governance, in the direction of developing a new system of values. The result was earth-shattering – the Soviet Union and the socialist bloc ceased to exist.

"In recent years, it has become clear to almost everyone that on the basis of the Western system of values, post-Soviet Russia by no means will be able to build a self-sufficient society – and in the best-case scenario, it will become an appendage of Europe and the USA. And at worst, a few appendages after breaking the country up into small(er) serfdoms.

"Today, global economic collapse is affecting the entire world. Financial problems in the West have become only part of the overall process, which is more and more reminiscent of the beginning of the Soviet collapse. The falling birth rate, a sharp increase in drug addiction, sexual degeneracies, a sharp drop in the level of education, and indeed, a categorical unwillingness to fight for an ideal, are becoming commonplace. If we add the inevitable destruction of state social-support systems in almost all Western countries, then it becomes clear that today's world and its system of values won't survive for much longer and will require far-reaching and sweeping planetary reform.

"The most important question that any researcher of human society faces, regardless of whether they represent a commercial structure that should build up its strategy for a sufficiently long time-period, whether state or scientific, is what forces will determine the direction of movement. And in what terms can they be described. All the examples described above are very indicative in the sense that they can be interpreted in entirely different ways, depending on which value/meaning system is used by the individual. And, if we take into account that each value system generates its own language (or rather, the interpretation of basic concepts, in other words, professional jargon), then how can we understand whether it is possible to adequately describe another value system in this language?"[1]

For example, one of the main terms of the "Western" value system is "freedom." But what does it mean? Does freedom of speech exist in the USA? At the propaganda level (in "Western" terminology), the answer is yes. And factually? Do we see any political mainstream support for Julian Assange or Edward Snowden? Or an across-the-board criticism in the

_____
1      https://khazin.ru/articles/10-vlast-i-obshhestvo/3820-o-problemakh-zapadno-go-global-nogo-proekta

mainstream press of the false chemical attack in Douma, Syria? No, they are considered to be "Putin propaganda tools against Western democracy and freedoms." What does "Western" freedom mean for Orthodox believers or Muslims? And for them, "freedom" in the "Western" sense implies the right to violate the biblical commandments with impunity, the first of which is the basic condition for the very existence of "Western" society – the abolition of the ban on usury.

And the second – automatically – the right of people professing "Western" values to choose independently which of the biblical commandments to fulfill and when. From the Christian point of view, this is pride, the worst of all sins, since these commandments were supposedly given by God, and it is not in the human right to make the corresponding choice. But to cover up such violations, the Western world coined the term "political correctness," the implementation of which is mandatory for everyone and which severely inhibits public discussion of such problems.

In other words, as Russian economist Mikhail Khazin explains, "instead of the biblical commandments or the "Moral Code of the Builder of Communism" (which, as we will see later, ideologically have much in common), the Western world offers its own system of commandments, the fulfillment of which is equally necessary: for example, "freedom," understood as the rejection of the value system of previous historical eras and "political correctness" is like a ban on discussing these very value systems. But there is also "democracy," "sacred law" of private property, "human rights," and much, much more."[2]

Note that the Western value system in itself carefully obscures its difference from previous systems. It (within the framework of the same political correctness) prohibits public discussion of the difference between the phenomenon of Protestantism and Orthodoxy or Catholicism – so as not to underline the rejection of biblical values. It makes tremendous efforts to whitewash banking activities as much as they declare it a "worthy and respected" profession in the entire history of mankind – although for 1,500 years of Christian and (partially) Muslim domination in Europe, the banker (usurer) could not be considered a respected member of society – since he openly and publicly violated binding biblical commandments.

Finally, the Western value system includes a carefully designed concept for the development of history, which derives the traditions of "democracy" from the Athenian "democracy" of Ancient Greece. I will forgo

---

2    https://khazin.ru/articles/10-vlast-i-obshhestvo/3820-o-problemakh-zapadno-go-global-nogo-proekta

the fact that all the city-states of Ancient Greece were slaveholders; I only note that they were pagan. And after the advent of Christianity, there was no longer any talk of any slave-owning democracies. Western historians effortlessly build a straight line of historical development, for which they use the somewhat amorphous, but pervasive term "civilization." This is done for a reason.

The fact is that although the value system within Europe has changed at least three times since the 16th century (and in different directions), the culture, in general, has maintained continuity. And for this reason, the primacy of Western historians defending their system of values clearly belongs to the cultural and not the "values" area, since it is more difficult to see the fundamental changes that have occurred over the past 500 years – and which we have shown previously and will show further later in the text.

And finally, the fundamental rejection of biblical dogmas, characteristic of Protestantism, makes it nevertheless closer to paganism. And in this sense, the choice of Athens as a model is an attempt to "obscure" the rejection of Christianity (and, in general, biblical values).

But the 16th century, on the contrary, is a century that Western historians love to discuss. Not because it marks the first fundamental change in the basic value system for a part of the population of Europe after the first one and a half millennia, but because they like this very system that arose at that time; that is, Protestantism, and its ideological derivative – "Protestant ethics." And in this place, a wonderful forgery is being carried out: the "Protestant ethic" itself is described in all its splendor. What is not mentioned is that from the point of view of the previous system of values (biblical, in the broad sense of the word), it is unacceptable because it is dangerous and aggressive heresy (what is called a "totalitarian sect" in the Russian tradition). At the same time, the opportunities that have arisen in connection with the abolition of the ban on usury, are actively promoted by "Western" propaganda, and it is unreservedly implied that they developed until the sixteenth century; only with the heyday of Protestantism did their development speed increase significantly.

Likewise, glossed over at best and ignored at worst, the real value system of socialist ideas,[3] which arose at the end of the 18th century as a response to the disdain of capitalist society, was an attempt to return the ban on usury in the form of socialization of the means of production. It should be noted that an "extreme" version of these ideas was implemented

3    https://www.cambridge.org/core/books/cambridge-history-of-modern-european-thought/european-socialism-from-the-1790s-to-the-1890s/175123179C134A5EC505A-E787A91632D

in the USSR. Success was grandiose, especially when you consider that, in retrospect, the USSR in the 1970s put itself in a position to win the Cold War and did not succeed only because the leadership of the country did not want to risk falling into the same trap that the USA finds itself in today. That is, in a situation where all the might of the country may not be enough to keep half of the world from falling into chaos, in which the bonds that provide control and order have suddenly disappeared.

"If we retrospectively examine the value models that existed in the Soviet Union, we can see that in the 20th century, at least two fundamental changes occurred. The first one was in February 1917, when the system of values of the "Orthodox empire" was rejected, which had existed in Russia with slight variations since at least the 15th century (and adopted from Byzantium). Moreover, the initial direction of this change was, most likely, towards the Western value system. This is evident both from understanding who really contributed to the February 1917 revolution (and there are very serious reasons to believe that it was organized by agents of France and, above all, England, who were very afraid of a unilateral truce between Russia and Germany in WWI), as well as by the one who, as a result, ultimately came to power.

"The differences between the Orthodox and the Western system of values turned out to be too pronounced, and Russia was not able to impose this model at that moment. And then, against the backdrop of an ideological vacuum, a group came to power that adhered to one of the radical socialist teachings. "Historically, Orthodoxy preceded the Western system of values, and socialism appeared later as an attempt to "return to place" a part of the biblical dogma rejected within the framework of the Western model. It is for this reason that in more than a few instances, the Christian and socialist value systems are very close, which allowed the Communists, led by Lenin, to "introduce" Russia to it.

"That said, the USSR had its version of history, based, naturally, on its system of values. The experience of the past 30 years (since 1991 and the collapse of the Soviet Union) has shown that the Western value system fundamentally contradicts many of the "cultural codes" of the Soviet (and Russian) people. We see it clearly in the example of the interview given a few years ago by the American President of Latvia, Vaira Freiberga, who sincerely believes in the triumph of fascism over communism and propagates this point of view with impunity in the framework of the Western paradigm. And the crisis of recent years, in particular, is connected with the fact that it is impossible to convince Russians that the USA and England, Soviet "allies" in World War II, defeated fascism; that living conditions in the former USSR were atrocious (now people live infinitely worse), that it was not possible under "socialism" for individuals to "freely" receive education and have access to culture, etc."[4]

That said, if we recall the socialist version of history, the description of the capitalist countries suffered serious one-sidedness as well. This is not accidental. As soon as the author of a historical (cultural, sociological, etc.) text chooses a basic system of values as his point of reference, he is forced to interpret all the events described and the consequences of them in its framework.

What is clear, for the society to move forward in the post-Bretton Woods world, a new value system needs to be designed on a planetary scale. For the past 600-700 years, Russia, as a project, has always had its system of values, although we could extend this period back another thousand years to the adoption of Christianity as a religious State. The same can be said for other global projects. So, what is a global project as opposed to a nation-state?

## Global Projects

Civilization is a lovely word. Most of the words incorporated into English from Latin sound beautiful. The combination of the two words "civilized" and "countries" more recently has become associated with something quite banal, using it for shining examples of successful business, the right policies, conditions, and circumstances of life of the representatives of the "elite." If the emotional element is put aside, a new topic comes to the forefront, which was again reinforced with a Latin root word – "globalization." It was assumed for a time that, with globalization in tow, a new Golden Age would come and people would finally begin to live happily and, if possible, equally well, perhaps forever after.

The central concept, is the "Global Project" (GP from now-on), which is the basis for describing global trends in the development of states, their coalitions, and civilizations (what it is now fashionable to call, "geopolitics"). A global project is a supranational idea, which, in principle, can become the basis for determining the value system of any person on Earth. At the same time, the crucial point is the voluntary choice of participation in a particular GP for each person. The basic concepts of any project must necessarily include the condition that its values should appeal to any person voluntarily, due to their universality and attractiveness.

4    https://khazin.ru/articles/162-global-nye-proekty/4268-o-global-nykh-proektakh-doklad-na-konferentsii-vsjei

I would like to clarify both words in this definition, so as not to fall into unnecessary analogies. The word "global" here should not be understood in the terms associated with the fashionable concept of "globalization." In our understanding, this term means that the Global Project initially assumes that its addressee is everybody, regardless of where and how he/she lives. However, as we will see below, each project forms its globalization system within the framework of which it builds a system of economic, political, cultural, and other ties based on project values.

As for the word "project," it does not mean that this education is created and supported due to someone's specific will. Instead, it implies that the idea underlying it is rich enough to structure the behavior and logic of its followers and allows them to sense and formulate the basis of their unity and common goals.

Even more precisely, the GP offers each person a particular value system that they can independently accept (or reject). "Moreover, the very concept of a "project" suggests that this decision should be made without violence. Violence itself, of course, also has its own, sometimes more, sometimes less limited place, however, either as part of the confrontation with other Global Projects or in the latter stages of the project, when the dossified mechanisms for "promoting" project values simply cannot keep up with the changing environment.

At the same time, of course, far from every idea that claims to be "supranational" and "global" can become the basis of the GP. Strictly speaking, only history – the event – is the tool that selects from the myriad of contenders an idea with a truly global reach.

"In addition to the idea which is the basis of the GP, it also includes a set of social, state, cultural, historical and other mechanisms and traditions that arise in the process of its functioning. And it is the interaction of these mechanisms within the framework of competition between individual global projects that determines the main streams of world history.

"Civilization (or its embryo), striving to formulate its own global project, must necessarily have at its disposal the "Great Supermundane Idea" as the basis for the project. It should be a real "Idea," capable of explaining the visible and the invisible world, from which the system of behavior and ethical rules are consistently derived. Moreover, this "Idea" should be exceptional, of universal appeal, in all corners of the globe and at all times."[5]

---

5      https://khazin.ru/articles/162-global-nye-proekty/4268-o-global-nykh-proektakh-doklad-na-konferentsii-vsjei

In modern marketing, this is called USP – a "unique selling proposition," which boils down to: *"Buy from us! Only we have the best!"* However, one idea is not enough. It is necessary that it connects with everyday life, incorporates customs, formulates a set of rules and procedures by which not only each person, but also the community of people as a whole must exist – that is, to develop the "Norm." The Norm is a buffer between the "Idea," as a set of unchanging dogmas, and everyday life. The Norm is fundamentally important from two points of view: First of all, in the Idea, as a set of source codes, nothing can be changed and corrected, but in the Norm, which has absorbed the harsh prose of life, it is possible to amend it and even modify it.

The development of such a Norm is normal for any multinational state, in which it is necessary to assemble a "completely unified denominator" out of peoples whose history and culture are entirely different from each other. This is one of the fundamental differences between communism and fascism, mentioned in the first part of this text: communism is a form of the "Red" global project, which not only proclaims but also ensures the equality of nations. But Fascism is an extreme form of racist nationalism, which simply despises and destroys any people except its own.

In the Christian Idea, usury is despised, but tolerated as a necessary evil in the normal life of Christian states, especially in those where Christianity is weakened by the propaganda of "Protestant ethics." The norm is not a written thing; rather, it is a complex system of meanings, which is the subject of tacit agreements. However, it is this "norm" that becomes the basis for creating rules and procedures that can be called laws, codes, instructions, ethics, mores, that is, various kinds of formalization of the Norm. All this is a practice that organizes daily and hourly complex interactions of the human community both within the borders of individual states and outside them.

It is here that the difference lies between the "system of meanings" and the "system of values," which I mentioned earlier. The value system is, in fact, the basic system of dogmas of the project. It is sturdy enough but cannot easily adapt to new prevailing conditions. The system of meanings is its adaptation to the real life of a particular nation, and it is with it that we deal in everyday life.

For example, the notorious monetization of benefits is not "bad" because it translates these benefits into material form; and not even due to their amount. In the Russian system of meanings of privilege, there is an expression of respect shown in the attitude of the state towards certain social types – veterans, disabled people, children, and so on. The material benefits may be small, but the fact of recognition of their involvement (in the war, for example) was more important to many than the money they received from the state.

It is safe to say that the global project takes shape precisely within the "Norm" of society. As devastation arises in the upper echelons of power, so the image of the future arises in the same echelons. It is there that a powerful charge of energy originates and matures, forcing millions of people to build their lives this way and not otherwise. But there should be no ambiguities and positions that were not thought out to the end: a global project should at every moment give each social layer an answer to the questions: why live and how to live.

Any project, even potentially claiming to become global, begins as a network. The cells of the supporters of the Idea are formed and multiplied, and the rituals are improved, the rules of behavior and interaction are formulated. Initially, the cells are not connected by subordinated relationships. They agree on fundamental issues (most often on the basis of imposing their own, common, design value system, on everyone else), but act independently. While the "Idea" itself is leading them, the "Norm" only then beginning to take shape. No societal idea survives its own implimentation.

At this stage, the development of the project takes place on the initiative of individuals, unrelated initiators and due to the activity of neophytes. There is no coordination center in the network stage; it is developing spontaneously, and in many directions, which allows it to quickly adapt to the needs, demands, and values of people in the system they accept, for a particular project.

As an example of the network form of the project, Christianity of the first centuries A.D., when thousands of preachers brought people the ideas of the new religion. "After Christ, Christianity was not rewritten, but created; the creation process lasted between 150 and 200 years (3rd-4th centuries A.D.) when a corpus of literature was created, and a hierarchy and territorial structure were built according to the model of the Roman Empire. A Biblical project was developed that was adequate for the new era. If before that, in the Mediterranean basin, social control was external in nature, the main elements of this social control were the "culture of shame" and external power control – the "Egyptian model," which found maximum expression in the Roman Empire and Roman law, then the changed conditions required more subtle and deeper, more internalized forms no longer just social, but socio-psychological control – from within. Hence the "culture of conscience."

"The "Red" communist project developed in a networked way in the 19th century, when thousands of its supporters brought to the masses a new system of values opposing the capitalist system of values. As soon as the number of supporters becomes significant, the political component is inevitably formulated. It is impossible otherwise: it is necessary to set house rules, define a management system, name friends and enemies.

"Furthermore, for a successful deployment, a global project must establish itself first in one country. This country should be large, powerful economically and militarily. Only a strong country, being the recognized leader of the project, can keep other project states from continuous conflicts among themselves and ensure that more and more participants (nations) join the project.

"In this process, it is vital to attract the elite or part of the elite of such a country. The elite, in turn, at times by persuasion, and at times resorting to violence, will achieve the support of the people for the new project. It is no secret to anyone that Russia's adoption of Orthodoxy was the result of a conscious political choice of the rulers."[6]

That said, we shouldn't underestimate the possibilities of indigenous population infiltration by the carriers of the Idea, followed by the accession of the population to it or its eradication. That is how Latin America was conquered, first by the conquistadors, then by the Catholics. Note that, although the Christian norm in Latin America of the 17th-18th centuries differed significantly from the European norm, today this region is the mainstay of traditional Catholicism.

From the moment when new norms are established in the supporting country, and it is strong enough to become a leader, the global project becomes hierarchical, managed from a single center, and openly expansionist. The state introduces the inherent managerial technologies into the practice of the project and uses its economic and military power to support it. It is fundamentally important, however, that the expansion of the project at this stage takes place predominantly peacefully, for the example of the embodied Idea is more reliable than bullets. One can only recall the speed with which the Russian state expanded after it became the supporting country of the "Byzantine-Orthodox" project in the 15th-17th centuries, or how quickly Catholic values conquered Latin America. No

---

6        https://khazin.ru/articles/137-arkhivnye-materialy/3745-o-problemakh-jelity-zapadno-go-global-nogo-proekta

weapon could provide such efficiency – ideas were the basis for the rapid expansion! It was guns, germs, and steel! What choice did the survivors have?

"At this stage of the GP, a relatively distinct and well-coordinated project elite is formed, which determines the direction of its development and, especially, the mechanisms of always-competitive interaction with other GP's. An example is the "Christian" project, which entered a hierarchical stage after become the State religion of Rome in 325 A.D. and on into the Byzantine Empire (note that the adoption of Christianity as a state religion in smaller countries did not affect its network nature) or, for example, "Red" (communist) project, which went into a hierarchical stage after the Great Socialist Revolution in November of 1917 (October, according to the old calendar).

"That said, the "Catholic" project went through the network stage as part of a single "Christian" project, in connection with which it immediately became hierarchical. At the same time, after Rome collapsed, this project's elite was scattered across different Catholic states, and it was united by the figure of the Pope (note that the activities of the Vatican state itself did not have a special relationship with the "Catholic" Global Project). Sometimes the hierarchical stage of the project begins almost immediately after its occurrence (as, for example, during the first implementation of the Islamic project in the 7th century A.D.), and sometimes it is significantly delayed (for example, the Buddhist project did *not* turn to the hierarchical stage, which may be connected with the specifics of its basic value system).

"The transition from the network stage to the hierarchical stage does not always take place painlessly for a project. Often during this period, individual elements of its network structure try to develop into independent (but related) projects. That is how the Shiite branch split from the general branch of the Islamic Global Project, and this is how the Catholic project split from the Orthodox Christian branch. At the same time, after the formation of the Catholic project, the common Christian project practically ceased to exist, since by this time almost all the activity of the Christian world was concentrated in the framework of competing Byzantine and Catholic projects."[7]

Furthermore, as soon as the project moves into the hierarchical stage, it begins to form a centralized structure that should support its mission-

7    https://khazin.ru/articles/137-arkhivnye-materialy/3745-o-problemakh-jelity-zapadno-go-global-nogo-proekta

ary activities and (if possible) regulate/control the structure remaining from the network stage.

Since a GP, by definition, involves expanding its zone of influence on all of humanity, these centralized structures also begin to play the role of headquarters, which use economic, cultural, political, military, and other levers to advance their projects. In other words, each GP creates its own construction of globalization, which it promotes as one of the main tools of its own expansion. At the same time, the material basis of any such globalization is the labor division system, which automatically links the project promotion system with the monetary, economic, and trading system. If the ideology of the project is in no way connected with economic activity (for example, with the Buddhist global project), this significantly slows down its transition to the hierarchical stage and further expansion.

An example of several alternative systems of globalization is the period from the 1950s to the 1980s, when two systems coexisted in the world – one within the framework of the Western labor division system based on the American dollar, and the other, respectively, based on the transferable ruble in the framework of the Council for Mutual Economic Assistance (socialist bloc). The Western system won. What are the practical implications of this victory? It means that it makes no sense for anyone who is not a part of the Western system to even try to influence the behavior and policies of the IMF, the World Bank, NATO, European Union, WTO, etc., like today's Russia or any other country non-aligned with the Western liberal-financier model, since these institutions are primarily the institutions of the Western global project, the control of which is carried out by its own elites.

With that in mind, thinking of influencing the West or winning arbitration hearings is absurd. Incidentally, this is also Donald Trump's problem, as the financial decisions in the Western world and its Bretton Woods-related institutions are taken by the global liberal financial elite of the Western project. Trump (alternative, murky global project), to push his policies through, first needs to dismantle the Bretton Woods economic model.

The development of the project in the hierarchical stage can continue for a sufficiently long time, especially if its elite is divided into numerous separate groups. An example of this is the Catholic project in the Middle Ages, when all the claims of the Pope or emperors of the Holy Roman Empire to monopolize the project ended in collapse. However, over time, the original spirit of the carriers of the "Idea" weakens, morality deteriorates, loosening in norms and rules is increasingly allowed, which means that both the supporting country and the entire project as a whole tend to decline. From this moment on, the supporting country is forced to behave like an empire or quasi-empire. This stage differs from the hierarchical stage by an even greater concentration of the elite, dossification of project mechanisms, and, most importantly, the transition of project management from sufficiently pluralistic elites to a rigidly organized imperial-style bureaucracy.

If the project is developed in a confrontation with other global projects, such a transition can occur very quickly. Thus, the "Red" communist project in the hierarchical stage existed for only a few decades, that is until the end of the 1940s, after which there was a transition to the imperial stage. There is reason to believe that Stalin in 1943 deliberately began to curtail the "Red" communist project, carefully positioning it towards the imperial stage, and increasingly strengthening the Orthodox-patriotic component in it.

The imperial stage of the GP is the last stage, followed by its disintegration or transition into a latent form. There are several reasons: firstly, the imperial bureaucracy categorically does not keep pace with the ongoing social, economic, and political processes in the world.

Secondly, the imperial consciousness prefers not to prove something, but rather to actively and forcibly impute the project value system, which sharply reduces the base for expanding the project and reduces the commitment to the project value system within the project countries themselves. Russian citizens are well aware of this mechanism, through the example of the activities of the Communist Party bureaucracy, during Gorbachev's "perestroika" period.

Thirdly, the adaptability of project values and ideological attitudes, which begin to lose the ideological war to competing projects, is significantly reduced. The ruling elites are not in a position to recognize the problems – otherwise, they are deprived of legitimation; they cannot take decisive measures – the rules of the game must be changed too much and their power will slip. To maintain the status quo, it becomes necessary to use violence both externally and internally on a wide-enough scale to cow the populace.

An essential part that determines the existence and development of global projects is their interaction, which is always fiercely competitive. Projects can be quite liberal within the internal project framework (public or even state), but this never refers to the values of alternative projects. For this reason, in no case should the terminology of a particular project be used to describe inter-project relationships – the ideology of any GP is monopolistic – alternative projects are always painted extremely negatively. This is clearly seen in the example of the ideology/doctrine of the modern Western project, which in exclusively negative tones describes both the "Red," Islamic, and even Catholic projects.

Seeing the world around us, it is difficult to resist the temptation to find a simple explanation (common denominator) for them. It is easy to say that the world is imperfect because democracy has not been established everywhere. Now, if and when democracy really takes hold, things will get better, conflicts will disappear, and the people will live happily ever after.

The thing is, that, isolated, observed phenomena or facts are only part of the system of meanings. In each global project, this set is unique, and each meaning exists exclusively in connection with others. When you try to change one of the elements, the system will either assimilate it or collapse. Here is an example: Did you realize that the position of the Central Committee of the Communist Party of the Soviet Union in the Soviet system of the 20th century was substantially closer to the position of the Boyar Duma in Russia during the 16th and 17th centuries than to the communist ideal? That is, the norm of the traditional Orthodox project absorbed and subsumed communism and not vice versa. Most likely, because the "Red" project simply did not have proven social mechanisms to function properly. In this sense, it is interesting to reflect on how the introduction of a security system that looks very much like the Soviet KGB will affect the United States – the leader of the Western project. The fact that nothing good will come out of it for the USA should be crystal clear to all. The question, thus, should be framed differently: what will prevail – the American system of meanings or an alien element within it?

There is, however, one more circumstance. The second half of the 20th century passed, in terms of war on the grand scale, relatively calmly, without the indescribable upheavals typical of its first half. The reason for this, strange as it may seem, is that there were three existing global projects at that time: Western, Red, and (hidden/latent) Islamic. Two projects inevitably collide, but three can create balance and harmony (Chinese methodology, which I will explain in greater detail later). The question is, with the Red project dead, if today's main adversaries are Western and Islamic projects, will China be forced to formulate its global project, as a counterbalancing act?

After the collapse of the empire, as the highest and last stage of the global project, chaos sets in. However, this should not be taken in a negative sense. Chaos is a natural and necessary stage, during which clarification of meanings, analysis of the past, accumulation of forces for the future take place. If the project is able to remain committed to the Idea, and to modernize the content of what makes up the Norm, then the possibility of its reconfiguration is very high. If not, then descendants will have to read about this or that bygone civilization in history textbooks, and when visiting museums, admire the highest culture of these dead systems.

Ideas tend to move from West to East. Chaos and renewal – from East to West. When the Soviet Union was strong and powerful, China was in chaos, groping for a new path. Now, China is on the rise, Russia is in chaos, but even she will find her way if she turns to the meanings that make up the Norm of Russian civilization. Then chaos will move to Europe, then to America, then it will come to China again, and the wheel of civilization will spin. The whirlygig of Time

# Chapter 3

# CHANGE THROUGH THE
# PRISM OF GLOBAL PROJECTS

The competition of projects, as described in chapter 2, takes place in three main areas, which, by and large, are independent and equal. And historical experience shows that if, in two of them, an apparent victory goes to one of the projects, then any superiority of forces in the third direction rarely plays a role. These three areas are Economics (of which military power is a derivative), Ideology, and Demography.

Demographics is not only the population but also its commitment to Project values; in particular, its willingness to fight and die for them. Thus, the complexity of the Western project in Iraq is primarily due to the fact that the home advantage of Islam in ideology and its superior population base entirely negates the overwhelming superiority of the Western project in the developed economic sphere (and, thus, military force).

The confrontation of the Western capitalist systems and Soviet socialist (plus satellites) system in the middle of the 20th century was due to the fact that none of them had a clear advantage (contrary to the ideological dogma of each of them): in the economy, the Western project was miles ahead; in ideology, the Red communist/socialist project had an initial lead. In demography, in general, it was a draw. And the defeat of the "Red" project at the end of the 20th century was due to the fact that in the late 1950s, the decomposed imperial leadership of the USSR abandoned the ideological war, moving to the so-called principle of "peaceful coexistence," and sharply weakened the demographic project component.

This was due to the fact that the slogan "building communism during the life of the current generation" led to the beginning of the realization of the principle "to everyone according to their needs." And this, in turn, led to a situation where a material reward was given to people, not for real achievements in the framework of the further development of the "Red" project, but simply because of their existence. Which, of course, could not but weaken the commitment to the design values of the next generation (the so-called "sixties"), who, became the "grave diggers" of the Red project and their country.

# Global Projects Today

"The first in written history was the "Jewish" (Old Testament) Global Project. It was this project that, for the first time, offered people not the power of weapons but a system of values. As expected, the initial try needed to be adjusted and improved; therefore this project, especially in terms of its ritual mechanisms, turned out to be extremely complicated. As a result, the number of adepts was extremely small. Note that I put the word "Jewish" in quotation marks, since this project is associated more with religion than with nationality. In this sense, Jews by birth, Baron Rothschild, the elite of the Western GP, are no less dangerous enemies for the "Jewish" project[1] than, say, neo-fascists. However, the name "Jewish" or "Israeli"[2] also does not quite fit the description, given that both modern Judaism and the state of Israel have a relationship to the "Jewish" project, but hardly coincide with it.

"Furthermore, one of the most important tenets of this project, the prohibition of usury, was applied only to representatives of its own project. Such a situation, as we will see later, had a fundamental impact on the entire course of the world process. At the same time, this very system of values turned out to be so attractive that a subsequent Christian project appeared, which, after the transition to the hierarchical stage, naturally became knows as Byzantine.

"The main difference between the Christian and the Jewish projects is not in dogma but in greatly simplified rituals. In addition, the ban on usury is universal, which led to the fact that already in the Middle Ages, a significant role in the control of the financial system was played by representatives of the "Jewish" project.

"Part of the network system of the Western Christian project in the framework of competition with Byzantium (as a state) ceased to exist, but one "splinter," in Western Europe, eventually developed into a separate, Catholic global project. Unlike the Byzantine Empire, which quickly acquired an imperial framework, the Catholic project, due to the political fragmentation of Western Europe, developed for a very long time within the hierarchical stage. Last but not least, the divergence of projects was also influenced by differences in the culture and mentality of the peoples that were part of the distribution area of the Byzantine and Catholic projects."[3]

---

1    https://www.jweekly.com/1997/03/21/the-rothschilds-generations-of-nurturing-zionism/
2    https://www.pewresearch.org/fact-tank/2016/03/08/in-israel-jews-are-united-by-homeland-but-divided-into-very-different-groups/
3    https://khazin.ru/articles/162-global-nye-proekty/3167-kako-global-ny-proekt-bu-

# 16th Century Europe

In the 16th century, after the catastrophic "golden crisis," which occurred as a result of a sharp fall in the price of gold,[4] a new, proto-Capitalist project, the ideological base of which was the Reformation, was born. "In doctrinal terms, this project moved away from the ideological base of the biblical system of values, abandoning one of the dogmas – the prohibition of usury – since the loan system became the economic base of the capitalist Global Project. The ban, of course, could not be canceled in dogma (and in Martin Luther's theses, for example, it is present in full), but was removed in the myth of the so-called "Protestant ethics." Note that the Capitalist project fundamentally changed the basic goal within the framework of the project value system. If in the Christian project, in all its variations, which did not even take the form of the GP, justice is the basis, then for the Capitalist system, it is self-interest and profit."[5]

This example shows that the biblical dogma system, which is the basis of almost all GPs in Europe, is not a mechanical sum of prohibitions and restrictions, but rather an essentially interdependent system of norms and rules, and this dependence is manifested through the whole life of people. From the point of view of a believing Christian (both a Jew and a Muslim), this is natural, and it cannot be otherwise since these dogmas were "given by God" and are not subject to revision by man. But a purely materialistic analysis shows that the rejection of only one of the doctrines inevitably led to a radical and fundamental change in life's goals and principles!

With the Capitalist project, with the presence of loan interest, another phenomenon of humanity is connected with the so-called technological society. No single state or civilization that does not approve of loan interest (especially Islamic) has been able to create a technological society on its own base (except for the Soviet Union).

"What's the difference between the Western Global Project and the Capitalist Global Project? Today the Capitalist project "in its explicit form" does not exist, since in the 19th century there were serious changes in its economic basis, which as a result, cardinally changed its underlying values. Only a few pieces of its former structure remained. The dogmatic structure of the Capitalist project was unstable and urgently required

det-sledujushhim
4        Chapter 7: Medieval Silver and Gold," mygeologypage.ucdavis.edu. Archived from the original on 2013-07-14.
5        Dyer, Christopher (1989-03-09). *Standards of Living in the Later Middle Ages: Social Change in England C.1200-1520.* Cambridge University Press. p. 219. ISBN 9780521272155.

a significant change, either towards a further rejection of biblical values (which was further strengthened because the "norm" in the new capitalist states was still largely Christian) or towards a return to the ban on usury. Characteristically, both of these ideas were realized.

"Both were born at the end of the 18th century, and what became the basis of the Western project, was the idea of how to realize the centuries-old dream of alchemists to create gold in vitro. It isn't difficult to understand the reasons alchemists were so eager to create gold – at that time gold was the Unified Measure of Value (UMV) for all humankind. But this idea, from which the mechanism of financial capitalism grew, and then the new Global project, was based on the fact that if gold cannot be created, then maybe it was possible to change the UMV?

"Today, the UMV is the American dollar, created, often out of nothing, by the US Federal Reserve, a private institution owned by the largest investment banks on Wall Street."[6] And the entire world financial system, with its institutions, such as the IMF, the World Bank, and many others, see as their primary task, the preservation of the Fed's monopoly on monetary proliferation.

Of course, without the presence of an interest loan, which was actively developing in the 19th-20th centuries, there could not have been a project. Its main stages were the creation of the first private state-owned bank (with the monopoly right to issue money) in England in the middle of the 19th century, the creation of the US Federal Reserve at the beginning of the 20th century, the Bretton Woods Agreements of 1944, the unlinking of the dollar to gold in 1971 and, finally, the collapse of the "Red" communist project in 1991.

And the change of name, from Capitalist to Western, is connected with the fact that the expression West, ingrained in the mainstream media, is usually mentioned to describe the design organizations of the Western state enterprise (countries such as the USA or Great Britain, and some purely Project entities, such as the IMF, NATO, etc.). Note that the basic system of values in the Western project compared to the Capitalist project has changed significantly. To the Western project, we owe the creation of the new "Sermon on the Mount" – the "Protestant Ethics," which de facto abolished the remaining biblical values.

True, the economy has undergone drastic changes since the main wealth began to be created not in the material sphere, production, or at

6        https://khazin.ru/articles/137-arkhivnye-materialy/3745-o-problemakh-jelity-zapadno-go-global-nogo-proekta

the expense of natural rent, but through the unrestrained multiplication of purely financial assets. This model has led to the fact that the share of financial values, which in the 19$^{th}$ century amounted to less than half of all human assets, today is more than 99%. Only the volume of financial futures, for example, oil or gold, exceeds the volume of physical oil (in price terms) by hundreds and thousands of times.

This way of creating assets through the printing press in the conditions of an already existing technological civilization made it possible to create the phenomenon of overconsumption when the development of a consumer credit system based on dollar emission allowed a sharp increase in the standard of living of a significant part of the population within the framework of the Western project.

At the same time, this significantly reduced their desire to fight for the implementation of project values, since such a struggle would inevitably reduce the standard of living. And if, before the collapse of the world socialist system, there was still an external threat, which rallied the rank-and-file followers of the Western project, then after its collapse, this factor fully manifested itself. As a result, one of the three main areas of inter-project struggle, demographic, turned out to be lost forever for the Western project.

Additionally, the aforementioned change in the main mode of production could not only seriously change the psychology of the project elite, but also sharply narrowed its managerial part: today, in fact, the main design decisions in the Western project are made by a narrow group of people consisting of several tens of thousands of technocrats.

"Furthermore, after the defeat of the "Red" project in the early 1990s, such a small elite and the absence (albeit for a short period of time) of real enemies on a Global project scale led to the rapid transition of the Western project to the imperial stage. And, as one would expect, the very first economic problems have caused problems for this "imperial" structure. Back in the first decade of this century, it was clearly visible that both the leadership of the European Union, primarily in Germany and France, and the US leadership (in the person of then-president George W. Bush) were seriously considering the possibility of leaving the structures accountable to them from the Western project and creating a supranational in the first, and national empire in the second case, with the return of the "old," capitalist in the first and even (partially) Catholic values in the second. Whether or not at least one of these attempts will succeed are yet to be seen, but one thing is clear – the sharp increase in terrorist attacks in recent years is significantly related to this crisis of the Western project, is an attempt by its split elites to shift the scales in their favor and to wrestle the control of the project from the Western elite circles.

"Outside Europe, in the 7th century, another project arose based on the biblical system of values – the Islamic project. It slowly developed within the framework of the hierarchical stage for almost 1,000 years, but the transition to the imperial stage within the Ottoman Empire practically led to the freezing of its own Islamic GP, its transition to the latent phase. And only in the 20th century, the attempts of the Western and Red projects to play the "Islamic card" in their interests led to its revival in the new edition, which today finds itself in a network stage. An essential factor in the revitalization of the Islamic global project was also the demographic dynamics, as a result of which the population of Muslim countries expanded rapidly.

"The leading quality of the Islamic project is its solid ideological component because the norms and rules, which are directly included in the dogma of the Koran, make active preachers of almost any project carrier. This significantly distinguishes the Islamic Project from all other GPs, which are only inherent in such activity at the very early stages of development."[7]

Asia also had its own global projects, which had not yet reached Europe, or rather did not have a critical enough mass of supporters, for example, Buddhists. It is precisely for the reason that their relevance is problematic for us today; we will not dwell on these projects.

The one exception to the abovementioned global projects is China. China today is at a crossroads: whether it will choose the path associated with raising the fallen banner of the Red project, or will it remain within the framework of a purely national, oxymoronic empire? A Capitalist economy in a totalitarian state, which in principle will not be concerned about processes that do not directly affect the purely national interests of ethnic Chinese and their vassality. There is enough evidence that points to the fact that communism, in its classical form, is not the goal of the Celestial Empire. In particular, communism has a negative attitude to usury, while China fully adapts capitalist tools, and communist paraphernalia is preserved only as a damper on system transformation.

To date, it seems that China is not interested in creating its own global project ("Datun," as I will explain later is a national project), neither on the "Red," nor on any other (for example, Buddhist-Confucian) basis, which significantly limits its own ability to control the world.

---

7    Mikhail Khazin: "Why it was not possible to create what is called a world government," Business Online, 26/0172013.

38

But back to the historical review. In the 18<sup>th</sup> century, almost simultaneously with the emergence of the idea of financial capitalism, ideas appeared in the works of Utopian socialists, which became the basis for the development of the "Red" Project. From the point of view of biblical dogma, this project was an attempt to return the ban on usury (in the form of socializing the means of production), but the ideology and technological mechanisms of this project have one crucial feature (compared with the previous ones) – a severe bias in the social sphere – the powerful development of social technologies.

The weak point of the "Red" project[8] is the complete absence of a mystical component in its practice (although it is present in dogma). At one time, in contrast to the Capitalist and Western projects, this was not as noticeable, but, as the alternative social projects borrowed the mentioned social technologies, this drawback began to play an increasingly important role. It is possible that Stalin's attempts to "reanimate"[9] Orthodoxy in the 1940s were connected with this particular flaw, but his death in 1953 ultimately stopped these attempts.

The Red project, which developed in the USSR in a rather sharp "communist" form, lost (for the reasons mentioned previously), but did not disappear completely, instead it switched to a latent form. Oligarchy/ Kleptocracy. The sharp decline in living standards in the base countries of the Western project after the inevitable and imminent global economic crisis will inevitably cause a powerful renaissance of Socialist ideas.

In addition, most likely due to problems with the dollar as a single measure of value, humanity (at least for a while) will objectively be seriously forced to consider the possibility of returning to life-practice the biblical dogma on the prohibition of usury.

It is here that it is time to recall the phenomenon of "technological civilization." The main problem of the Islamic project, (in comparison to historical Europe and the West in general) is the complete incapacity to build a modern technological structure on its own, medieval base.

The industrial society of expanded reproduction and accumulation of capital, having emerged in the West in the throes of the Netherlands (1566-1648) and English (1640-1660) bourgeoisie revolutions, went through three stages of a progressive increase in wealth. On the "lineal progress" these stages are marked by a measured step of improving energy and production technologies.

---

8    https://vk.com/@manjagin-rossiya-posle-stalina-kto-unichtozhil-krasnyi-proekt
9    http://www.odnako.org/blogs/rossiya-i-globalniy-krasniy-proekt-istoriya-padenie-i-budushchee/comments/page-14/#613758

1. Manufacture on manual textile machines – Dutch stage: 18th century. The first technological paradigm.

2. Factory mass production, where a person became an appendage of a steam engine – the British stage: the 19th century. The second, coal – and the third, electric engines, technological paradigm.

3. Conveyor production, the internal combustion engine, and microelectronics – American stage: 20th century, fourth – oil; and fifth – computers, super-technological structures.

Thus, it is evident that Islam cannot use the experience of the Capitalist and "Western" projects; loan interest in Islam is strictly prohibited. The only case in history when a technological society was built without using loan interest is the USSR, that is, the base country of the "Red" project. For this reason, the penetration of Islam into Europe may begin to take on a significant socialist connotation, which will inevitably correlate with the rise of similar sentiments in the context of an acute economic crisis.

# Problems for the Elite of the Western Global Project

Any global project, and especially one that has entered the imperial stage, not only actively promotes its project values and principles, but also creates a stringent system of control over their implementation. Such a system operated in the USSR, and today it operates in the USA and other countries of the Western project.

Due to the imperial stage, the control system is quite bureaucratized and formalized. For example, there is an unwritten rule in the West about how corporate media presents the information. In other words, everyone knows what they can and cannot say in public (without being told overtly) and the consequences one suffers if they break this rule. You can recall the story of journalists who, on September 11, 2001, questioned the official narrative of the terrorist attacks in New York City. Or of those scientists who rejected "generally accepted" concepts of the Twin Towers collapse or the dangers of "Global Warming," newspapers that, on command, began to carry the same nonsensical version of events with terrorists and box-cutters, bin Laden and the Taliban, This was also obvious during the West-orchestrated dismantling of Libya. I am not saying that there is a little green man in a spacesuit who gives orders to politicians, economists, journalists and opinion leaders to behave in a particular way. No, they themselves know which position is a "correct" position that can further their careers and which position is an "incorrect" position; why an opinion leader cannot write glowing articles about Syria, Iran, Venezuela, or Russia, why you cannot criticize Obama and compliment Trump, and so on and so forth. I repeat – the elite of the Western global project strictly make sure that people who do not reflect the interests and principles of this project are excluded from climbing a career social ladder or in the opposite case, lose all their privileges and become invisible, such was the case with the Nobel prize-winning economist Joseph Stiglitz, or one of the "fathers" of Reaganomics, American economist Paul Craig Roberts. Nothing surprising or incomprehensible in this, but today this situation has become dangerous for the elite of the Western project. The fact is, the current crisis is not just a crisis within the framework of the normal development of the model that has become the basis for the Western project. It is a crisis of the model itself, which no longer provides a resource not only for its development but even for normal existence of the project. In other words, it is necessary either to seriously reform the Western project, or else it must disappear.

"A similar situation existed with the Islamic project in the $18^{th}$–$19^{th}$ centuries – since the rapid technological growth of the West did not allow the Ottoman Empire, which at that time was the base of the Islamic project, to expand and compete with the Western Project. The limitations of technological growth are an essential part of the Islamic project, in which the economic model of the $7^{th}$ century is included in canonical texts. In any case, the impossibility of development led to the destruction of the empire and the return of the Islamic project to the network stage. If today or tomorrow there is, within its framework, a direction that will overcome this dogmatic problem, then the Islamic project can quickly be restarted in the future; otherwise, it will gradually fade and disappear.

"Today, the United States finds itself in an identical situation. They must fundamentally change the model of their development, start looking for new approaches, in particular, drastically change the social structure. Instead, state control of government apparatus is being toughened (to the levels of the Soviet KGB of the 1970s and pre-collapse 1980s), the US becoming a Prison Planet ready to crush everyone willing to stand up to them internally (Julian Assange is a good example).

"As a result, all potential reformers are almost automatically marginalized, and instead of reforming, the elite of the Western project is destroying the system that prevents them from turning it around. This is a fairly typical situation, we can recall the last decades of the existence of the Russian Empire pre-1917 (and the last years of the USSR pre-

1991), but it makes it impossible for a peaceful way out of the general economic crisis."[10]

The elite of the Western project, terrified of losing its privileges and positions, are engaged in actively fighting those who, theoretically, could become its saviors. This behavior can be understood: there are no resources to preserve the elite of the Western project on the current global scale. And those who suspect that they may be forced out of the elite group are desperately fighting against any attempts to reform the system, as this will only exacerbate their withdrawal from the elite. Moreover, the rigidly institutionalized and dogmatized imperial structure helps the Western elite in its struggle against any attempts to reform the existing system.

All this is very clearly visible in the quality of Western political elites, incapable of finding a solution, and even more incapable of even more or less clearly articulating the problems that their countries are facing. There is little doubt today that the Western project, just like Thessalian King Erisychton from Greek mythology, is beginning to devour itself. And when you consider that the crisis will only deepen, the short-term situation becomes completely hopeless and untenable.

## Ares, Athena and Apollo wars

When we discuss conflicts, we often talk about geopolitical players, projects, macro-regions, etc., but how do we differentiate players from the regional power, a local elite group, people, etc. from global players? The answer is simple – the geopolitical player must be a subject and be able to wage all types of wars.

Currently, the era of the unipolar world is ending, the age of the dream of the "golden billion" – the period exemplified by the joint dominance of Western global and capitalist elites. What are some of the obstacles that the old and the new geopolitical players will have to deal with in order to be able to redefine their future?

Of the existing descriptions of the different types of wars, the following typification of wars, first coined by Russian futurist Sergei Perespegin, is closest to me – Ares (armed struggle), Athena (trade and economic struggle), Apollo (psycho-historical struggle). A typical mistake in considering different types of wars is the idea of hierarchy and increasing complexity; it seems to me that we should talk about a closed scheme of the type "rock-paper-scissors," where the warrior loses to the merchant, the merchant to the priest, and the priest to the warrior. Plus, long-term confron-

---

10  https://www.business-gazeta.ru/article/73923

tations, conflicts at the player level have always been on all three fronts; the only difference is that in different periods of history, the significance of the wars of Ares, Athena and Apollo on the overall result is different.

It follows that if a player cannot wage all three types of wars, then, in the long run, he is doomed to fail. For example, where is that Japan from the 1980s that prophesied world domination? Did a giant GDP help China in the mid-19th century? The answer is a resounding no on both counts. Thus, for a long-term presence on the geopolitical scene, a global player must have the necessary resources to wage three types of wars:

a) armed forces for global, regional and local conflicts;

b) financial and economic system with a high degree of autonomy and significance within the world;

c) unique, significant for the world ideology/projection, as re-sources for a psycho-historical war

Let's call this combination a "geopolitical triad."

## The Ideology of a Global Player

If the resources for the war of Athena and Ares are understandable, then what about the war of Apollo? In the coming historical peri-od, the central front of the struggle will take place within the field of meanings and psycho-history.I have often described the classification of projects along two axes: conservative-liberal, right-left. I consider it nec-essary to introduce another axis: "national - global," i.e., how much the ideology proposed by the project is acceptable/attractive for the whole world (ordinary people and elites), and not just a specific people or reli-gious group. Islam offers the idea of justice, but only for Muslims. "More precisely, it is declared, of course, for everyone, but what matters is not how it is declared, but how the rest of the world perceives it. You can talk about the Chinese proposal of a shared fate as much as you like, but for now, most of the neighboring countries will perceive this solely as fulfill-ing the philistine dreams of ordinary Chinese and guaranteeing crumbs from the table to the surrounding barbarians, if they certainly recognize the Celestial Empire as the center of the world, the situation will not change. Do you seriously think that the same Islamic peoples will do this with an open heart and will not try to rob and kill their benefactor at the first opportunity?"[11]

11      Pereslegin Boris, Suma Estrategia, Guerra de Ares, https://litresp.com/chitat/ru/%D0%9F/pereslegin-sergej-borisovich/summa-strategii/147

The current transition period, from a unipolar world to a world of pan-regions, will be short, and everyone who wants to participate in the future "Great Game" must be prepared for what's coming. Thus, the formation of a geopolitical triad (resources for all three types of wars) is the primary task of every global project in the struggle for its subjectivity. In the following section, I will explain the winning strategies of individual global projects and their function from a psycho-historical perspective in the post-economic collapse world.

*****

Ours was the greatest civilization in history, so advanced and powerful, it dwarfed anything that came before it, but like other great societies, it did not last. To have lived, and then to have died is not to be absent but to become absent, to be someone and then go away – leaving traces. How could the civilization that had mastered the planet, suddenly collapse?

Now, image the following…we are in the year 2020. Decay is rampant and unavoidable. Businesses are failing, and companies that remain in business face shortages and delays. People respond with a helpless sense of doom. The anxiety leaves one gasping for breath and represents a declaration of defenselessness before a force too terrifying and massive to combat or even comprehend – pervasive hopelessness and loss of spirit.

Great cities lie abandoned, incredible feats of engineering left to ruin. A collapse that caused the greatest disaster in human history – our extinction. If you are trying to assembly a multi-dimensional case, to understand what kind of a force drives events: a collapse of civilization, happening it seems with the precise stroke of a diamond cutter's knife – a pogrom of demand destruction designed to reduce the world's population in order to preserve for the elite the ever-diminishing natural resources. This single piece of the puzzle was what started to make everything else resonate and make sense of the hidden dynamics.

We know what a collapse looks like: Budapest's cobbled streets – a war zone. Protesters armed with blocks of ice caught on film smashing up Hungary's finance ministry. Thousands are trying to force their way into the legislature. This is real. In the year 2020, the economic collapse is hitting hard in every industrialized country in the world. Around the world, emerging financial markets are imploding at the speed of light. The meltdown has hit turbocharge in Europe as a result of a two-month-old lack of Russian natural gas.

Triggered by the economic collapse and compounded by human suffering in unheated, near-zero weather, riots have erupted from Latvia in the North, to Sofia in the South. Around the world, from China to India, to Europe, industrialized nations are frantically preparing for civil unrest. This is not some piece of fiction. This is not *Atlas Shrugged*. This is about now. It affects all of humanity.

Another image: Ordinary people enraged by austerity cuts and draconian wage deflation, their hard-earned savings reduced to nothing under forced government devaluation, fighting for their survival. Civil unrest now moves from the back to the front burner. Political leaders and opposition groups from as far away as Belarus, South Korea, Turkey, Lebanon, Hungary, Germany, Italy, Spain, United Kingdom, Austria, France, Mexico, and Colombia are calling for the dissolution of national parliaments or new Parliamentary elections.This is madness, but it is real. It is all around us. We see it on a daily basis on television, read about it in the press, and see it with our own eyes. The European Monetary Union has left half of Europe trapped in a depression. Bond markets in the Mediterranean region are at all-time lows. S&P has downgraded Greek, Spanish, French, German, British, American debt to junk, and the country's social fabric is unraveling as the pain begins.

The Spanish, Portuguese, Italian and Irish, American and Chinese governments are balking at paying their short-term debt, putting at risk the solvency of the world's financial system. Most of Europe is being bailed out, its citizens prohibited from withdrawing savings in a desperate effort by the European Union to stave off collapse. A great ring of EU states stretching from Eastern Europe down across Mare Nostrum to the Celtic fringe are either in a 1930's depression already, or soon will be. Each state is a victim of ill-advised economic policies foisted upon them by elites committed to Europe's monetary project – either in the European Monetary Union or preparing to join – the states are trapped.

However, the economic aspect of it is just one area. This is as much about geography as it is about politics. A new order is being created where geography and money are proving to be the ultimate trump cards: geography becomes the governing economic decision-making factor.

Geography is giving us our first major political tectonic fault line. From the Baltic south, through Greece, into Turkey, then fanning out across the Middle East. This is the new frontier of soon-to-be flaming unrest. A snake eating its own tail for nutrition. It is the way money works … for now. The scope of the crisis, as we are discovering, is simply beyond one's comprehension. Our collective impotence to address an entirely new conceptual set of nation-threatening issues runs the risk of being seen for what it is – trying to fix the unfixable.

Knives are coming out, and points of no return are fast approaching. If our situation goes much further, we will soon know whether the United States and the rest of the world lives or dies. Moreover, we will know whether a civilized society is an option or an untenable dream. If it is not, then the barbarians at the gates will come, and they will bring with them mighty appetites.

First stage: Systemic breakdown that will cripple the economy. The world economy comes to a screeching halt. No welfare checks, no Social Security, no health care benefits, no food stamps for the poor, and no money to pay the millions of government employees.

Panics would, within a few days, drive prices significantly skyward. And as supplies no longer meet demand, the market will become paralyzed by prices too high for the wheels of commerce and even daily living. The trucks will no longer pull into food stores. Hoarding and uncertainty would trigger outages, violence, and chaos. Police and military will be able to maintain order for only a short time, if at all. The damage that several days' shortage and outage will do could soon wreak permanent havoc that starts with companies and consumers not paying their bills and employees not going to work. This would be the second stage.

The poor will be the first to suffer, and they will suffer the most. They will be the first to die. Death of hundreds of millions. That's the final stage. It is excruciatingly painful to get one's mind to accept this reality, but Mother Nature does not grant many time-outs.

The problem is, humanity has no Plan B, and it is now also too late to come up with a Plan C or Plan D. Cultural progress is what brings light out of darkness, civilization out of disorder, prosperity out of poverty. All of these essentials are being challenged and threatened. Wars, famine, disease, droughts, social unrest, depleting natural resources. How often have we chased the dream of progress only to see that dream perverted? Technology offers us strength, but strength enables dominance, and dominance paves the way for abuse.

Technological advancements are not the end of the world, merely seeds for change and change never comes without pain. It's in our nature to want to rise above our limits. Every time we have met an obstacle, we've used creativity and ingenuity to overcome it. And isn't achieving a dream, worth it? Society needs laws and regulations to protect it. And if the elite need to work in the shadows, pulling strings to enable us to head in a safe direction, would supporting them be all that bad?

Creation comes from cognition, and cognition is impossible without words that describe each project as spheres within the contours of the universe. Let us begin.

# 1. STRATEGY USA (ALTERNATIVE PRO-TRUMP ELITE)

What strategy would certain American industrialists (the immensely rich circles behind Donald Trump) propose; in other words, strategies focused on preserving the country at the cost of destroying the global economic system in the post-Bretton-Woods world.

In domestic politics, the United States is approaching a civil war, the beginning of which is predicted for 2020-2021. Every 80 years, there is a reload of meanings, principles of management and strategy (1775-1783, 1861-1865, 1941-1945, and, now, 2021-2025).[12] Over a three-cycle period, the United States went from a recalcitrant young colony to a world hegemon – and wants to remain a key player at the table of history. But at present, the dominant paradigm doesn't seem to have the resources nor Grand Ideas/conceptualization; in other words, high specialization is very beneficial in conditions of stability, but extremely dangerous in an era of change and transformation.

"Almost the entire financial elite (young money), bureaucracy, intelligence agencies, military, academics, the press, the artistic elements within our society have achieved success within the framework of the Bretton Woods economic model. All their influence and assets are associated with the financial sector. These people will not be able to maintain their position within the framework of a trans-industrial society; assets are depreciated (who needs derivatives and obligations of bankrupt companies). What is urgently required are managers and specialists of industrial and space programs, not financial-services gurus.

"An even bigger problem, in addition to the devaluation of all previous achievements and assets related to the paper wealth of banking financiers, is the understanding that the transition will be made, in great part, at their expense. "Thus, in the next 20 years, the United States (or whatever they will be called after the second Civil War) is waiting for the construction of a new economy, society, and the acquisition of higher meaning (conceptualization) through the assets of financiers. For the United States to maintain its leading world-power position, it is imperative that during this

---

12    https://nvspb.ru/2015/06/10/19302010-e-istoriya-povtoryaetsya-57922

time, no other hegemon appears in the world. In other words, while there is still strength, influence, and resources, they need to prepare for what's coming."[13]

For, as contradictory as it may seem, the actions of Donald Trump and the elite circles behind him have a clear sequence and logic – foreign and domestic policy is unchanged and, for the most part, successful. Their final goal was surprisingly truthful: "Make America Great Again." Can this goal be achieved without the destruction of the financial sector? No, it can't. Is it possible to turn yesterday's elite into a "nothing burger" without considerable bloodshed? Also, absolutely not possible. Paradoxical as it may seem, the civil war in America is beneficial to the elites behind Trump and strategically beneficial to America. Let me explain.

## National policy

One gets the impression that Trump's actions are aimed at tightening the contradictions – on his part, there are practically no attempts at rapprochement or compromise; he is ready to bide his time. Preparations for an active confrontation are underway, and the only question remaining to be answered is when, and what excuse will be used to start the civil war. Paraphrasing geostrategist Andrei Shkolinikov, this is one of the scenarios providing casus belli at a specific time.

Step 1. Let's suppose, Trump wins the 2020 elections.[14] Liberal financiers have decided to play their only card: global market collapse (according to the scenario of the beginning of the Great Depression of 1929). In response to the collapse, Donald Trump accuses the democrats of everything under the sun and urgently imposes temporary restrictions via executive order, equivalent to the repealed Glass-Steagall law, to combat the crisis. In parallel, the process of returning permanent restrictions through Congress is being launched.

Step 2. In a wave of mass bankruptcies of investment banks and financial corporations, countless paper millionaires and billionaires become instantly impoverished. Supporters of financiers begin to dispute and demand the lifting of restrictions, as abuse of authority, raise a new wave with demands for impeachment for everything Trump has done or might do, at once.

In response, the Trump Administration reveals the results and details of investigations against individual heads of the intelligence agencies, the

13    Сергей Переслегин: «Апокалипсис – это необходимая часть развития мира», 15/11/2015Подробнее на «БИЗНЕС Online»: https://www.business-gazeta.ru/article/145484
14    As a point of reference, my publisher received this manuscript in early January 2020

leadership of the Democratic Party, and the previous Administration regarding violations of laws, corruption and commonplace criminality. Formal accusations are brought before the previously eligible members of the elite; high-ranking democrats are placed under arrest.

Step 3. A wave of multi-millions in protest demonstrations sweeps through the largest cities of America; representatives of Hollywood, Silicon Valley, the media, and Wall St. stand out amongst the crowd. The Republican states (territorially most of the country), on the contrary, back Trump's proposals.

Step 4. Individual states begin to adopt unconstitutional acts aimed at disobeying the White House. The Supreme Court, controlled by conservatives, supports the President, causing even more hysteria. Democratic crowds led by Hollywood actors, politicians, and media representatives across the country demand "popular impeachment." Pro-Trump conservatives are ready to hang liberals on poles.

Step 5. A large number of weapons in the hands of the population (360 million guns in America) lead to victims on both sides. Troops are brought into the cities; the death toll climbs to thousands. The country is plunged into complete chaos.

Step 6. States controlled by financiers (mostly democratic enclaves on the East and West Coast) impose martial law, refuse to obey the White House, and organize parallel government bodies. Part of the army, navy, and intelligence agencies are moving to their side. As a result, an almost complete destruction of the financial sector and services; falling living standards; loss of some territories (Alaska, Texas); a significant part of the losers escape to Canada (in the future, the USA will absorb Canada into a Greater North America). Others flee to Latin America. The USA discards the weight of the past cycle and begins a new cycle – space development, additive technologies, etc. That said, the United States cannot start a period of internal transformations without ensuring external security. The danger? Over the next 15-20 years, a new global hegemon might appear that can prevent the revival of the USA.

## 2. EUROPE'S STRATEGY

What is Europe's "winning strategies" in the coming years? The focus is on the conservative forces of Europe. "Their task is to save and preserve European civilization, no matter what. With a high degree of probability, they won't have the time to do anything, but that said, Europe should never be underestimated. On the continent, there are still relics of previous eras and traditions that, with due attention, can turn into seeds and give healthy shoots.

"If, for the conservative elites of the United States, the strategy was the key element of their survival, then their European counterparts, whose current situation is untenable, at least short-term, will need to focus on survival strategy and internal restructuring.

"What is today's Europe? Its meanings and ideas are fully exhausted, the cultural code non-existent – a combination of the effects of birth control, social change, political progress, and economic necessity has produced a tipping point."[15] In other words, the bio-social system has lost basic instincts and is not capable of reproduction. The attempt to integrate urban neo-barbarians failed – the newcomers from Africa and the Middle East were not ready for anything constructive. If existing trends continue, then in the coming years, Europe will be thrust back to the Dark Ages (the period shortly after the collapse of the Roman Empire).

Thus, the crisis is evident and seems inevitable, but the question arises – can Europe manage the crisis? After all, people have learned how to manage individual crises, a collective crisis, crisis of a small country. So why not take another step – to learn how to manage crises at the level of peoples/ethnic groups and super-ethnic groups?

# Image of Europe of the Future

Today, the construction of Europe on liberal principles is no longer a tenable option. Some European regions can still maintain liberal principles (peoples of the sea, northern countries), but the continent as a whole will only be able to reassemble itself based on conservative principles. Ideologically, we are looking at competition between the left - communist idea and the right - nationalist. In the history of Europe, there existed an interesting plan for the preservation of European culture and meanings – the Roman Empire or, as its main fragment was later called – Byzantium; a kind of reserve, repository and museum, where peace was respected while the rest of the continent was bathed in blood and chaos. "There was only one strategic problem – Byzantium had no concept of the future; it lived in the past. But this is the second stage of the problem. Between death, and stagnation with unclear prospects, stagnation is better; biding your time to find a better way.

"Thus, for Europe to survive, it is imperative to create a New Byzantium, where Vienna will play the role of old Constantinople. Who will

---

15      https://www.youtube.com/watch?v=2HIEXKUszQU, Studio Aurora, 22/02/2020

become a part of the New Core of Europe? Those who have at least some passionality, traditional values, and readiness to fight."[16] These are:

> Group 1: Austrians, Hungarians, Serbs, and Croats; East Germans; Czechs, Slovenes; Bavarians, Northern Italians. The Poles are destined for the role of the counter-nucleus, a sort of a perpetual contrarian. Over the past few decades, Britain has played this role in the EU.

> Group 2: Scandinavia, Holland, and several other maritime powers will maintain liberal values and will build the New Hanseatic League. Britain will partly enter New Hansa, partly try to revive its empire – but that's another story.

> Group 3: The rest of the European countries will become peripherals, no man's territories that will gradually be reconquered by forward-looking nations. The empire will try to defend itself against external barbarians at the expense of barbarians who settled inside its borders earlier. The last time this happened, they were only able to delay the destruction (Rome was destroyed, Italy depopulated, imperial regalia sent to Constantinople). One hopes that perhaps this time, it will start a new European cycle without the Dark centuries.

# Key Steps

Step 1. Against the backdrop of a worsening economic crisis and falling social standards of living, the level of fear, and a feeling of lack of comfort among the population are growing. A new military agreement is concluded in Vienna on the formation of a pan-European force (the Vienna Treaty). Headquarters and controls are located here. Military units are formed according to the territorial-national principle.

Step 2. There is active sabotage of existing European Union mechanisms. The Visegrad group acts as a brake on all undertakings, and centripetal tendencies are actively supported. Gradually, in almost all continental countries, conservative forces come to power, and thorough cleansing of national liberal bureaucratic structures begins.

"Camps are created for refugees and migrants outside the EU – vast spaces to accommodate extraterritorial refugee towns. North Africa, Turkey, Ukraine, etc. The external borders are not guarded; if you want to, leave. These are slums with free food. All new refugees are sent to these towns, and they are no longer allowed to enter the EU."[17]

---

16      https://www.youtube.com/watch?v=2HlEXKUszQU, Studio Aurora, 22/02/2020
17      https://www.youtube.com/watch?v=2HlEXKUszQU, Studio Aurora

Step 3. The complete paralysis of pan-European institutions – the refusal of national governments to obey, the veto on everything, the threat of a massive exit from the EU, etc. Events are gaining momentum under the pressure of another wave of migrants from the Middle East, Turkey, Africa. Migrants cause a new wave of violence in cities and paralysis of the governance system in a number of the most developed countries, due to the inability to give an adequate response to terror.

Step 4. Overcoming the Great schism: the restoration of the Eucharistic communion of Rome and the Eastern churches. "Under the slogan of "returning to tradition," the Catholic Church rejects almost all liberal innovations and accepts the Creed of the Orthodox Church. "Two rites – one faith." Only the weight, significance, and resources of the Vatican are incommensurable with the rest of the churches.

"The process of unification of dioceses and the unification of peoples separated by faith (the process meant to last several generations) is launched. Both churches return to the principles of non-money-grubbing – gaining moral authority, which is especially important in times of crisis. The policy of Brussels (European Union) over the past decades is condemned as anathema, as it destroyed European culture – the Church enters into a fierce open confrontation with EU governance structures."[18]

Step 5. The dissolution of the EU.[19] While maintaining the "Vienna Treaty" for the countries of the New Core (unified command), at this point, most of the military units are from/on the territory of the former Austria-Hungary. Almost all of Europe's old money and aristocratic families (Guelph aristocracy) find themselves on the territory of the New Core or in the immediate vicinity.

Step 6. In the countries of the New Core, a severe anti-migrant sweeping operation begins. It consists of:

> 1. Cancellation of all social benefits for those who have not worked for more than three years and who have no disability (locals can go into the army or police; this route is closed for migrants);

> 2. In response to the wave of crimes (no free money, no income), the principle of "zero tolerance" to crimes is adopted (maximum sentence, expedited trial, use of weapons during detention, the death penalty, etc.);

---

18    https://www.youtube.com/watch?v=2HlEXKUszQU, Studio Aurora

19    "The End of Europe: Dictators, Demagogues, and the Coming Dark Age," James Kirchick, *Foreign Affairs Magazine*, May/June 2017, https://www.foreignaffairs.com/reviews/capsule-review/2017-04-14/end-europe-dictators-demagogues-and-coming-dark-age

3. Introduction of troops into the cities to restore order (almost all military personnel appear on the territory of the New Core and consist of the local indigenous population);

4. Loss of citizenship for any criminal offenses by a court decision and eviction of refugees outside the boundary of the former EU;

5. Forcing out disloyal populations from the countries of the New Core.

Against the background of this struggle (the image of the enemy is crystal clear), poverty and fear, the establishment of "National Communist" regimes is everywhere. Restriction of property rights (property is sacred, only, for the time being, used for the good of society), new principles of social justice, etc.[20]

Step 7. Local wars and redistribution of borders are gaining momentum. The fundamental principle is "blood, soil, history" – a maxim of Black International (colours red and black). The genocide of Albanians, Bosnians, Turks, Arabs, etc. begins. A mass eviction of peoples is launched to prevent future conflicts. At the same time, chaos in the countries on the periphery is taking place – all dissatisfied are evicted. There are practically no combat forces in the countries of the perimeter. They have no money and no weapons.

Step 8. The political union of the countries of the New Core. It is based on the principles of peaceful and respectful coexistence of all indigenous peoples, but a complete ban on national autonomy and identity for all visitors. The rejection of a national/religious tradition is tantamount to a rejection of the future in the state. There is a copying of the principles of Israel as a state of the Jewish people.

Step 9. The cleansing/integration of European countries of the new periphery begins with the eviction of non-indigenous and disloyal populations (liberals, renegades, and parasites). All these events are accompanied by processes of ethnogenesis - the emergence of new peoples.

# Foreign Policy

The most crucial external risk for Europe is Russia, which plans to take Eastern Europe for itself (without which, the whole strategy is not feasible). At the same time, Russia has retained stronger imperial and conservative traditions than the peoples of the New Core.

"As part of the conservative strategy, one part of the European elites (linked to the Vatican) will have a separate line – that Moscow should become the new Constantinople, and Russian right-conservative circles will actively contribute to this. But for Russia, this is a strategic loss – the "Byzantine trap," the rejection of development, etc. Revived Austria-Hungary is attractive to Russia as one of the regions of the new Eurasian state, without any burden in the form of the ruins of Western Europe and the Vatican with Guelph elites. In other words, the revival of Russia should take place at the expense of the future of Europe, and not vice versa.

"This is the best-case constructive strategy scenario for Europe. Does Europe have the necessary time to implement it? After all, the gap between the present time and the beginning of the Dark Ages is too small, the level of passion and energy among European peoples is too low. The most important thing is not to repeat the fate of Byzantium, which preserved the European heritage and culture, but died, having received a stab in the back and betrayal instead of gratitude and help."[21]

## 3. STRATEGY FOR THE RIGHT-WING LIBERALS/GLOBALISTS

This section describes the strategy of the right-wing globalist forces, also called the financial international (Finintern). I'll remind you again that this is not about the forecast, but about the strategy, i.e., how these elite circles see their way to victory at the global gaming table, and what they will do to achieve it.

*****

In the 1970s, the Western world finally came under the control of financiers implementing the right global project, which was embraced by all elite groups – capitalist, old aristocratic elites, etc. After 1991, with the collapse of the Soviet alternative socialist project, the territories of the former Soviet bloc passed under the control of the financiers. According to futurist Sergei Pereslegin, right-wing globalists have achieved the goal and began to build their new world order, the world of the "end of history." This was based on four pillars of power:

1. Armed forces (resource for the Ares war);

2. International law (a resource for the wars of Ares and Athens);

3. Bretton Woods financial and economic system (resource for the Athens war);

4. Information and psychohistory - the media, IT, the "dream factory" (a resource for the Apollo war).

The introduction of the right global project is clear – control over the world where state bodies of metropolises/neo-empires become corporations, in what is known as One World Company Ltd. This concept was developed for the first time in 1968 at the Bilderberg conference in Mont Tremblant, Quebec, Canada.

But, then, in 2008-2009, the system suddenly broke down, and by 2012 it became clear that nobody knew how to fix it. What were Finintern's Strategic miscalculations?

1. Key elements of the control system (armed forces, financial centers, and institutions, information control functions, etc.) have not been taken away from the control of the United States[22] and have not been broken up into thousands of pieces;

2. The increase in the costs of world governance turned out to be too high; the world turned out to be a very complicated place, and the simplification, the unification of the world went extremely slowly;

# Strategic Options (methods of reaching objectives)

According to geostrategist Andrei Shkolinikov, "the key to the implementation of the right global project is the change of elite leadership. IT-employees are replacing financiers. The application of the strategy will move in the following direction:

1. Creation of a new information-digital society and network management systems (existing financiers' operations are in deep crisis);

2. Preparation of the scenario "Overload" (last chance) for the degradation of civilization and the destruction of traditional and archaic elements.

"The allies of financiers, in addition to investment banks and financial corporations themselves, are the liberal elites of the United States (not only those affiliated with the Democratic Party but also from the Republican Party), the EU leadership, Saudi Arabia, some Jewish elites, the IT industry (Silicon Valley), Hollywood, and the world media.

"Opponents of financiers (they do not have to be allies among themselves) are the US conservatives (capitalist project), the conservative

---

22      The bankers and financiers tried to take the issue of global currency out of US hands and into the hands of what was expected to become the 'central bank of central banks'. It would be a supranational institution that would have the exclusive right to print the global currency during the financial crisis. The US dollar would remain a national currency, and its issue would be limited to the amounts set by the 'central bank of central banks'. At the G8 and the G20 meetings at the time, it was decided to set it up under the IMF, and debates of shares, purely technical deliberations, were already underway. But then came the Strauss-Kahn scandal, and the theme disappeared from the media and internal correspondence between national leaders. The US did not let the issue of the global currency slip out of their hands.

elites of the BRICS countries, the conservative forces of Europe (the Vatican, Guelph elites), Britain, left globalists, network structures."[23]

# Modus Operandi of the Financiers (Strategy 1)

We are talking about a suicide attack to destroy and defragment the world. For the liberal elite to prevail, the United States, as a singular force, must be destroyed, and the valuable elements of command and control spread around the world. Again, for the liberals to succeed, Armed Forces, Silicon Valley, Hollywood, media, etc. cannot be controlled by the structure of US isolationist/industrialist leadership. A similar policy applies to other nation-states and empires.

Step 1. The provocation of wars and conflicts throughout the world. Any resources and actions are acceptable for the sake of regaining control of the White House and the Federal Reserve. We can talk about the physical destruction of members of other elite groups. Finding an excuse for *force majeure* to write off debts of the global financial system.

Step 2. Transfer of the IT industry to India (caste system, as an image of the future for all humankind). "The transfer of Hollywood to New Zealand, the institutions of the Bretton Woods system to the EU and China. The launch of the Central Bank of Central Banks project (today's Bank of International Settlement, BIS) with the final desperate intent to wrestle control of the USD from the United States."[24]

Development of the technology of "big data," social ranking, control, etc. All that makes up an "electronic concentration camp." Development of principles and launch of pilot projects of network management instead of the state-bureaucracy.

The launch of global Internet access, bypassing state regulation – mini-satellites, almost-free communicators with access to the network – every peasant has the right to read and watch the "correct" (to brainwash and dumb down the population) information.

Step 3. The provocation of internal conflict in the United States, the outbreak of terror, ideally, all this combined with an armed conflict with China in the South China Sea. For the liberal elite to survive, first order of business is to dismantle the United States (controlled today by the industrialists with Trump as the face of the project).

The military conflict between the USA and China will lead to the cessation of maritime trade for the latter, which will entail a collapse of the

---

23      https://www.youtube.com/watch?v=B47AxC6Mx3g

24      A geostrategic vision of the future of the world and of Russia, Andrei Shkolinikov, Politizdat Publishing, p.294, ISSN: 0869-4435, 2019

export-oriented economy, which depends on imported raw materials, an internal social explosion and military defeat – China also needs to be divided into several smaller territories.

Step 4. Interception of cash flows from drug trafficking to states and "privatization" of intelligence agencies (CIA, Mossad and MI-6 control most of the global drug trade).

Step 5. Implementation of the economy of efficient consumption, i.e., consumption remains one of the pillars, but regulation with the help of social indices appears, i.e., behavior management. The transition from money to barter chains – for specific purchases/sales, liabilities/bills are generated (the same blockchain technology), couples are selected for exchange (a rough example: multi-component alternative transactions in the real estate market), the processes grow until there is a closure (all recorded using blockchain).

"Global control is ensured by control over the mechanisms of generating exchange chains and the information environment. Thus, the degree of danger of the actions of "programmers" should not be underestimated, their actions can completely change humanity and not for the better – a caste society plus mind control; from the point of view of Christianity... we are staring Satanism in the face. And, let's not forget about transhumanism, it will bloom here in full color and all its brightly toxic variety."[25]

# 4. ISLAMIC WORLD STRATEGY

In recent decades, the Islamic world has played the role of a junior partner to other global forces, allowing itself to be used as a cover and a bargaining chip. But will the project agree to remain on the sidelines in the future, or will it try to achieve victory at the round table of global projects? This text contains the "victory strategy" of the Islamic world, and it is by no means a forecast.

*****

For a Christian, the understanding of Islam is initially tricky, since a conceptual apparatus is needed that contains a unified religious, economic, social, and cultural meaning. Strategic problems of the Islamic world can be summed up in the following way:

The absence of a single spiritual center, capable of speaking for the majority of the Islamic world. No single religious structure recognizes more

25    A geostrategic vision of the future of the world and of Russia, Andrei Shkolinikov, Politizdat Publishing, p.318, ISSN: 0869-4435, 2019

than 20% of the Ummah. There are several competing political centers, reflecting the degree of contradiction between them:

1. Crisis of traditional Islam;

2. Erosion of forms of national identity in the framework of aggressive globalization and radicalization;

3. A large number of counter and anti-systemic projects within the Islamic world.

Existing trends (the most probable development of events) are more likely to lead to the following changes:

1. The fall of the Saudi regime – for almost all external and internal players this is beneficial;

2. The transition of Iran and Malaysia/Indonesia to the sixth technological paradigm, as elements of its periphery, and as a result, a significant change in their self-identification;

3. Economic and managerial integration of Pakistan and a large part of Afghanistan back to Greater India;

4. Degradation and collapse of state structures of other Muslim countries;

5. Acting out the ideas of pan-Arabism; degradation of Islamic banking; the collapse of Islamic network structures.[26]

An essential problem of the Islamic world is the religious rift; the most promising political center, Shiite Iran, is less than 20% of Shiite Muslims. It cannot be recognized as the existing Sunni world, but the direct conflict of the Persians with the Arab countries or Turkey will be tragic for the latter.

For many years, Saudi Arabia acted as the unofficial spokesman of the Islamic world, which was included in the world elite along with the Finintern and the Western capitalist elites. Still, the time of the Saudis is ending, Islam needs a new leader. There are several options:

# Leadership Transition to Turkey

"One of the prevailing ideas about the prospects of the Islamic project is the generally accepted opinion of high chances for the future success of Turkey, be it the new Ottoman Empire, the Turkic Kaganate, or the Islamic Caliphate. I do not agree, since the complexity and

---

26    A geostrategic vision of the future of the world and of Russia, Andrei Shkolinikov, Politizdat Publishing, p.34, ISSN: 0869-4435, 2019

scale of the tasks facing Erdogan and/or his successors are many times harder than the tasks facing Russia. Let me give you an example:

"Imagine, the Bolsheviks lost the Civil War in Russia, all the tributaries except the indigenous European territories were torn off from Russia's control. For several decades, the country worked diligently destroying cultural and national diversity, "convincing" the Volga peoples and Ukrainians that they were, in fact, descendants of nomadic Russians speaking unknown languages (as Kurdish was often denoted in Turkey). After a century, this national Russia suddenly declares that it plans to revive past greatness. Three competing principles of integration are advanced: pan-Slavism, the revival of the empire in its old borders, and messianism ("Moscow, the Third Rome," we are the leaders of the Christian world).

"Today, Turkey, vying for supremacy and leadership of the Islamic world, comes up with three conflicting projects – pan-Turkism, neo-Ottomanism, and pan-Islamism. The problems with this scenario are, neighboring nations do not see the Turks at all as an older brother, historical memory, unclear prospects, and the integration of national elites into other blocks and structures create a gap between dreams and reality.

"Thus, the strategy of Turkey as the leader of the Islamic project does not have long-term prospects in the real world; you need a "Miracle" with a capital letter or a sharp change in the rules of the geopolitical game. A special piquancy of the situation is given by the need for Turkey to play all-in, since almost any loss or passive position will lead to disorganization and disintegration of the country."[27]

In the aftermath of WWI, Turkey firmly established itself within the framework of the "Western" global project. Moreover, at the first stage, in the form of an absolutely impoverished appendage (in the 1970s, Bulgaria's industry was more extensive than that of Turkey and Greece combined). With the beginning of "Reaganomics" in 1981 (that is, a sharp increase in corporate control in the USA and other countries of the "golden billion," or, in other words, developed Western countries), Turkey gained the right to enter the fast-growing EU market and began to sharply increase its economic potential.

From the point of view of control over the infrastructure created in Turkey and which allowed it entry to the EU market, it was carried out by the elite of the "Western" global project, that is, by the financiers. The fact that Turkey was a member of NATO, that is, a project managed at the

27      A geostrategic vision of the future of the world and of Russia, Andrei Shkolinikov, Politizdat Publishing, p.115-116, ISSN: 0869-4435, 2019

national (USA) level, did not play a unique role since the US leadership was also under the ideological control of financiers.

The situation began to change drastically[28] after it became apparent that Turkey would not be accepted into the European Union.[29] Since it became obvious to everyone that in the event of serious economic problems, the EU will simply close off its markets to external participants (and even if that was not the case, then, all the same, Turkey couldn't compete with China). At that moment, a serious question arose of what to do next. Since the crisis was looming on the horizon, and no one wanted to see it, Turkey began to gradually build its own regional project[30] that did not contradict the general principles of the "Western" project: either the new Ottoman Empire (that is, trying to control the markets of Islamic countries), or "the great Turan," that is, trying to unite the Turkic speaking countries under the guidance of Turkey.

Truth be told, "neither the oil sheiks nor the leaders of political Islam liked either one of the ideas. The Turkic nations weren't particularly excited about the Union with their former Big Brother and protector (they had developed their own regional alliances and hoping for a future union of questionable benefits wasn't in their cards). But then a crisis struck; and it became clear that something had to be done quickly. And suddenly, the ideas of the Eurasian unification turned out to be stronger and more attractive than the Turkic union, and political Islam began to play such games that the question arose, not how to build it in itself, but how to make sure that in the process it didn't destroy Turkey itself. And the ever-pragmatic Erdogan began to change the concept and instead of his own project decided to join one that has clearly started to take on real contours."[31]

At this point, another interesting event occurred: Trump's victory in the US presidential election. As I explained in my previous book, *In the Shadows of a Presidency*, Trump represents not the "Western" liberal-financier project, but the capitalist global project, another fascinating contradiction arose: the trade and foreign economic infrastructure of Turkey and its lobbyists are pulled in one direction, and Trump with the NATO infrastructure in the other!

Moreover, they aggressively attack each other. In any case, Turkey's internal problems only worsen as a result (since the support of these struc-

---

28      Options for the  EU-Turkey relationship, Marc Pierini, Carnegie Europe, 03/05/2019 https://carnegieeurope.eu/2019/05/03/options-for-eu-turkey-relationship-pub-79061
29      https://carnegieeurope.eu/2019/11/07/can-turkey-s-prickly-relationship-with-eu-be-repaired-pub-80296
30      https://www.brookings.edu/project/the-turkey-project/
31      A geostrategic vision of the future of the world and of Russia, Andrei Shkolinikov, Politizdat Publishing, p.127, ISSN: 0869-4435, 2019

tures in the Turkish elite is quite significant, it was they who shaped its policy for decades).

Erdogan has three choices in this situation:

- Bet on the "Western" project (with preservation, if only for a while, of EU markets and conflict with NATO and Trump);

- Bet on the Capitalist Project with Trump (with the inevitable and relatively quick loss of EU markets and, in general, the absence of a clear economic perspective);

- Or bet on the Eurasian Project, in conflict with both Brussels (NATO alliance) and Trump. Perhaps the unlikeliest option we need to consider is Turkey joining China's Silk Road. It is noteworthy that the New Silk Road is not so much a transport corridor connecting China with Europe, but an economic development zone under the protection of China with a guaranteed return on investment in USD. Under this project, with a capital investment capacity of up to $8 trillion in 2015, the Asian Infrastructure Investment Bank (AIIB) was established. It is quite obvious that during the crisis of the world credit and financial system based on the US petrodollar, the Chinese project of the New Silk Road Economic Belt and the 21$^{st}$ Century Sea Silk Road, act as a way of geopolitical demarcation of land globalization led by China and globalization of the sea, led by the United States. With the transition of world leadership from the American cycle of capital accumulation to the Chinese cycle without collapsing markets (without the collapse of the dollar).

Today, 16 countries belong to the Economic Belt of the New Silk Road, 12 of which belong to the World of Islam. Both the economic belt and the sea route must pass through the zone of interests of Turkey. "Historically, Turkey has always been a "buffer" of the Silk Road, because neither the Ottoman state nor the Seljuk Turks were members of the family of nations of Genghis Khan, neither during the time of Ilkhan Khulagu, nor later under the control of the Silk Road by Timur. Today, Turkey claims to have a special place in the capital of the Economic Belt and a special role in ensuring the safety of the belt and path.

"It is essential that the current leadership of Turkey, step by step, carries out the Islamization of the secular state of Kemal Ataturk,[32] intending to recreate the red Turkish Caliphate sufi tarikati. And the President of the Republic of Turkey Erdogan is the recognized leader of all non-clerical political Islam."[33]

The solution to the issue of restoring the Caliphate under the leadership of the Turks (and the Turkish sultan of the Ottoman Empire was the last caliph of the faithful until 1924) is connected with the succession of the dynasty in the absence of the law on succession to the throne. According to official Turkish documents, with the end of the Ottoman dynasty, rights to titles pass to the dynasty of Crimean khans Gireev.[34] Thus, the peaceful and safe development of the Islamic countries of the New Silk Road Economic Belt requires the restoration of the Caliphate. And the restoration of the Caliphate is impossible without determining the role of Crimea in the project "One Belt, One Road."

When, after the coup in Ukraine, in March 2014, the Republic of Crimea returned as the subject of the Russian Federation, the self-governing body of the National Assembly of the Crimean Tatars, the Mejlis, recognized by the Verkhovna Rada of Ukraine, turned out to be outside the legal field of the Russian Federation. Furthermore, the spiritual connection of the Crimean Tatars with Turkey has never been interrupted. And the former (in 2015) Prime Minister of Turkey and the leader of the then-ruling Justice and Development Party, Ahmet Davutoglu, in the roots of the clan, is the Crimean Tatar.

In other words, the Republic of Crimea as part of the Russian Federation has become a place of confrontation:

1) Turkic project of the New Caliphate.

2) Project of the New Crimean Khazaria of Ashkenazi Jews (continuing the Molotov-Lozovsky line for the creation of the Jewish Soviet Socialist Republic of Crimea).

3) Putin's Russian Orthodox project: Sacred Crimea is the site of the baptism of Prince Vladimir, where Chersonesus is as Holy as the Temple Mount in Jerusalem for Jews and Muslims.

Against this historical and political background, on November 22, 2015, Crimean Tatars on the Ukrainian side undermined power lines, which deprives the Republic of Crimea of light and water supply. And on November 24, 2015, by order of Prime Minister Davutoglu, in the sky over Syria, the Turks shot down the Russian front-line bomber Su-24.

---

33      https://www.rand.org/content/dam/rand/pubs/research_reports/RR2200/RR2273/RAND_RR2273.pdf

34      The *Crimean Khanate* was a Turkic state existing from 1441 to 1783, the longest-lived of the Turkic khanates that succeeded the empire of the Golden Horde.

If you do not take into account the interests of control over the exit of the "Belt and Road" from the countries of the World of Islam to the European expanse (and we are talking about control over the eastern part of the Mediterranean Sea from the Suez Canal to the Greek port of Piraeus and, through the Bosphorus Strait, to Crimea and Ukrainian and Georgian ports of the Black Sea) then these events are not connected. But if we take into account the strategic interests of the three political forces fighting for a profitable place within the "one belt, one road" project, then the warning signals sent by the Turkish military and Crimean Tatar must be examined in a different light.

# 5. LATIN AMERICAN STRATEGY

The collapse of the world into pan-regions is becoming more and more apparent, and Latin America has emerged as one of the potential centers of a future global project. For a while, it looked like Brazil, as the most economically powerful and largest state, would play a central role in the formation of a new macro-region, consisting of Iboroamerica, but today's reality doesn't meet these expectations.

Brazilian elites, like any other country in the region, were incapable of building their own subjectivity. As I have stated before, a geopolitical project needs an ideology that is immanent to the population, and in this case, it is leftist and mostly liberal, and the ruling circles, largely due to the age-old pandering to the USA, are strongly right-leaning.

"The Latin American region is mostly unique in its unity and diversity. On the one hand, the integration of language, religion, and history; on the other, many elements of Native American cultures, national states, and a constant search for ethno-cultural identity. A large area and population, even in comparison with a similar Arab world, is characterized by less internal stress. At the same time, unlike Europeans, Latinos are characterized by clanism, they can be considered conservatives only in comparison with the democratic population of the United States (for example, look at the dynamics of the growth of Protestantism among Ibero-Americans). Since the days of Simón Bolivar, Latin America has been moving towards a community of peoples, a mestizo synthesis (as opposed to a melting pot and multi-culturalism), unification with the spirit of freedom, and the unification of Latin America was a prototype of the unification of all mankind.

"Latin America has every chance to raise the fallen banner of left globalists, be it Bolshevik-Leninists or Trotskyists. The left-liberal geopolitical project was strongly marginalized and almost entirely destroyed by the Western (as a left project) and Soviet (as a liberal project) elites. With the reformatting of the world beginning in 1991, the external economic, ideological and military pressure of the world hegemon is declining, and the snake of the evolving Trotskyism from Ernesto Rafael Guevara de la Serna on the banner can again break free with new forces and meanings.

"Attempts to create a geopolitical project in Latin America on a different ideology from the left-liberal ideology are doomed to failure, as they will be inorganic and secondary. If you look at the history of Latin America over the last century, it was either a right-liberal to the left-conservative version, Today attempts to form a right-conservative project will lead to dependence on the Vatican (Black International/continental elites of Europe), which is clearly not the image of the future for an independent geopolitical project.

"Thus, one should not expect any reasonable and productive actions to gain subjectivity from the leadership, most elites and modern political institutions of the countries of Iberoamerica. It is for this reason that I don't have any illusions about Brazil's membership in the BRICS. The elite of the Latin American project is not yet visible, it has not formed in a volume sufficient for self-awareness, but its contour is already quite discernible."[35]

## The Elite of Latin American Project

The final appearance and subjectivity of the elite of the future Latin American left-globalist project will only become possible after the outbreak of civil war in the United States when America's elite will focus inward, and a significant part of the liberals will flee the country. What will the Latin American geopolitical project look like? It will be a grass-root movement, truly leftist, but possessing the necessary military, financial, and ideological resources for victory in the internal struggle. I'll clarify right away that there will be no forces and resources for external conflict for a long time, i.e., without territorial remoteness and weakening of other players, the project in question simply does not stand a chance.

## Structure of the Future Left Global Elite

Left globalists will not need to seize power in different countries and then, unite them; they will create meta-state structures outside of official structures, diverting resources into their own circuits, and turning existing state structures with their outdated institutions into empty, impotent shells.

35    A geostrategic vision of the future of the world and of Russia, Andrei Shkolinikov, Politizdat Publishing, p.275, ISSN: 0869-4435, 2019

As the saying goes, "production forces overtook production relations, which became a brake on development," only the revolution will be of an unusual kind. Yes, there will be a change in real power, names, property, borders –but official authorities are "asleep at the wheel" and can't grasp the dizzying changes around them.

"The basis of the global meta-state, social institutions, and the economy will be network principles; it will be an entirely new type of organization. The key in this system is the automation of processes, strict and generally accepted protocols for the interaction of enterprises, an open network of trading floors. Such management and organization are necessary for the transition to robotization of production, and yes, this is where the question arises – how to occupy and what to do with 95% of the population?

"The organization of the "information society" based on the traditional dictates of right-wing globalists does not lead to development, but to "digital dementia" among the younger generation. The pros and cons of the described system versus classical planning are understandable; everyone can take them apart."[36] Still, for the left-liberal global project, such a management system will be natural – there is no single center, anyone can join (network principles, self-organization), a kind of "conga line-dance principle."

# What Should Be Done

Step 1. Increasing the autonomy of US intelligence agencies (many functions have long been self-sustaining due to drug trafficking), controlled by globalists, in Latin America.

Confronting any unifying initiatives and/or the emergence of influential political leaders in the countries of Iberoamerica – financial problems, growing protest, riots, partisan movement, worsening crime situation, physical extermination of individuals, etc. Influential politicians and political groups should not appear.

Development and launch of prototypes of IT systems in the framework of the Dark Web Internet to service the functions of the criminal world of Columbia and Mexico.

Step 2. After the outbreak of civil war in the USA and the collapse of statehood in a number of European countries, the organization of the resettlement/flight of globalists of leftist views to Latin America. Evacuation of intelligence agencies and parts of Silicon Valley.

---

36      A geostrategic vision of the future of the world and of Russia, Andrei Shkolinikov, Politizdat Publishing, p.311, ISSN: 0869-4435, 2019

Preparation of bases for the evacuation of naval units oriented/controlled by liberals, the latter taking control of the Panama Canal.

Step 3. Actively weakening and undermining the work of state institutions throughout the Continent. Even now, the situation is deplorable – the leaders of drug cartels and partisan/paramilitary detachments (often the same people) at the provincial level are much more respected than the official authorities, and in the conditions of a permanent crisis it will only get worse. Widespread promotion through non-governmental channels of networked open systems for managing and organizing economic processes (see the section above).

## Creation of the Basic Structures of a Meta-State

Step 4. The actual formation and self-awareness of the elite of the left globalists, the emergence of subjectivity; up to this point, there was only one-directional movement of various groups due to the coincidence of interests. This is the weakest point of the strategy; without self-awareness, a global left-liberal project will not be formed. All previous actions were just a long preparation.

Step 5. Elimination of official state structures and institutions from the life of the majority of the population. Transfer of almost all financial flows of the continent to network structures (no financial flows, no taxes, no state power). The capture and subsequent almost complete abolition (they are simply outdated and no longer needed) of the weakened organs of traditional states by network structures. The formation of the combined armed forces to counter other geopolitical projects.

Step 6. The creeping spread of network structures, penetration around the world, into the territory of competing geopolitical projects; a revised and evolved principle of permanent revolution in life.

The beginning of a long exhausting military, economic, and psycho-historical confrontation with the revived United States, which also stepped into the sixth technological paradigm.

## Conclusion

Unlike other geopolitical projects, Latin America has not yet outlined the contours of its future, not to mention the appearance of the subject. Brazil, like any other state in the region, was not able to take a step forward to take responsibility for the combined future of the Continent. What must be done? Wait for the appearance of a left-liberal, globalist project, natural for Iberoamerica. The construction of this project will be orchestrated from the ground up, contrary to the will of the ruling elites.

If a left-globalist project is created, its global significance and influence will be foremost, and the attractiveness for the population is very high since its primary struggle resource is located on the field of psycho-history (the central front of the new era). In the future, the significance of this project for humanity may turn out to be comparable with the communist movement of the 19th and 20th centuries.

Unlike many other projects, left-wing globalists are looking to the future, creating an organic part of the sixth technological paradigm – the trans-industrial economy. The weakest point of the strategy is a complex multi-way combination in the initial stages, even before the appearance of the subject. In this period, external actions can destroy the very possibility of the presence of this geopolitical player, depriving humanity of a crucial development scenario.

"In a multipolar world, the left-globalist project can even act as a permanent ally of Russia. Can a left-liberal path be adopted in Russia? Doubtfully. Russia is a conservative country, so the direct implementation of a left-liberal project will be disastrous for Russia's psychosocial sense. How many people want shocks on the scale of the post-Soviet 1990s?

"Thus, the geopolitical project of Latin America can be exciting and promising, only the window of opportunity for its creation is very narrow – 10 to 15 years maximum; that is until the United States returns to the global round table after the conclusion of its Civil War."[37] What is the main conclusion? A leftist conservative project should be built in Russia and replicated as a counter-balance by a leftist liberal project in Latin America. A left-wing conservative project in Russia should survive to the moment when only three poles of power remain. The second conclusion is that for a long-term perspective, Russia in the world needs a robust Latin America as its counterpole.

# 6. BRITAIN'S STRATEGY

The strategy of Britain is multivariate, but in many ways banal, and what you want is a maritime power that benefits from trade (read robbery) of colonies/partners. The true heiress of Venice, there are no permanent allies, all projects are limited in time, and the world has become too open to rob someone for centuries. Despite this, Britain has

---

37    A geostrategic vision of the future of the world and of Russia, Andrei Shkolinikov, Politizdat Publishing, p.236, ISSN: 0869-4435, 2019

good prospects to become a geopolitical player. This section examines two of London's most apparent and probable strategies – the re-creation of the British Empire and the invasion of barbarians in Europe.

The main question of the British strategy can be formulated rather simply: "Whom to rob?" And depending on the answer to the second question - "For how long?," the strategy becomes short, medium, or long-term. In recent decades, Britain has been limited in its appetites and resources, the result of societal and elite degradation.

Today, Britain is openly moving towards the behavior of the times of Morgan, Drake, East/West Indian companies, and the Opium Wars.

## Current Situation

In recent decades, Britain has been a part of the world elite in a privileged position, which was primarily due to history, the voluntary surrender of the status of great power and the system of reproduction of the elite. Instead of colonial robbery, London has become one of two centers of financial theft. That's just the ongoing breakdown of the world into pan-regions, primarily reflected on the world elite, quarreling among themselves. The resources collected were sorely lacking to maintain the system, and the plans of each member of the privileged club consisted exclusively of salvation at the expense of others. Then, came the schism within the elite circles.

Paraphrasing Shkolinikov, the elite broke up into two ideologically positioned forces – global financiers (Finintern) and the isolationist, industrial elites of the United States. The question is not even the dominant right-wing liberal principles, but the lack of a future for Britain in the conservative camp. What does Britain need to do to be a geopolitical player?

> 1. Ares war: The ground army is traditionally weak, the fleet is a mockery of the status of the mistress of the seas, the dependent defense industry – tight integration with the United States and Europe. All that remains is a small and outdated nuclear arsenal and the cynical ability to fight through proxies;
>
> 2. Athena's war: Britain is a maritime power, at the heart of its economy is trade, the legacy of Venice. All the power of Britain was based on a nonequivalent exchange/robbery of colonies/"partners";
>
> 3. Apollo's war: Besides history, "the white man's burden," myths about aristocracy, and pirate traditions, there is nothing to offer the surrounding nations as far as psycho-historical image is concerned;

4. Passionality: Of course, more than on the continent, yet the system of reproduction of the elites makes itself felt; but still, on a much smaller scale than 200 years ago.

In general, the picture is not very joyful, but unlike the continental countries of Europe, immersed in Arab/African invasion, Britain has several viable options:

1. Elite reproduction system, including willingness to sacrifice oneself;

2. Territorial isolation/natural border with Europe;

3. Willingness to create a pan-region anywhere in the world, as a result of the marine type of power;

4. Acceptance by the whole society of primordial inequality – an estate society; readiness for cruel and cynical actions.

The most important long-term civilizational problem in Britain is the lack of psycho-historical meanings and unifying ideas. Her whole story is based on the creation of short-term unions solely on the principles of economic benefit. By the way, Britain is an excellent example of reliance only on the economy and ignoring the meanings. As long as economic wars were at the forefront, Britain had no equal. As soon as the role of meanings grew, there was a transition from the status of the only superpower to the position of a middle European country, a loss of position, even against the backdrop of formal victories.

To rephrase it, maritime power can afford short-term alliances and betrayals – the whole world is their oyster, whereas the continental world is limited by neighbors; you cannot backstab the entire world and hope to get away with it forever.

# Britain's Options

The choice of the future of Britain is in many ways similar to the choice of Russia; there is no dominant strategy, but there are several strong competing ones. The difference between the islanders is a weak psycho-historical component, but this traditionally does not bother them; treachery, selfishness, and cynicism have long been the hallmark of their politics. It must be said that all the strategies of Britain have an attractor the transfer of the center to New Britain, that is to the Asia-Pacific region. There remains only a related question; who will be robbed for them to achieve this end?

As soon as it became clear in *Perfide* Albion that the world could not be kept in the current configuration, they were the first to react. Spend resources on maintaining a dying system, or try to snatch a piece first? The choice is obvious.

Work in Britain is going on several fronts simultaneously; this is clearly illustrated by the example of the royal family. That's how the blood of the Merovingians now flows in the veins of Saxe-Coburg-Goth (along the lines of Diana Spencer, a Cinderella who just wanted family happiness and love, etc.), King David (without comment), but recently they "discovered," that the Prophet Muhammad was the ancestor of the Queen.[38]

In general, Britain is ready to switch to any development option. Two scenarios have already been discussed within the framework of other strategies. The first is an attempt to preserve global peace after the self-removal of the United States, in alliance with Finintern and China. The second option is a worldwide catastrophe.

We will analyze the remaining strategies in more detail, not forgetting that Britain's midterm task is to form its own pan-region of at least 300, optimally 500 million people.[39] Further, it will be necessary to rob their victims as much as possible, and switch to the sixth technological paradigm for the resources received.

None of the strategies is long-term, one or two generations, and the definition of "friends" needs to be redefined, along the lines of united, robbed, framed, and abandoned. This is what a common scenario of "Anglo-Saxon friendship" looks like.

## Exit to New Britania

When analyzing the strategy of Britain, one should not forget that in spirit, they are not the successors of the Plantagenets, for whom the continent is the center of the world, but the followers of the Vikings, Venetians, and pirates. Life is trade and/or robbery; we live but once.

A possible limitation for Britain is likely climate change, both warming with rising sea levels and crowds of neo-barbarians; and cooling, in the absence of proper infrastructure, is changing the economy and social structure completely.

"All of Britain's development strategies have one thing in common, an attractor to which everything converges – the transfer of the political, administrative, financial, etc. center from Europe to the Asia-Pacific region

---

38      https://www.history.com/news/is-queen-elizabeth-related-to-the-prophet-muhammad
39      https://www.ecfr.eu/article/britains_role_in_the_world_after_brexit_and_the_pandemic

– Australia and New Zealand. Western Europe is becoming too turbulent, the central policy is being transferred to the Pacific Basin, and Australia is more promising for development than a small squeezed and robbed island with a neighboring shelf. Well, it's easier to look for new "friends" there. Why Australia and New Zealand, not Canada? Canada will always be in the shadow of the United States, due to different proportions, and even a civil war in the states will not radically affect this.

"Thus, a significant part received in the framework of a nonequivalent exchange of resources will be directed to the creation of territories of the sixth technological paradigm in Australia and New Zealand. This will be accompanied by the transfer of the political center and the launch of the relocation/exodus of the most valuable population from Europe."[40]

## The Strategy of the New British Empire

This strategy is the most historically sound and straightforward. Based on the revival of the British Empire on the right-liberal principles of Britain, Canada (until the United States or whatever is left of it after the Civil War turns Canada and parts of Northern Mexico into Greater North America), Australia, New Zealand, and Greater India.

Why is an alliance with Britain beneficial to India's caste system? She needs protection and time to start in the 2055-2060 project – transhumanism to create super-Brahmanas, a new kind of people. The role of Britain in this alliance is a trade and management center, military defense. India: the primary production and consumption, Australia: the resource base. The total population will exceed 2 billion people. This is more than enough to create a pan-region, even taking into account the pre-industrial lifestyle of the majority. According to geostrategist Andrei Shkolinikov, Britain would need to devise a plan based on the following steps:

## Territories of Expansion and Cooperation of Britain

Step 1. Economic isolation from continental Europe, European Union institutions, and the USA. Launch of programs to revive the merchant and military fleets, fleet bases. Assistance to Finintern in transferring resources, structures, technologies and assets to overseas Britain from Europe, and the USA. Strengthening ties with Overseas Britain by fortifying the structures of the British Commonwealth.

40    A geostrategic vision of the future of the world and of Russia, Andrei Shkolinikov, Politizdat Publishing, p.236, ISSN: 0869-4435, 2019

Step 2. After the outbreak of the US Civil War and the identification of the winner, providing asylum for the losers, as well as bases for the "escaped" ships. The latter will be the basis of Britain's new supremacy at sea. The conclusion of a union with India, unification into a single state with overseas Britain.

Step 3. Launch of the exodus program to "Overseas Britain" (see above) with the resettlement of the population and the creation of territories of the sixth technological paradigm.

Launch of a mass training program for the highest castes of the Brahman (from the age of six) in England, together with the local elite. In fact, we are talking about the future merger of the British and Indian elites.

Launching the defragmentation of India on a regional basis through infrastructure restructuring. A typical coastal region will look like this: a "port city," roads, pipelines, etc. coming from it, cover only your region and do not intersect with similar systems in neighboring regions. After the degradation of the "unnecessary," previously created end-to-end infrastructure, and this with the proper ability to wait a short time, transport connectivity will go only across the sea. Communication of internal regions through separate transport corridors with the same ports. Involvement in the pan-region of other territories and countries as exploited colonies.

Step 4. Taking control of the principle world trade between the pan-regions, forming military bases on key sea routes. The transformation of India into enclave territory, the promotion of cultural isolation, and internal conflict. The connivance of several local civil wars, up to genocide. The torpedoing of any biological and medical research, development, and production in India.

Thus, this strategy is a repetition of past centuries, and the life of the new Empire, by default, is no more than 30 years. The only option left, is to become one of the centers of the tripolar world and have time to wait for the children brought to power in India; that is, raised as a part of the English elite.

# African Resources

The main task is to take control of the resources and potential of France, Spain, Portugal, the countries of the Greater Maghreb and the Gulf of Guinea. In this scenario, the navy is also of crucial importance, the traditional role of Britain is management, trade, and ... robbery. The controlled part of Europe is turning into the battlefield of Arab and Black Africa for the future.

The transition to the sixth technological paradigm for Europe and Africa is not actionable; there is no intellectual and technological base, the newcomer population is painfully backward and uneducated. Significant resources will go to the outcome in Overseas Britain. The remaining resources will be claimed for:

a) preservation of post-industrial structure in European territory;

b) minimum control of migration flows and restoring order;

c) creation of transport infrastructure focused on export through seaports;

d) robbery of African territories.

The military wager will be made on the ordinary non-Muslim black population of the Gulf of Guinea, with white officers and sergeants from Europe. We have seen this model before in British colonial India.

Step 1. Obtaining and strengthening informal control over the countries of Western Europe in alliance with the United States. Liquidation of European Union structures as a stronghold of liberals, together with the liberal financier USA (anti-industrialist group) and continental elites.

The formation of the land colonial-police forces from the population of the former African colonies (Gulf of Guinea), mainly non-Muslims. The merger into unified government with overseas Britain.

Step 2. Organization/ provocation/ non-resistance of a wave of aggressive and warlike neo-barbarians to Europe, primarily from the Arab countries. The motive: from massive hunger due to climate change, wars and economic hardships. The goal is the maximum dismantling of statehood on the Old Continent.

The fleet creation policy is similar for all strategies of launching construction and providing a base for the losers in the US civil war.

Step 3. The entry of colonial-police troops into Europe, the cleansing of territories from Arabs under the slogans of protecting the local population. Capturing the maximum area, delimiting zones of influence with the continental elites of Europe. The announcement of protectorates and the establishment of their own authorities in Europe.

Step 4. Gradual capture of the territories of the Greater Maghreb and the Gulf of Guinea using support bases and colonial armies. Launch of the exodus to Overseas Britain (see above). It's impossible to stay in Europe – whoever doesn't leave, after half a generation, will dissolve in the new population, and it's okay if they are at least black or brown *Christians*.

Otherwise, the great monuments, cathedrals, museums, and other relics of the European religious heritage will be turned to dust.

Step 5. Formation of coastal enclave cities in controlled territories. Suppression of non-Anglo-European cultures and languages in controlled territories. Integration of the white population into the English ethnos, with relocation to Overseas Britain. The transfer of the capital to the Pacific Ocean.

Thus, at the exit, we get the outcome of Britain to the Pacific basin, the complete barbarization of Western Europe, and the pitting of Arabs against black Africans. All this is done to facilitate the robbery and export of resources.

Why not start an "exodus" without an accompanying mess? Because Western Europe alone is not enough to create a pan-region, and they won't voluntarily go to London. There is no logic in pitting a few Arabs or Negroes against each other, London needs a conflict that can be controlled. How else to "persuade" all these people, most of whom live in the pre-industrial world, to share resources with Britain?

# Conclusion

The ongoing collapse of the global economy, like any crisis, leads to an intensification of deep, archetypal reactions. Most managed to forget that under the veneer of correctness, the City of London hides the temper of the Venetians, pirates, and employees of East/West Indian companies. If it were not for the British educational system, this would not have happened, but, in a zero-sum game ... any gain is a loss, any loss is a gain. The key questions as far as British strategy is concerned, who we rob, and for how long. The deeper the archaization of the world goes, the stronger British positions become.

The destruction of the world elite has opened many paths to the *Perfide* Albion. Almost all of these strategies do not exceed one and a half generations. Britain does not have the necessary army and navy; traditionally, there are no psycho-historical meanings, but this is not a condemnation at all.

Almost all strategies contain the key element – the transfer of the center of gravity to the newly created "Overseas Britain" (Australia, New Zealand) and the creation of the sixth technological paradigm economy there. Everything else is aimed at solving secondary issues – whom we will rob/who is going to be our temporary "friend"/patsy.

The New British Empire and African Retribution strategies address the issue of sacrifice in different ways. However, in both cases, Britain becomes a natural adversary of Latin America, which I will discuss later.

# 7. Global Project USSR-2

Amongst a myriad near-term projects involving Russia, the most likely scenario is Global Project USSR-2. The new Soviet project (Putin openly referred to it in his December 2019 international press conference) will be fundamentally different from the original version, as it should be built on a dialectical contradiction with the post-industrial society, which will try to build the "Third Rome" (affinity to Vatican and European elite), and not on returning to the industrial Soviet Union. Following the results of recent decades (1989-2019), today, Russia needs a radical modernization of the social, political, and technocratic spheres in the post-liberal, Western consumer-oriented society. To become a geopolitical player, the USSR-2 must:

1. Possess a strong army (Ares war);

2. Become a self-sufficient large economy, i.e., a population of at least 300, preferably more than 500 million people (Athens war);

3. Have strong and stable internal values (Apollo war).

With the Ares war, everything is clear – the need to develop the existing armed forces. On the second point, it is also clear – the revival of the economy, the "integration" of the surrounding territories. However, with the third point we walk into a minefield because the primary loss of the Soviet Union was precisely in the area of psycho-history.

"The issue of ideology of meanings is very critical. Built on the principles of Eurocentrism and Protestant work ethic, Marxism was not sufficiently stable in the fight against capitalism. Success in the "Russian world" requires the integration of spiritual and moral Orthodox foundations, with the cleansing of the latter from ecumenism (the influence of the Vatican), money-grubbing, and a separate rethinking (assessment of the opposition red-white, monarchism, etc.). This is a prerequisite for separation and delimitation with a much more powerful geopolitical project in terms of economics – China.

"The Soviet Union lost the war of meanings, the "new man" never appeared, "mine" became higher than "ours," but it should be the other way around. In addition to strengthening the spiritual and moral influence of the Orthodoxy, supra-economic higher goals for society and the ideas of messianism are necessary."[41]

---

41       https://www.youtube.com/watch?v=-6vE86hcMJM

USSR-2 carries another important construct: the revival of ideological control and the limitations of political activity. The priorities of these policies should be:

1. Isolation and strengthening of economic independence;

2. Transition to post-capitalist relations;

3. Integration of new territories into a single system (destruction of internal borders);

4. "Trans-industrialization," in the sense of a transition to the sixth techno-structural paradigm using the fourth as the basis, and the fifth, as infrastructure;

5. The disproportionately high development of the military-industrial complex and army.

Supporters of this strategy within Russia are that military-industrial complex, a significant part of the security forces, the technocratic and scientific elites, builders, metallurgists, and others involved in the creation of infrastructure and megaprojects.

The primary directions of expansion within the framework of the USSR-2 strategy are the European territories of the former Soviet Union, the Far East, the Russian north; the auxiliary directions are the Balkans and Asia Minor.

When implementing the USSR-2 strategy, the structure of contradictions in the world has Continental Europe as the main loser, as it will not be able to turn its full attention to the Russian threat. "The central conflict will take place between Russia and Finintern (international financiers), whose assets will be used to develop Russia in the future. The contradictions with Continental Europe and China will be in the nature of the struggle for control over the adjacent territories that Russia needs to form its economic zone, the pan-region."[42] Thus, the launch of the USSR-2 strategy requires the solution of several mandatory issues:

1. The creation of a new "theory of the construction of socialism as post-capitalism," as a synthesis of political economy and the spiritual and moral Orthodox foundation;

2. The issue of education/creation of a "new person" is essential;

3. The formation of supra-economic higher goals for society;

42    Андрей Школьников: СССР -2 Стратегия России -Государственный капитализм с социализмом, https://www.youtube.com/watch?v=wBrGcpG42Q8

4. Reservation and strengthening of the army and military-industrial complex;

5. Creation of an economic zone of 300 to 500 million people;

6. Transfer of full power for 15-20 years in domestic politics to a brilliant practicing economist and patriot, with a team of like-minded people.

In addition to the initial requirements, it is necessary to take into account other risks.

# Key Pitfalls of USSR-2 strategy

The implementation of the USSR-2 strategy is widely regarded as revenge for the collapse of the country in 1991 and dismantling of liberal, West-oriented policies of the past 30 years. In the wake of attempts to restore the "socialist homeland" there is a great risk of destroying the elements of the post-industrial economy that have developed in the country. These are inhabitants of large cities, the so-called "creative class," speculators, non-productive forces, and parasites. The natural outcome of this scenario is a civil war, which will lead to the destruction of existing economic and political relations, the loss of part of the territories, the decrease in the current and medium-term potential of the country, the decrease in internal diversity, the establishment of new psycho-historical meanings.

Will there be an opportunity to win back losses? The United States, with its current situation, can take a chance by making a sacrifice in the short and medium-term for long-term gain, but Russia does not have this luxury. Too much has been stolen, lost, and given away to the West over the past 30 years. Russia has destroyed its industrial base, and only rapid reindustrialization can save the country. What are the possibilities to prevent civil war?

For development, you need to build a sixth technological paradigm, and not slide down to update the fourth, with the complete demolition of the existing elements of the fifth. This development is fraught with the economic and social crises in large cities, egged on by the liberal Western enemies of Russia and with the impending danger of a slide towards civil war. There will be a conservation of technological lag and semantic dependence, i.e., 20 years of a quiet life, and then a strategic loss and decline.

"The question of materialism vs. Orthodoxy is also a key element to consider. The need to develop a "theory of building socialism as a post-capitalism," where the key is the issue of educating a "new person," was noted earlier. It is for spiritual and moral education that it is proposed to consider the synthesis of Marxist theories and Orthodoxy. The need to abandon purely materialistic principles is determined not only by the indicated problem, but also by the presence in the immediate vicinity of the materialistic and socialist China – they say so themselves.

"In the potential confrontation, China's much stronger economy is partially offset by a lingering military vulnerability to Russia's nuclear arsenal, lower military spirit, and a lack of experience in real combat over the past decades. The field of psycho-history is becoming a vital issue. What are the prospects of the confrontation between the two materialistic socialist ideologies, one of which were the designated losers in the Cold War, and the latter with claims to be a world hegemon? In a look at the domestic supporters of the socialist path of development, most of them rapturously talk about the Chinese experience, right down to worship. Is Russia ready to exchange the Washington Consensus for Beijing? For those who are ready, I would like to advise reading the strategy of China and recall that the latter does not have younger partners, older sisters, but only pets. Does Russia want to be China's pet? I doubt it.

"Thus, the restoration of the USSR based on a materialistic Marxist ideology carries the risk of entering the zone of influence of China. Without changing the psycho-historical component, this scenario is even worse than the "Third Rome" – China's resource appendage and the latter's expansion territory."[43]

# The Formation of the Economic Zone of Russia

An equally important issue is the formation of the monetary and economic zone. Let me remind you that the minimum number is estimated at 300 million people, but an economic area of 500 million is much preferred. With a smaller population base, it is impossible to form a closed system of division of labor.

USSR-2 is very attractive to the ordinary population of neighboring countries, as a left-conservative project that stands for justice. However, for national elites, the image of USSR-2 is revolting and horrifying. USSR-2 rebirth will significantly affect wealth levels of the "privileged" class, that is, those who have profited enormously from the liberal financier policies (gangster capitalism) since the new Russia's former leadership under

---

43    A geostrategic vision of the future of the world and of Russia, Andrei Shkolinikov, Politizdat Publishing, p.307, ISSN: 0869-4435, 2019

Yeltsin in the 1990s. Why would the Oligarchs want to lose a significant share of personal savings (stolen from the population) and dramatically lower their outrageous standard of living? If not socialism, then at least state capitalism with vibrant elements of socialism will have to be built by Russia's allies. Entering into the economic and technological zone of the USSR-2 for other territories and countries will be very difficult.

What are the prospects for the expansion of Russia's population beyond the current 145 million people? In the first place, the periphal territories of the "Russian world": Ukraine, Belarus, Kazakhstan, Transcaucasia, Moldova, the Baltic states. How this will happen is a separate issue, however, these territories would be re-integrated into greater Russia, in some cases via organic integration, in other circumstances as a result of a loss of markets (European markets mainly) and in some rarer cases, when feasible, as a result of military force. Thus, we can add an additional 80 million people. There are questions about Kyrgyzstan, but there is a policy of Salafi Islamization, and the longer it continues, the closer they will be to the fate of Afghanistan.

The next territory is the Asia-Pacific area: Japan, Korea, Vietnam, and Philippines, and Indonesia. All these countries have one important need – not to be absorbed by China. They all need protection following the United States withdrawal from this region. There are no prospects for creating their own pan-region in these countries. Are they afraid of socialism? The short answer is no. Historically, these nations have been inclined towards collectivism, and the structure of the economy is far from liberal-western. Will Russia's Orthodox foundations strain them? No, we are not talking about a complete duplication of Russia's path. The question arises whether Russia can provide protection to these countries, and the answer is obviously yes… if it does not become a vassal of China. Who wants to be a junior partner and subordinate of your historical adversary? Anybody?

Two more groups of territories remain – Turkey and anti-Turkey (Balkan Christians, Kurds, and Syria). The scale of the contradictions here is understandable, the problems of alliance with the Ottomans, with their historical acts and ambitions, are the same. The inclusion of these territories in Russia's pan-region will be accompanied with great difficulties and limitations. Furthermore, Russia's implementation of the USSR-2 strategy complicates the game of rebuilding the Middle East by dividing Turkey and Saudi Arabia, which is also not something that Russia should look forward to in the long run.

Thus, remaining on materialistic principles, Russia risks falling into vassal dependence on China and losing the prospect of economic and ideological expansion into the Asia-Pacific countries. The maximum economic zone will be 395 million people; well over the minimum, but lower than the recommended number. And if you introduce adjustments for migration flows in the light of geopolitical processes, then the actual number will be even less. In the case of building "Orthodox socialism," the expansion potential will amount to more than 700 million people. Thus, the need for the creation of Orthodox/Christian socialism turns out to be one, if not the most potent, strategy.

# Conclusion

One of the key elements in the implementation of the USSR-2 strategy is the need to create a new value system. Although the value base of "Soviet man" and "Orthodox" is mostly similar, this was not enough. It is necessary to move away from materialism to greater spirituality and moral development. At the forefront are justice, service (preferably heroic), and sacrifice.

Will the new society look like the USSR? Yes, in the post-WWII period. The stability of this system will be quite high, and the main mistakes of the previous state system have been taken into account.

Key conditions for implementing this strategy:

a) political will to launch a strategic plan;

b) creation of a "theory of building socialism/post-capitalism," especially regarding the spiritual and moral education of a new person;

c) strict ideological isolation from China, the best option is the integration of Orthodoxy and socialism;

d) The presence of a brilliant economist-practitioner with a team in power.

# 8. CHINA'S GLOBAL STRATEGY

Modern China can be divided into three economic contours:

1. Agrarian: (zero technological paradigm) and textile (first technological paradigm), which makes up the majority of the population (almost one billion people), of which 300 million are illiterate and in terms of the division of labor and income correspond to Soviet Russia of the 1930s, or even earlier;

2. Industrial China: the dominance of industry of the second, third and fourth technological paradigms, which corresponds to the division of labor in the cities of the USSR in the early 1980s (350 million people); and finally,

3. Post-industrial China: Hong Kong, Shanghai (financial centers, 150 million people).

The agrarian, China consumes little and is practically not connected with the world – the most they can hope for is to buy a shovel, a bike, etc. The post-industrial paradigm is also understandable in Marxist-Leninist terminology; a classic parasite from the era of monopoly capitalism. The whole problem is in the industrial part; this is the part that does not allow all of China to become self-sufficient and move forward.

The United States faced the problem of specialization in the fifth technological paradigm, for the shedding of the shackles of which it faces civil war. China is overloaded with production from zero to the fourth paradigm; moreover, if it developed with a focus on the domestic market, i.e., increased domestic demand, then there would be no problems. Stalin, conducting collectivization,[44] created a consumer of agricultural machinery, and an excess of the population went to work in the cities. China did not bother with this – almost all products were sent to the foreign market. Therefore, if we take the structure of the distribution of the population via different ways of production; for example, the European Union as a standard in a developed country, we will see a wild bias. It takes decades to get rid of this imbalance.

This is far harder than it appears. How many doctors, teachers, engineers, scientists, etc. are there, not in absolute numbers, but as applied to the large base population of China? How many people with specialized secondary and higher education are needed instead of semi-literate peasants? How long does it take to create a system and give the right training to hundreds of millions of people? Where do you turn to acquire enough natural resources to make this transformation possible? I think it's evident that for a properly high domestic demand, there must be high productivity and a high division of labor in the country as a whole. The key question is, what led to such an imbalance?

# China's Strategic Mistakes

To date, China has made two strategic mistakes, that have given it a substantial advantage in the short and medium-term; but have turned into insurmountable problems in the long run. As a result, today's China is at a crossroads:

1. China believed the United States and built its economy based solely on foreign markets – they forgot Mao Zedong's teachings;

2. China believed liberal economists in 2008 that the crisis was cyclical in nature, and instead of urgent economic restructuring, they began to create additional production capacities and increase domestic demand with infrastructure projects of the industrial era – not paying heed to Rosa Luxemburg's work;

3. China believes in the union with London and the Rothschilds by trying to build liberal globalism II, altogether rejecting the works of Lenin and Marx.

Much has been said about the pursuit of rapid growth (via industrialization and infrastructure projects) and ignoring internal problems for decades; it seems that the state was simply afraid of social riots and unrest – all to keep the economy growing.

There is a myth about the great benefits of public investment in infrastructure, except that the investment should be directed to industries with the maximum multiplier. And if in America of the 1930s, the infrastructure was the basis for moving to the fourth technological paradigm, then, as we are about to enter the sixth technological paradigm, limitless investment in infrastructure is not optimal and even counterproductive to inject unlimited funds into the infrastructure for the fourth technological paradigm. By the way, those who will point out that China rail is a technological marvel, I remind you that high-speed passenger trains are not a scientific, but rather a purely applied-engineering task.

The question we must ask, what is the price for strategic mistakes at the wrong time of human development? China's economy is built on a surplus in foreign trade and wild public investment. What is the scale of the problem?

"Over the years, investment in fixed assets in China has been 42% -43% of GDP, while the world average is 20%-22%. If it were a one-time surge, this wouldn't be a problem, but in China's case, this was an exercise lasting several decade. China's problem is that a significant part of investments make no economic and/or social sense. We add exports in the amount of 20% of GDP, and we find that the minimum drop in the Chinese economy after the disappearance of the global market, the transition to the pan-regions, and the termination of unreasonable invest-ment will be from 30% to 50%. Can China survive such a drop intact? Quite unlikely."[45]

# Important Figures on China's Economy as a Percentage of GDP

What will happen to the population after such a collapse of their economy? The brunt of the collapse will bear the urban population, today China's middle and upper-middle class are used to the comforts of spacious apartments, cars, smartphones, etc. Will they be willing to forgo their middle-class existence and return to their villages, surviving on $1 per day? Quite unlikely.

It should be clear why China suddenly became a champion of globalization, albeit with a Chinese specificity. A severe decline in the standard of living of the urban population, an internal social explosion (as witnessed in semi-internal Hong Kong since summer-fall 2019), a period of fragmentation. And then again, unification? Quite unlikely. The world has become smaller, distances have narrowed, contradictions have become more acute. Will external players give China a chance? I see several scenarios:

# Strategy 1

The essence of this strategy is to dominate the world and preserve China as an exporter. It is only in conditions of the collapse of the world economic system, more precisely, the self-removal of the United States, the erosion of authority and significance of world political institutions and financial structures. What needs to be done? According to Shkolinikov, the establishment of a new world money-issue exchange center based on the gold standard.[46]

Step 1. Conclusion of trade and investment agreements in the framework of the concept of "One Belt – One Road." The goal is to open markets for China's products previously sent to the United States (mainly #'s 2-4 techno-paradigm), a reverse flow of resources, technology (5-6 techno-paradigm), and food.

The conclusion of an alliance with the right-wing globalists/Finintern and Britain. Here is the weakest point of the strategy; it implies self-re-

---

45      Три стратегии Китая, Андрей Школьников, https://www.youtube.com/watch?v=H-jlc5n38C2w
46      Ibid

moval and/or consent of the United States for subsequent actions, and this is wishful thinking. China will not be able to wait for the start of a civil war in the United States as part of this strategy, since its ally, the right-wing globalists, will not let it sit in the trenches. Time is short, and they simply don't have the luxury of waiting.

Step 2. Ensuring the safety of the Indian Ocean shipping lanes by creating a network of controlled and allied naval bases (China already prowls the Straits of Malacca, Sunda, Hormuz, Bab-el-Mandeb, Sosinsky as well as Australia as its leading South East Asian partner and port of Gwadar in Pakistan). Actively penetrating the affairs of Europe, the Middle East, and Afghanistan, supporting efforts to destroy/dissolve NATO. A united Europe without military forces would fall under the shadow of China and Russia (initially).

Land routes to Europe should go through the territory of weak countries/satellites. The route through Russia is not acceptable – Russia is too strong militarily.

Building up a powerful Naval Force, ideally two times more powerful than the United States. All of this takes time, but time is unavailable to China against the backdrop of global economic collapse. Risky operations are not China's strong point – and waiting for an ideal moment is a luxury they do not have.

Step 3. Creating the contour of a new financial world, with an emission center in London. As a result, China will have a controlling stake. The establishment of a new world monetary equivalent ("world" currency) with a soft peg to gold. Lending by the emission center to buyers of Chinese goods, intergovernmental settlements, and loans in the new international currency (Central Bank of the Central Banks project).

Step 4. Preservation by China of its production with a surplus in foreign trade. Redirecting the flow of goods from the USA to Europe, Russia, Turkey, etc. These are products that were previously sold in the USA.

Active "assistance" in the de-industrialization of Russia, the destruction of the military-industrial complex, the space industry, and the nuclear industry through the creation of joint ventures and cooperation. In the future, Russia should play the role of a military mercenary without its defense industry and technology.

Since this will be a neo-colonial system, rent for the maintenance of China will gradually be included in the price of goods. The rent for the "maintenance" of the emission center will be charged in the form of interest on loans. The trade surplus of the Middle Kingdom will only grow, which will lead to an increase in production and an increase in imbalances.

Step 5. Continuing the policy of artificially increasing domestic demand through subsidies and public investment in infrastructure, building up domestic debt and destroying the value of projects. The standard of living of the population of China will gradually increase due to artificial events, while other countries will decline.

Strengthening the policy of nonequivalent exchange, i.e., pursuing a policy of monopoly capitalism/imperialism. Is such a scenario possible? Of course, usury is natural for the Chinese – rationalism, practicality, prudence, the desire to capitalize on everything, and live at the expense of others.

Does such a China have a future? No, the window of opportunity for change is short-lived, China could not prepare in advance, and then there is the continuation of the policy of accumulating and transferring problems to the future. Who is the primary beneficiary of this policy in the short term? Britain. The financial international, in fact, is their scenario.

## Strategy 2: USA minus 70 years

China's next strategy is to prevent a social explosion within, but this time, without an alliance with right-wing globalists. It is necessary to move away from a positive trade balance and become an emission center. To do this, it is essential to solve the Triffin paradox[47] – to achieve a negative trade balance due to the limited production of lower classes; to feed and clothe the rural population, then move towards Great Unity – Datun.

Step 1. Any vigorous economic action before the outbreak of the US Civil War is pointless. Therefore, there is a long positional struggle with everyone else in the world to strengthen their positions. In the Celestial Empire, there is a proverb – "It's not scary to go slowly, it's scary to stop," so work will continue along these lines. This approach is appropriate in stable conditions, but during whirlwind change, it is more likely to lead to a strategic loss. Increasing shadow influence in international institutions, elites, and counter-elites of almost all countries of the world (from Latin America to the Middle East and Europe).

## Strategy 3: Active Growth of Naval power

Step 1. Taking control of key straits and waterways by force, via China's fleet and the army. To the Chinese, anything that contributes to the prosperity of China and the increase in territory controlled by the Emper-

---

47      Conflict of economic interests that arises between short-term domestic and long-term international objectives for countries whose currencies serve as global reserve currencies.

or is permissible. Do you think the conflict in the South China Sea, where all world laws require its equal division, is a problem for China? No, they are stronger than their neighbors, and their actions are morally justified; thus, they "teach a lesson." Isn't it, ironically, in tune with Kipling and the "White Man's burden"?

Step 2. The transition to trade only for the yuan; in fact, the creation of its own global emission center. A gradual introduction of social subsidies (both direct and through the purchase of agricultural products) of $1.5 - $2 thousand (in yuan equivalent) per year-per person, exclusively for the purchase of food through cashless payments, coupons, etc. Mass purchase of products in the agricultural sector abroad, primarily meat, for distribution to the population. The standard of living of the rural population is growing, the country's trade balance is becoming negative, and the yuan becomes world reserve currency.

Step 3. Launching new internal infrastructure programs under the guise of an "Asian mode of production." Launch of humanitarian programs for the strict assimilation of the surrounding peoples and national minorities.

Step 4. Carrying out internal reforms to gradually bring the structure of the economy to the reference structure of developed countries (a minimum of two generations will be required). The withdrawal of enterprises focused on the export of lower products outside of China (metallurgy, heavy engineering, etc.). Re-orientation of part of the production to domestic needs.

Imposing a policy of limiting technological development on other countries. China should become a leader, and since it cannot go faster, others must be slowed down. The methods will be a repetition of US policy, only in a much more stringent and uncompromising version.

Step 5. Beginning of the New Phoenicia mass resettlement program – the creation of enclave cities[48] around the world in places convenient for trade. A couple of million Chinese from the village and simple industries are exported to territories "bought" or "rented for 99 years" on the coast of the seas and/or along the trade routes near the bases of the Chinese fleet – Europe, Africa, Australia, Central Asia ... Russia. All world trade must go under the control of Greater China.

Step 6. Creation of "cities of the future." Some of the funds previously allocated for infrastructure projects should be transferred to the creation

---

48      The Takeover: "China Is Building Enormous Self-Sustaining Chinese Cities All Over The African Continent," Michael Snyder, December 30, 2019, http://themostimportantnews.com/archives/the-takeover-china-is-building-enormous-self-sustaining-chinese-cities-all-over-the-african-continent

of cities for students, scientists, and engineers. Granting (matching the middle-class living standards in developed countries) to almost all gifted students, graduate students, and young scientists in the world (hundreds of thousands of people). Creating an analog of regency courses at seminaries, i.e., a flood of these cities by young Chinese women whose purpose is to marry a foreign student and tie him and his children to China.

The Chinese are characterized by the desire to absorb innovations to overcome backwardness, to reinforce a sense of national exceptionalism and superiority, and if for this purpose it becomes necessary to assimilate several hundred thousand people from across the globe, so be it. The development of technologies of the sixth and seventh technological paradigm based on these cities.

Thus, we are talking about repeating the US strategy of the middle of the last century. Can China pull it off? I don't think so. There is simply not enough time, as other players/global projects/regional powers will react quickly and decisively. Unfortunately, China will ignore these risks and systematically attempt to create its own world, trying to impose on others its idea of correctness. Even when the meaninglessness of this path becomes apparent to everyone around them, the Chinese will not back down. They can't. It has been their modus operandi for the past 3,000 years.

When, with a high degree of probability, a disruption of plans occurs – by the time China begins to seize the bridgeheads, it suddenly turns out that the world has almost broken up into pan-regions. Each market has its top owner, who has gained control and blessing/recognition from the post-civil war USA. If China can take the second step, then resistance will only increase; everyone has their own plans and they will not have a global Chinese nationalist world.

What is the reason for underestimating opponents? The cultivation and maintenance of ideas of exclusivity for two millennia led to a low level of critical thinking, reflection, neglect of negative historical experience and other people's traditions. We combine this attitude with ugly pragmatism; and are not surprised that the surrounding peoples are not at all eager to embark on the "One Way."

Step 7. Choosing the enemy. China faces enormous social problems; it is no longer possible to avoid the inevitable. The generalized economic collapse will result in a 30%-50% drop in the Chinese economy. The key task will be to maintain unity through internal mobilization. How? Focus on an external enemy to unite the country.

Military, economic, psycho-historical confrontation, within the framework of which an adjustment will be made. The enemy must be strong enough so that the struggle is long, weak enough to be defeated "heroically," and sufficiently principled so that he won't surrender. Options:

1. USA: not suitable; too strong and, with a high degree of probability, will launch nuclear missiles if seriously threatened;

2. Russia: an ideal option, if not for its formidable nuclear arsenal;

3. Europe: far away and not a subject; it is a battlefield, not an adversary;

4. Japan: an ideal option; in a matter of weeks, it can manufacture several nuclear bombs. You can fight with Japan for a long time, incurring losses, the enemy is principled. Because of this, Japan will seek the protection of Russia;

5. Britain: a possibility if the Rothschild/China deal falls through and especially if control of Australia is the prize of victory;

6. India: weak and disorganized, but with a population base of 1.5 billion people combined with nuclear weapons, not a wise choice for an opponent.

7. Islamic world: struggle for Indonesia, Malaysia, Central Asia, Pakistan, and control over Persian Gulf reserves. To fight on this front, a strong psycho-historical component is needed – Confucianism, Taoism, and a Chinese understanding of communist ideas are a weak option.[49]

China needs:

Adoption of an Ethno-oriented religion (shift ideology to the right); revive communist ideology and revolutionary enthusiasm (to the left).

Religion must meet Chinese specifics – a strict hierarchy (a tradition of complete dependence on the bosses), externally spectacular rituals, the absence of external control (attitudes can only give their own), the presence of a historical precedent, the possibility of correction ("right" is necessary only in old age). Well, there must be high spiritual energy.

The only thing that comes to mind and satisfies all the requirements is the revival of Arianism or another ancient Christian movement under its guise, with a separate patriarch and Chinese characteristics. The adoption procedure is understandable; competent comrades who have retired are baptized, take the dignity, their crypto-Christian biography becomes

---

known. The Chinese are easier to indoctrinate in the team psychology, compared to Europeans.

Step 8. The trigger for the start of an active phase is the American Civil War and the withdrawal of their troops from other regions of the world. Promotion of conflict with the chosen enemy, the beginning of an active confrontation. For most people, it may seem savagery, the deliberate planning of victims in tens of millions (nuclear bombs will have to be destroyed), but in the Chinese tradition, the combination of cruelty, deceit, cunning, and resourcefulness sets completely different boundaries of what is permissible. Pragmatism is at the heart of everything. The army in China is a very conservative institution; with the cultivation of nationalist and traditional values, give it an ideology, and an enemy, and they can do wonders.

# Conclusion

The disappearance of the global market threatens China with a 30% -50% economic decline, a social explosion, and collapse, with a high probability of breaking up into several smaller territories. Also, China cannot stop or slow down its development, the economy and society are imprisoned within the contour of constant growth: there is no growth. Social contradictions are aggravating, falling – we are meeting a social explosion. China has three viable options and one historical misión, which I will examine separately:

1. An alliance with the Finintern in the present tense provides short-term benefits, but a strategic loss;

2. A partnership with Britain and the creation of its own currency zone after the outbreak of civil war in the United States, with due luck, gives a quiet and well-fed life for 10-15 years, but then leads to a loss;

3. A high-risk scenario of overloading, by removing internal tension from an external military conflict, a collapse in the standard of living, and reformatting of the cultural canon.

# Chapter 4

# THE ORIENT'S HISTORICAL MISSION WITHIN
# THE CONTOURS OF METAPOLITICS

Historians have explained the post-WWII Cold War geopolitical confrontation from the perspective of dialectics, as the struggle of the opposites: the USSR against the USA and the blocs of the Warsaw Treaty and NATO alliance led by them. However, I would like to break the tradition of analytics and give an assessment of the Cold War from the perspective of the Law of Changes in a combination of three forces: the USSR, the People's Republic of China, and the USA, with emphasis on the lessons of history.

According to the sinologist Piotr Gvasikov, the ternary approach: "Us – our enemies – our allies" is typical for evaluations of global processes by Chinese strategists. This approach is based on Chairman Mao Zedong's Theory of Dividing the World into Three Parts, which Deng Xiaoping in 1972 called "the greatest contribution to the treasury of Marxism-Leninism."[1] For biblical binary logic reigns supreme in Marxism: "He who is not with us is against us," and "the third is superfluous, the third doesn't count."

The fundamentally different result of geopolitical analysis and metapolitical assessment of events comes from the relation to the category of time. It is about linear progress (geopolitics, two opposite forces) versus changes in cycles (metapolitics, three forces in a bundle).[2] In the Great Game models, this concept is represented by confrontation on a "great chessboard" between the "white" and "black" in their forward movement versus the "card table of history" (game of Bridge), where there are three or more players, and the moves follow in a circular pattern.

In geopolitics, time is only an arrow-shaped duration from the past to the future (progress), plotted on a line of dates (numbers). In metapolitics,[3] time is also the order of events in the cycles of Being. History is the

1       https://www.fmprc.gov.cn/mfa_eng/ziliao_665539/3602_665543/3604_665547/t18008.shtml
2       The Three World Theory and Post-Mao China's Global Strategy, Herbert S. Yee *International Affairs (Royal Institute of International Affairs 1944-)*, Vol. 59, No. 2 (Spring, 1983), pp. 239-249, Oxford University Press on behalf of the Royal Institute of International Affairs DOI: 10.2307/2619937
3       The Metapolitical Structure of the West, Roberto Esposito, *Qui Parle,* Vol. 22, No. 2

sum of waves of different periods of time. And the historical choice of the path is connected with the "window of opportunity" to catch the phase of the cycle and "saddle" the wave of the ebb or flow of the life energy, which has cosmic foundations. These grounds come from the influence on the life on Earth of the energies of the Sun, the Moon, and the stars.

## Short History

To effectively use the lessons of the Cold War to anticipate the future fought within the contours of a Third World War (Hybrid warfare 5.0), one should understand: when, how and in what way the confrontation between the USA and the USSR grew into a union of three forces: USA-China-USSR. And also to explain where, when and why the USSR lost the Cold War, the United States became the nominal winners, and the lead country of the Third World – the People's Republic of China – turned out to be the hidden recipient of the main benefit from the clash of the two "superpowers."

It is officially believed that the Cold War began in 1946, after Churchill's speech on March 5 in Fulton (USA), where the idea of creating a military alliance of the Anglo-Saxon countries to fight world communism was proclaimed. It is important to note that in 1946, the People's Republic didn't exist; and China was not a pole of power in what the Anglo-Saxons call the Great Game.

The end of the Cold War was officially announced on December 2, 1989, at the summit of the leaders of the USSR (Gorbachev) and the USA (George H.W. Bush) in Malta. What the Soviet propaganda at the time presented as a great diplomatic victory of "new thinking" was, in fact, a complete and unconditional surrender of the USSR to the United States.

Towards the end of the Cold War, following Mao's theory of dividing the world into three parts, in 1969 breaking the friendship with the USSR, and in 1979 establishing relations of "constructive cooperation" with the USA, the PRC became an independent pole of power in The Great Game. The wise monkey (China) looked at the "battle of two tigers in the valley" (the USA and the USSR) and, at the end of the Cold War in 1989, came out on the side of the winner.

The end of the Cold War is a point of predestination (the convergence of the waves of history of different periods) that has changed the balance of power, trump cards, and the further role of the PRC in the Great Game.

In 1989, against the backdrop of the failures and difficulties of perestroika in the USSR, the PRC forced the Soviet Union to remove the

(Spring/Summer 2014), pp. 147-161, Duke University Press

three obstacles to normalize Sino-Soviet relations (the USSR withdrew troops from the border with China; withdrew troops from Mongolia and Afghanistan; and forced Vietnam to withdraw armed forces from Cambodia). In June 1989, China fought off the US attempt to carry out in China a liberal, non-violent "Velvet Revolution."

The "counter-revolutionary rebellion" of students and intellectuals in Tiananmen Square (Gate of Heavenly Peace) in Beijing was crushed by the forces of the People's Liberation Army. After that, the configuration of forces in the USSR-China-USA triangle changed. The USA became an adversary, and the USSR became an ally of China. The formula of Deng Xiaoping's policy was: "Carefully observe, defend our positions, decide things calmly, hide our potential, wait for an opportunity to act, then pounce and destroy."[4] The bottom line for the Chinese: in a fight of three forces, take a passive position (Law of Change).

Mathematically, two versions of the Law of Changes[5] are written by the Buhl algebra: $(1 + 1) + 0 = 0$ and $(0 + 0) + 1 = 1$. The first option: when two forces are active, and one force is passive, a mixture of three forces is turned in favor of a passive force. In Chinese tradition, this option is called "A wise monkey looks from the mountain to the battle of two tigers in the valley." The second option: when two forces are passive, and one force is active, a union of three forces is turned in favor of an active force. This option is called the "Almighty Dragon."

Therefore, in the confrontation between the PRC and the USA, "China" wins at the expense of the efforts of our ally – Russia.

In 1989, the United States won the struggle for the political resources of the Russian Federation as a partner in the Great Game. New Russia, in 1994, an extension of Western liberalism ("partnership for peace"), was admitted to the "pan-European house." And in 1997, to the G8. The United States won as Russia made a financial commitment to the Washington Consensus.

The Washington Consensus is a rule-book for those who were building the new economic model in Russia and other countries of the defeated socialist bloc. The idea was to ensure complete and unconditional transition of those countries towards the Western financial and economic system, which by that time had acquired a dominant position in the world. Therefore, there were several basic binding principles, and no alternative option was allowed whatsoever.

---

4      Deng Xiaoping, *Collected Works*, vol. 3 (Beijing: People's Publishing House, 1993).
5      https://www.ancient-origins.net/artifacts-ancient-writings/ching-0011652

First and foremost, only the dollar was to drive growth. The countries coming into the orbit of the Bretton Woods system could not have any internal sources of growth not tied to the dollar. The idea behind it is that a country is allowed to have only as much national currency as can be exchanged for real currency, primarily the dollar. Second, foreign investments were to be given top priority. They were supposed to be the sole source of growth, and, at the same time, to guarantee that the added value formed within the country could be easily transferred abroad.

Thus, in 2020, as the battle for the survival of the Bretton Woods economic model is in its endgame, the United States (bankers-financiers) will not allow Sino-Russian full-fledged cooperation without a fight. Despite the statements of the leaders of the Russian Federation and China about "comprehensive strategic cooperation," all levers of influence (Russian friends of the US dollar), as well as tough economic policies (sanctions) diplomatic (freezing relations) and military (breaking agreements) pressure on the Kremlin are activated to the fullest.

## Mao's Strategy and the Chinese Dream

According to well-informed sources, who were on the rostrum of the Tiananmen Gate on October 1, 1949, Mao Zedong, after declaring the PRC in a confidential conversation with Prime Minister Zhou Enlai, touched on the idea of building a state of New China.[6] Regarding international relations, Mao firmly said that China "becomes an ally of the USSR only for a while."[7]

"Thus, from 1949 to 1959, the rivalry of the USSR and the USA during the war in Korea (1950-1953) in the status of an ally of the USSR under the Treaty of Friendship, Union and Mutual Assistance from February 13, 1950, was indirectly carried out by the People's Republic of China. The PRC took on its shoulders the primary responsibility for the ground war, accepted all the risks and significant losses. In contrast, the Soviet Union took full advantage of the global consequences of America's disastrous war in Korea.

"The death of Stalin in 1953 to the Caribbean crisis in 1962, was the period of Khrushchev's thaw. Shortly after Stalin's death, Mao Zedong began his departure from copying the Soviet experience of socialist construction ("The Great Leap Forward") and charted the course toward independence from the USSR while maintaining a confrontation with the

---

6        Mao Zedong, Zhou Enlai and the evolution of the Chinese Communist Leadership, Thomas Kampen, Nordic Institute of Asian Studies, p.66, 2000.

7        https://www.wilsoncenter.org/blog-post/sino-soviet-alliance-70-years-later

United States (manipulating the mutual fear of nuclear superpowers) in 1959 (Lushan Plenum of the CPC Central Committee)[8] when the United States was declared to be a "paper tiger." The fear of a nuclear war against the PRC was called psychological loyalty to the enemy.

"Khrushchev, on the contrary, visited the United States in 1959 with the proposal of a peaceful co-existence of socialism with capitalism. Mao Zedong made the final creation of the USSR-PRC-USA triangle by securing the role of an independent player in the Great Game for the PRC in 1969, via a slyly organized split with Soviet Russia in the form of an armed border conflict in the vicinity of Damansky[9] (Zhenbaodao) Island on the Ussuri River near Manchuria in March 1969; and at the Zhalanas-hkol Lake (Dzungarian Gate) in August 1969. After that, the PRC turned from an ideological ally into a strategic adversary of the USSR. The West, on the contrary, has opened access to credit and technology for the PRC. Hostilities between the USSR and the United States escalated.

"On the other hand, the relations of "constructive cooperation" between the PRC and the USA were cemented, when the functions of an ally of the Middle Kingdom passed to the North American United States, took place in January 1979 during the visit of Deng Xiaoping to Washington and his meetings with President Carter. The conspiracy took place against the backdrop of the Islamic Revolution in Iran, which weakened the position of the United States."[10]

Twenty-year agreement was signed in February 1979 and later extended in Beijing by President Bill Clinton and Jiang Zemin for another 20 years. The terms of cooperation were fulfilled by both parties, with the agreement expiring in January 2019. These were 40 years of the most-favored-nation status in China's trade with the West. And 40 years of success in the policy of "reform and opening up" (pragmatic enrichment) by Deng Xiaoping.

The constructiveness of cooperation with the United States was confirmed by a "counterattack for self-defense" on Vietnam, which China launched on February 17, 1979. By April 3, 1979, Chinese troops occupied the centers of three border provinces. After the direct route to Hanoi was opened and general mobilization was announced in Vietnam, China

8        Lushan Huiyi Shilu (The Veritable Records of the Lushan Conference). By Li Rui. [Beijing: Chunqiu Publishers; and Changsha: Hunan Jiaoyu Publishers, 1989. 377 pp.]
9        The Sino-Soviet Border Dispute: Background, Development, and the March 1969 Clashes Thomas W. Robinson, *The American Political Science Review*, Vol. 66, No. 4 (Dec., 1972), pp. 1175-1202, American Political Science Association
10       Gvasikov, Piotr "Exploring the future in the context of globalism," Bookvenir publishing, p.41, 2017

considered that the psychological blow had reached its goal, announced the cessation of the offensive, and began the withdrawal of troops. On December 25, 1979, the USSR, competing with the United States in the Great Game, sent troops to Afghanistan. The Afghan war lasted 10 years (1979-1989) and ended in the collapse of Soviet power and the dissolution of the USSR.

Thus, the Chinese "wise monkey" on the mountain received the main benefit from the battle of the "two tigers." For the "skin" of the defeated "Soviet social-imperialism" in the form of the republics of Central Asia was the natural course of a Chinese vision (in the form of the SCO, the Shanghai Cooperation Organisation).

"American imperialism," having exhausted the "energy of the West" and leading the unipolar world, entered a crisis of "limits of growth" and now, in the course of the "clash of civilizations" in the Third World War of a new hybrid type, the Trump administration is looking for ways to "Make America Great Again." The path to realizing the Chinese dream of a great revival of the Chinese nation in practice started from the outcome of the Cold War, reformatting the link between the three.

The strategy of "manipulating barbarians" in the conjunction of the three forces of Mao Zedong on the scale of three generations of the Chinese 60-year cycle (grandparents, parents, children) was crowned as a complete success. The roles of the USSR and the USA with respect to China were reversed. A union of three forces turned in favor of China. After which it became possible to implement the doctrine of trinitarian harmony – the transition to the "Great Unity – Datun" of the countries and peoples of the world around the "Middle Kingdom of yellow people."

What analysts of European education and mindset consider "monstrous mistakes" ("Great Leap Forward," "Cultural Revolution") in the PRC's political practice was an implementation of Mao Zedong's theory of dividing the world into three parts. After all, Mao, the "Great Helmsman" (who must cope with the waves of history) was first of all a Chinese way, and only secondarily Marxist.

"That is why not a single Western theory can fully explain what is happening in China, either in the economy or in politics. The West doesn't understand how, in China the dialectic of progress is combined with changes in the cycle, how capital is adjacent to the Asian mode of production, how the eastern despotism gets along with democracy. Mao's theory: the one separates in two, but changes occur in the union of three forces. Analysts of European education and viewpoint, however, see the first part of the formula (universality of contradiction) and do not see the second (cycle of history)."[11]

## Trinity is Universal

Trinitarian harmony is a key concept in understanding the universe beyond Western two-dimensionality. The world of signs and symbols. The Universe is orbits, trajectories, waves of rotational motion of celestial spheres. Whereas earthly progress is a progressive movement in segments, stages from the beginning (alpha) to the end (omega) of direct steps (stages) forward and upward.

It is noteworthy that an accurate knowledge of earthly events is always an analysis: the dismemberment of the whole, measurements, and numbers. Whereas the understanding of cosmic foundations is always the assessment of a single Divine presence, proportionality of the threefold/ternary harmony of the inseparable and non-merged Trinity; Logos – full of symbols, images, and similarities of analog processes.

The trinity of being is the exchange of substances, energy, and information. The trinity of quantities in the universe is the amplitude, frequency, and phase. As applied to time as astronomical cycles of sunrises and sunsets, phases of the moon and the motion of stars when sweeping cycles in a wave line, the ancient Greeks called the amplitude "Kronos" (duration), the frequency "cyclos" (sequence), and the phase – "kairos" (the moment of arrival) of the event. And in the spirit: Jing – the spirit of space \ Shen – the spirit of time\Qi – the energy of life.

When applied to man, the trinity is the body, soul, and spirit. And the civilization code is triple-wired in a number (genetics of the body), color (filters of the resonances of the soul), and tone (music of the spheres – Spirit). In the application to society, trinity is power, honor, and conscience. The power is divided into conceptual – priests, monetary – dealers, and the prevailing physical coercion – warriors.

The Jews are divided into (Pharisees\Essenes\Sadducees). The Orthodox, into (Judaizing\non-possessors\Josephites). Islam, (Sunnis\Sufis\Shiites). The Communists, (Trotskyists\Leninists\Stalinists). And the financiers are (interest-holders\money changers\appraisers). Also, the peoples of the biblical Mediterranean civilization, the descendants of Noah, were divided into three branches: Shem (Asian East-Jerusalem); Ham (south of the Old World-Babylon and Egypt); Japheth (European

11     Gvasikov, Piotr "Exploring the future in the context of globalism," Bookvenir publishing, p.89, 2017

West-Rome). Shem is a priority of spirit and will. Ham is the instincts of the body (satiety and comfort). Japheth is the logic of the mind and fiber of the soul (science and art).

Trinity, in matters of power, is most evident in the example of the biblical Mediterranean civilizations of Babylon, Egypt, Greece, Rome, Jerusalem. As an appendix to the house of Jacob, threefoldness is manifested in the division of the elites of the kingdom of Judah during the Maccabee dynasty (2nd century B.C.) into three conceptual parties: the Pharisees, Essenes, and Sadducees.

Whereas the earthly duality is manifested in the fact that the house of Jacob is two sides of the same coin: The Communist International of the proletarians of all countries and the Financial International of the monetary authorities of all countries. Let's examine the evolution of the conceptual trinity of the house of Jacob.

# Living Roots of the Tree of Israel

The Pharisees: a religious and political party of the middle-income strata of the urban trade and craft population (shopkeepers) in ancient Judea. They proclaimed themselves wise (self-designation "rabbi"). Not being priests, they emphasized the casuistic interpretation of the Oral Torah of the legislator Moses. Adherents of formal piety, they were, in a figurative sense, hypocrites. The founders of the religious legal system of later Judaism, designed in the secret part of the Talmud-Mishneh. Rationalist jurists.

The Sadducees are a priestly-aristocratic party of the land nobility and the higher priesthood. Conservatives. Adherents of the letter of the Law of Moses. They combined secular and spiritual power into a symphony. They rejected the Oral Torah and accepted only the Written, or Tanah, which only priests could explain. They based their teaching on three principles: The Old Testament, or Tanach, the temple, and the clergy. From the Greeks was perceived the need for luxury in the nobility. And Roman-imperial influence was expressed in the function of "slaves of the treasury." Masters of money affairs.

The Essenes are an ancient Jewish ascetic sect in Palestine (Canaan). They gave the teachings of Moses a proto-communist interpretation, denied luxury, slavery, and lived in co-operative communities. They influenced the emergence of the first Christian communities (Judeo-Christians). They relied on the disadvantaged masses: landless common people, poor artisans and lumpen proletarians (have-nots). The way of the Essenes is the way of non-possessors.

In Holy Russia, starting from the 15th century, the trinity of the conceptual foundations of real politics manifested itself in the three branches of Orthodoxy.

The Judaizers (Sharia, Metropolitan of Moscow and All Russia Zosima, the doctrine of "Moscow – the Third Rome") are a branch from the Pharisees, on which individualists grew up with the idea of personal salvation of the soul, human rights in the world, and the soulless dictatorship of the law. Liberal Democrats and Trotskyists. Talmudists. Progressive globalists.

The Josephites (followers of Joseph Volotsky, the doctrine of the "symphony of power") are a branch from the Sadducees, on the tenets of which stands a vertical hierarchy, all the same the Pope or the "father of peoples" Stalin. Clerics and Imperials. Zionist Mondialists.

Non-possessors (followers of Nilus of Sora, elders) is a branch from the Essenes: Collective salvation, mutual responsibility in the community, horizontal networks of the international Bolshevik-Leninists, Chabad.

# Interest-Holders, Appraisers, Money Changers

In finance, there are three ways to get something "out of nothing": loan interest (interest) – the fruits of Pharisaism, capitalization of expectations (appraisers) – historically, these are Sadducees and the exchange rate (money changers) – these are now Essenes-internationalists. In modern business, the trinity is symbolized by a bunch of 3Rs: Rockefellers, Royals, Rothschilds.

Interest-holders are the Rockefellers. The current US Federal Reserve rules. Yale illuminati.

Appraisers are Royals. Indulgences. Now antique property. Goodwill. Bank of the Vatican. Prelature Opus Dei.

Money changers are the Rothschilds. Gold. Order of the Bnai-Brith.

Symbolically, the Trinity is: a "Point" (Pharisees with the individualism of the rights of an individual person) – "Vertical line" (Sadducees with a hierarchy) and "Horizontal line" (Essenes with network structures).

The "point" (.) is defined as individualism, human rights, the letter of the law. In biblical civilization, these are the heirs of the Pharisees. Adherents of the casuistic interpretation of the Law of Moses and formal piety. In a figurative sense, hypocrites-Talmudists. The founders of the religious and legal system of later Judaism, designed in the oldest part of the Talmud-Mishneh. Pharisaism is the conceptual foundation of modern globalism; the carriers of which are the Anglo-American bourgeoise. In finance, these are the "interest-makers," forging wealth at the expense of loan interest on credit. In politics, these are the Illuminati Masons in the USA, concentrated under the wing of the Skull & Bones Order and in the Rockefeller banking group, which has been dominant in the US Federal Reserve since 1972. An instrument of monetary power here is the issue of USD.

Horizontal line (–) is a network structure, a commitment to the energy of disadvantaged masses. In biblical civilization, these are the heirs of the Essenes, a Hebrew sect that gave the teachings of Moses a communistic interpretation. They relied on the destitute masses: landless common people, poor artisans and lumpen proletarians (have-nots).

Out of the Essenes came the internationalists. The conceptual basis of the international is the provision that the homeland of the Jews is the whole world, and the mission of the Jews is "to shepherd the nations of the world, like countless herds, according to the Testament of the Most-High." In global finance, these are money changers who receive wealth grown from nothing due to the exchange rate of currencies. This is the Financial International of the banks of the Rothschild group with such instruments of monetary power as gold, diamonds, drugs. In politics, they are masons under the wing of the Bnai Brith Order ("Sons of the Covenant"), conceptually nourished by Kabbalists.

The vertical line (|) is a hierarchy, a commitment to the strength of the state and the church. In biblical civilization, these are the heirs of the Sadducees – the party of the land aristocracy and the highest priesthood in ancient Judea (2$^{nd}$ century B.C.). They relied on the propertied sections of the population, combining secular and spiritual power; initially, as opponents of Greek merchant capital. Then they came to a compromise with foreign influence – Hellenistic (commercial and monetary with the satisfaction of the needs of the feudal nobility in luxury goods) and Roman-imperial (as "treasury slaves").

Mondialists came out of the Sadducees. The carriers of the ideas of mondialism nowadays are the Old European, mainly Romano-Germanic, clan aristocracy. In world finance, these are master appraisers of a group of Catholic banks, who receive wealth from nothing by capitalizing on expectations (indulgences – "should not," now – goodwill, antiques). In politics, this is the world elite, nourished by the Vatican.

## The Perspectives of a Hybrid War

Western analysts should remember that since Sun Tzu, high-level Chinese politics have been "an endless path of cunning and deception." At the same time, the Chinese "path of victory" by non-military means (keys to the civilization code) is a treasure that cannot be disclosed either abroad or within China.

The Soviet "military Sinology" of the time of the Comintern and the Socialist Camp of Stalin coped with the decoding of the stratagem[12] of Chinese politics. Khrushchev, within the triangle of relations with the United States and China, has already "played in a play written by other people" (Kissinger's words about China spoken in 2011). And Gorbachev and the Ideological Department of the Central Committee of the Communist Party of the Soviet Union, who completely switched over to chess schemes (War of Opposites) in the Great Game, demonstrated a complete misunderstanding of the "Chinese specificity."

Seeing the Sino-American contradictions regarding the conclusion of a new agreement on cooperation between Xi Jinping and Trump and delving into the analysis of the "trade war" (cover story) between the USA and China in spring 2019, the Russian security apparatus took up arms against the USA and joined forces with the PRC.

President Putin's speech from the rostrum of the St. Petersburg International Economic Forum on July 7, 2019, was sent to the media as an announcement that "Russia no longer recognizes the current system of US world domination. Moreover, Russia poses a total challenge to this system and in this confrontation, essentially unites with China and the rest of the world – with those parts of it that have not lost their will to save from the American dictate and are looking for a force that they could join in this confrontation."

Literally, Putin said: "We are not creating military alliances with China. Yes, we are strategic allies. We are not working against anyone. We are working for the benefit of ourselves and our partners." Translation: the Kremlin still has a strategic assessment of the new alignment of forces of the Great Game and a crafty choice of one of the three options for the course and the final outcome of the hybrid warfare.

Option one: With the announcement by Xi Jinping in 2012 of the path for the Great Revival of the Chinese nation, the PRC, in conjunction with the three forces, for the first time since the middle of the 19th century, took an active position. Now, to execute the "Almighty Dragon" scheme: $(0 + 0) + 1 = 1$, the PRC needs both the United States and the Russian Federation to take up a passive position. This, however, is unrealistic be-

12    Soviet Sinology and Two Approaches to an Understanding of Chinese History, Alexander Pisarev, *China Review*, Vol. 14, No. 2, Special Issue: Doing Sinology in Former Socialist States (Fall 2014), pp. 113-130, The Chinese University of Hong Kong Press

cause of 1) Trump's ambitions (Make America Great Again) and 2) Putin – wounded by the sanctions of the "national pride of the Great Russians." And if it were possible, then this option of a combination of three forces would threaten Russia at the exit from WWIII with the loss of sovereignty and, in the new post-industrial world order, falling completely under the dictates of the "Chinese Dream."

Option Two: Russia, in the confrontation with the United States/Western Europe, continues to take an aggressive position, which, with the annexation of Crimea, began in 2014. Further, the international situation with the participation of Russia in Syria can develop according to the following scenario:

> a) The terrorists of the banned Islamic State of Iraq and the Levant from the territory of Afghanistan are preparing a full-scale attack against the post-Soviet republics of Central Asia.

> b) In Ukraine, the confrontation between the "people's republics" of Donbas and the Armed Forces of Kiev is escalating.

Russia is drawn into a large territorial war on three fronts against the United States and its regional partners. China supports Russia in the UN Security Council; but does not intervene in hostilities (takes a passive position/wise monkey on a mountain, Syria, Crimea, Ukraine). Here, China repeats the Cold War scheme: $(1 + 1) + 0 = 0$.

The United States is actively building the "... New World Order against Russia, on the wreckage of Russia and at the expense of Russia," as per Zbigniew Brzezinski's doctrine explained in his "The Great Chessboard," and relying on technological superiority in the hybrid offensive. Russia, unable to fight the Hybrid warfare on three fronts, is forced to repeat the Cold War scheme with an "arms race," loses, and moves from the federal structure of the state to the Confederation of Moscow Russia (loss of territory, prestige and psycho-historical relevance).

China, according to this scheme, completes the hybrid war on the side of the winner. And the territories of the Far East and the Arctic (the Center is prevailing over the North, according to the Chinese Law of Change – more on that later) are objectively included in the Chinese "Sphere of Economic Welfare of Northeast Asia" (the plan for creating such a sphere was announced by Chairman Xi in September 2018).

Option three: Russia gradually slips out of the ambush of an active confrontation with the United States and takes up a passive position, while cleverly playing in its favor the scheme $(1 + 1) + 0 = 0$, where China is actively fighting with the United States for world leadership.

Raising the banner of globalization in Chinese (creating a "community of a single destiny of mankind") and proclaiming the project to implement the "Chinese Dream" of Great Harmony Datun, the PRC cannot sacrifice principles, because it "will lose face." In the Chinese strategy and Chinese mentality, it is acceptable to intentionally leave the territory and cut any material and human losses; only moral damage is absolutely unacceptable.

In summary, Russia is China's rear, and vice-versa; their geopolitical "back-to-back" position in Siberia, the Far East, the Arctic, and Central Asia can either be a chronic headache, or offer a major strategic advantage, depending on their political relationship. Co-operation allows Russia to enter the New World Order together with China, on the shoulders of China, and at the expense of China as the point man (the antithesis of Brzezinski's doctrine). In terms of military art, "on the shoulders" means: advancing behind China, not against it, using the path it paved. The rear is what is behind the front. This is where reserves, resources, mobilization, design and production bases are located. Militarily, the rear is something you never give up. However, to take advantage of this option of a combination of the three forces, Russia must still have an independent conceptuality of their future as a Global Project.

# Great Game 2017-2020

Any knowledge about the intentions, possibilities, and worldview of the participants of the Great Game, to be used effectively, requires conceptualization in the form of a Global Project. If geopolitics is the doctrine of space, the confrontation of land and sea and the relevance of the strategic interaction of partners in the Great Game, then, the Asian perspective is the doctrine of time, the long game, the cosmic foundations of change, the trinity of harmony and the timeliness of players' actions on a scale of globalism. Based on the concepts of meta-politics for countries and peoples of non-Western civilizations – the heirs of the United Kingdoms of Genghis Khan (First Horde) and the pseudo-Socialist Empire of Stalin (Second Horde), the world project "Big Eurasia – Third Horde" is developed.

What can be expected from Sino-Russian relations, which, according to their respective leaders, are "experiencing the best period in history"? The answer is contained in the official statements of the parties. We are talking about "comprehensive strategic cooperation" (good neighbors in confronting common threats); "New era" (post-industrial information society of Artificial Intelligence, digital economy, and 5G communication format); and, most importantly, "decisive support in matters relating to the fundamental interests of each other" in the new, "difficult and far-reaching international situation."

The main characteristic of the "new starting point" in a relationship between the PRC and the Russian Federation is that 75% of their payments in international trade are made in US dollars (China-US trade turnover is $600 billion a year,[13] and China-Russia only $100 billion). But the most dangerous thing for the further greatness of China and the Russian Federation is the fact that the accounting unit of the personal wealth of the Chinese "development activists" and Russian oligarchs and officials, is USD.

This is where the ambiguity of the international situation arises when the states of China and Russia oppose "economic sanctions" of the USA in the "trade war" of a new hybrid type. And government officials and the whole of business are concerned about how not to lose their hard-earned USDs, stored in cash and in the accounts of the banking system controlled by the Americans.

It is this contradiction of national and personal interests on the part of the US dollar that causes a split in the elites in China and Russia and forms a staunch opposition, in the "Friends of the US dollar," to the comprehensive strategic interface between the PRC and the Russian Federation in their quest for survival in a new technological era.

The science of all sciences – history – teaches that the resolution of such a contradiction is possible either by forceful coercion (short of physical elimination) by the State, of persons who have embarked on the path of "betrayal of the homeland" (collaboration with the Americans). Or through a "transit of power" from the anti-American front to a regime of "constructive cooperation" with the United States. On this path, starting with the publication on February 11, 2019, of the manifesto of the current government, "The Long State of Putin," Russia has been pursuing market liberalism.

In any case, the resolution of contradictions within the people is based on the external relations of the opposing elite groups. It acts as part of the Great Game of global projects. China has such a global project (the historical name is "Datun-Great Unity"[14] of countries and peoples around China). Russia does not have a global project. And with national projects in practice, no matter how forward-looking they are, it acts only as a pas-

---

13      https://ustr.gov/countries-regions/china-mongolia-taiwan/peoples-republic-china

14      The Great Union of the Popular Masses, Mao Tse-tung and Stuart R. Schram, *The China Quarterly*, No. 49 (Jan. - Mar., 1972), pp. 76-87, Cambridge University Press

sive partner in a strange game. Around the world, "tectonic processes of global transformation"[15] are taking place, which the well-informed Pope Francis called the Third World War on September 19, 2014. Any war, even a new hybrid-type of conflict, ends with a winner. Victory should look like a "new currency world" with the return of "old money" (gold) and the removal of financial speculators of "new money" (Wall Street banks) from leverage in five critical countries of world liberalism: the USA, Britain, France, Russia, and Israel.

A vivid intelligence sign of the global transition of mankind to the "new currency world" and "new world order" was the announcement of the Bank of International Settlements controlled by the "Sons of the Testament" (New Jerusalem global project, capital London) about the entry into force of the Basel III rule[16] on March 31, 2019 (on the transfer of metallic gold from the status of raw materials to first-class asset status) deferred until the end of 2021.

In other words, in three years 2019-2020-2021, a ticking financial revolution should occur, where the PRC will be the depository of banking gold of the world (at least 30,000 tons returned to China by the Rothschilds as a reparation for the 19th century Opium Wars),[17] and therefore the leader of the New World Order (community of peoples of one destiny). Since it was not possible to agree on a phased peaceful withdrawal of financial speculators of the US petro-dollar, the return of gold, as the principal investment resource of the economy of the 6th techno-paradigm, will be the result of *force majeure*, which has always been the war of arms.

## Red Dragon and Black Belt

In 1987, the Chinese put forth the concept of transferring the three-sphere strategic border of China beyond the boundaries of the national territory – on land, in the oceans, in the polar regions and space. In 1993, the Military Council of the Communist Party of China Central Committee adopted the secret doctrine of "Three Norths. Four Seas."[18] And in

15 ▪ https://www.chathamhouse.org/sites/default/files/public/Research/International%20 Economics/0713r_industrialtransformation.pdf
16 https://www.armstrongeconomics.com/markets-by-sector/precious-metals/gold/will-basel-iii-changing-golds-status-as-a-reserve-asset-for-banks-change-the-future/
17 What is the Rothschild Role in China's Gold Accumulation & Price-Fixing Scheme?, Anthony Boyd, March 6, 2014, http://www.24hgold.com/english/news-gold-silver-what_is_the_rothschild_role_in_china_s_gold_accumulation___price-fixing_scheme_.aspx?contributor=Charleston+Voice&article=5265537798H11690
18 China's Strategic Shift towards the Region of the Four Seas: The Middle Kingdom Arrives in the Middle East, Dr. Christina Lin, ISPSW Strategy Series: Focus on Defense and International Security, Issue 226, April 2013

2013, Xi Jinping came up with the "New Silk Road" initiative, which by 2019 had grown into a strategy for China's victory in the Third World War of a new hybrid type by non-military means, "Belt and Way." And all this is included in the Chinese globalization project with the historical name "Datun" (Great Unity), which since 2013 has been called the "Community of the Unified Fate of Humanity."

According to the sinologist Piotr Gvasikov, "Four Seas is a spatial coverage: from the Arctic Ocean in the North, to the Indian Ocean in the South; and from the Pacific Ocean in the East to the Atlantic Ocean in the West. And the "Three Norths" are territories with a population subject to overcoming by non-military means. For, on the cosmic grounds of the Law of Changes, the Center occupied by China (the Navel/Epi-center of the Earth) in the turns of history is dominated by the north (the west is defeated by the east; the south is defeated by the west; the north is overcome by the south; and the east by the center)."[19]

The first north is Siberia and the Russian Far East.
The second north is the North Atlantic Alliance (NATO).
And the third north is the North American United States (USA).

It is evident that the opposition of the New Liberal Russia to a democratic (pro-Western) choice of peaceful aggregate power of the PRC by peaceful means is almost impossible. The Armed Forces of the Russian Federation do not have the military ability to deter China via conventional methodology. A nuclear missile in opposition to China's peaceful overcoming of Russian resources beyond the Urals in a hybrid war is absolutely useless.

And the way out of the situation is suggested by martial arts schemes (sambo, judo), where you succumb to the onslaught of the enemy and turn the vector of his strength in a favorable direction to you with a rotational movement. The schemes for intercepting the enemy's energy by translating translational motion into rotational are well known to Vladimir Putin from the physical culture of a black-belt judo master (translated as "soft way" from Chinese).

These schemes – to succumb and turn the vector to his advantage – President Putin has been applying, starting with the 2001 treaty on the good neighborly relations of liberal Russia and the People's Republic of China. As for the Belt and the Way, the interception of the vector of change

19       Gvasikov, Piotr "Exploring the future in the context of globalism," Bookvenir publishing, p.236, 2017

by Russia (the Chinese Center prevailing over the Russian North), took place in 2013. And in a speech at the first Forum in 2017, Putin firmly urged China to develop the Northern Sea Route.

The Chinese icebreaker *Xuelong*[20] (Snow Dragon) first explored the Northern Sea Route in August 2012. After that, China became a participant with a 20% stake in an integrated project for the production and supply of liquefied natural gas from the Sabetta seaport at the mouth of the Ob River – Yamal-LNG. In August 2017, the first cruise of the Christophe de Marjorie ice-class gas tanker took place along the NSR, where, in some places, a unique vessel overcame ice fields 1.2 meters thick.

And this is in August, while in winter, the ice thickness in the eastern part of the NSR reaches 4 meters. The air temperature drops below -50°C. And the ice situation is changing, so that the icebreaking pilotage for 3 days is forced to stretch to 20-25 days. That is, the shortest route is not the most comfortable nor the most profitable. And the NSR is needed not so much for the logistics of the Chinese "New Sea Route of the 21st Century," but mainly for short-distance shipping within the Russian North (Northern delivery for 20 million people and covering forces). At the second Belt and Road Forum in 2019, China got a 20% stake in the Arctic LNG project on the other side of the Gulf of Ob. And the creation of Greater Eurasia is a combination of the EAEU and the concepts of the Belt and Road.

# Historical Perspective of Sino-Russian Relations

The history of the betrayal in the middle of the 19th century by the West of Chinese Christians of the "Heavenly State of General Prosperity" and the subsequent "century of shame" associated with the humiliation of Chinese sovereignty in colonial enclaves have made, and are making Russia and China, as heirs of the United State of Genghis Khan, natural partners; having "common roots" and understandable to all "principles and values."

Since 1923, the leader of the bourgeoisie revolution and the "father of the nation,"[21] Sun Yat-sen, has been implementing the concept of "unity with Soviet Russia," and Mao Zedong, after the formation of the PRC, first obtained from Stalin the conclusion of the Soviet-Chinese treaty of friendship, union, and mutual assistance. But the "white" Sun Yat-sen and

20      The Role of the Arctic in Chinese Naval Strategy, Ryan D. Martinson, China Brief Volume: 19 Issue: 22, The Jamestown Foundation, December 20, 2019
21      Bruce A. Elleman, Soviet Diplomacy and the First United Front in China, Sage Publications, Inc., Vol. 21, No. 4 (Oct., 1995), pp. 450-480.

the "red" Mao Zedong pushed to this strategic step – the Western policy towards China: in 1923, European powers surrounded the government of Sun Yat-sen in Guangzhou after the decision to return customs to China. In this connection, Sun Yat-sen stated: "We will no longer rely on the West, we will have to unite with Soviet Russia." And Mao Zedong, in the conditions of economic blockade and embargo from the West for 10 years, received enormous financial and military-technical assistance from the Soviet Union.

Moreover, neither the "unequal treaties" of tsarist Russia with China, nor the "insidious recognition of Outer Mongolia by Soviet Russia," nor the Soviet-Japanese Neutrality Pact and the Soviet-Chinese Treaty in August 1945 following the results of the Yalta agreements that were concluded with damage for the sovereignty and territorial integrity of China, nor the occupation by the Soviet Union of Xinjiang in 1939-1942 and Tannu-Uryanhai (Tyva) in 1944 prevent China from pragmatically solving its tasks. The harm caused to red China is well known and remembered.

"The Big Eurasia" mentioned by Putin in his speeches, is the Third Horde project. "It is important to note that the main point should be sought not in what Putin said, but in what is not stated. So, in his speeches at the second Forum in Saint Petersburg, Putin never mentioned "the soft power of culture where the Spirit of Victory lies." The People's Republic of China, having taken up the enormous task of creating a community of a unified destiny of mankind, does not have this Spirit. But Putin knows for sure from the Law of Changes (the east is overpowered by the center) that China can receive the vaccination of the spirit necessary for the Datun project only from the correct Eastern teaching of primordial Russia."22

# Change of Epoch 2020-2021

The Chinese write in hieroglyphs. Hieroglyphs depict a specific thought: symbolic pictures, acting as a direct code of consciousness, while letters record the sounds of speech. This phenomenon of writing determines the specificity of the thinking of the Chinese. One such concept is "Socialism with the Chinese characteristics of the new era"

"In 2017, by the decision of the 19th all-China Congress, recorded in the charter of the ruling party of the country, according to which the nation, since 2018, adopted the order of life based on the original tradition of civilization of yellow people. For the fact that the translation is perceived as an abstract concept – "socialism" – an educated Chinese, relying

22    https://www.youtube.com/watch?v=LVXlsJM81ec&t=214s

on the meanings of each hieroglyph, is able to imagine how: "the union of clans around the ancestral throne in the colors inherent in (those are) the Middle Kingdom." These colors are red, yellow, blue, white and black.

"It is crucial that, to the Chinese, black is a color of the sky. This is what is called cosmos in science, and the Bible calls it "darkness above the abyss." White, however, symbolizes the invisible world: "The world beyond." Whereas, red is the color of blood: a person in wealth, glory, and wisdom (correlates with Confucianism). Yellow is the color of the soil: racial distinction, health, and culture of the Han people (here is the doctrine of the eternity of Buddhism). And blue is the color of harmony (Taoist teachings).

"In the twentieth century, the symbol of red was replenished with "ideas of Mao Zedong" – Chinese Marxism – that began to dominate the conceptual power of the Middle Kingdom, and under the name "Maoism" began to capture the minds and hearts of the revolutionary outskirts. The yellow color remained with the Chinese nationalists. And under the blue stood the Chinese liberals, champions of freedom and "human rights." Character Transformation: From the Yellow Qing Empire, through the Republic to the Red Gong Empire.

"Clans in China are formed by family, relatives, countrymen, and class-mates.[23] Clans are established in one generation of peers with obligations that extend to children and grandchildren. An individual in China is not a single person and not a cell of the community, but the "iron screw" of a bureaucracy machine, where movement requires "stretching ties" and lubricating friction and plugs with a bribe. It is the clans who zealously monitor the conformity of the evolution of society following the agreed course, line, and state policy. A serious departure from this, at least three generations of a state line worked out and coordinated for the future, is punishable not by disgrace, but by prison and death; you can't pay off with money; the shield of glory does not help either."[24]

The privileges of officials are not inherited and the full renewal of pow-er by the "active" members takes place in the bureaucratic cycle of five generations. Thus, in China: the first generation of leaders is connected with the name of Mao Zedong, the second with Deng Xiaoping, the third with Jiang Zemin, the fourth with Hu Jintao, the fifth with Xi Jinping. With the proclamation of Xi Jinping of the Chinese Dream, as an ideal

23     The Growth and Decline of Chinese Family Clans, John C. H. Fei and Ts'ui-Jung Liu, *The Journal of Interdisciplinary History*, Vol. 12, No. 3 (Winter, 1982), pp. 375-408, The MIT Press
24     Gvasikov, Piotr "Exploring the future in the context of globalism," Bookvenir publishing, p.236, 2017

replacing the "ideas of Mao Zedong," the ousting of older generation rev-
olutionaries from power is now nearing completion.

Inside the country, the red revolutionary symbolism is increasingly replaced by the yellow National Socialism. But at the same time, on a global
scale, the blue clans (liberals) who received the name "Komsomol members," remain in an interlocked external relationship with the USA and the
European Union. "The current "clan alliance" was formed in 1989 after
the pacification of the counter-revolutionary rebellion of the Chinese liberals. It was an attempt of the "color revolution" initiated by the West; a
peaceful protest of students on the Tiananmen Square in Beijing, which
the nationalist Deng Xiaoping, heading the Military Council of the CPC
Central Committee (the pinnacle of power in China), ruthlessly crushed
by force.

"The Clan Alliance of 1990: the heirs of Mao Zedong – red party members; the successors of Zhou Enlai – are blue Komsomol members; and
the heirs of Liu Shaotsi and Zhu De are yellow dragons. Then, in 1989,
after the failure of the attempt to turn China onto the path of liberalism,
ternary harmony in society was achieved on the conditions of the winners
– Chinese nationalists of the "dragons."

"Via an agreement, lasting 10 year, the levers of power were given to
the political heirs of Mao Zedong, to the Shanghai group in the person of
Jiang Zemin. It was the Reds who, through the practice of "triple representation" (of the rich, smart and the whole nation), legalized the transfer
of development money by the Party to private hands, and the intelligent
youth were sent to study in the United States with the task of settling there
to understand the secrets of high technology."[25]

Then, over the next 10 years, power passed to the heirs of the blue line
of liberalism, Zhou Enlai-Komsomol members. The "Blues" proclaimed a
course towards harmony and scientific development of the country, which
justified the "borrowing of the beneficial fruits of Western culture" and
thus ensured an unprecedented breakthrough in the Chinese economy.

"Finally, under the task of victoriously completing in 2019, the year
of a yellow pig (a symbol of well-fed Chinese) of the "Xiaokan" cycle of
"small prosperity," begun by Deng Xiaoping in 1979, the "dragons" returned to power."[26] Historically, the "Dragons" are deep-seated military
clans in mainland China, Taiwan, and the overseas diaspora that developed during the Opium Wars of the mid-19th century and have solid

---

25    Gvasikov, Piotr "Exploring the future in the context of globalism," Bookvenir publishing,
p.176, 2017

26    Ibid

foundations in the nether world. Paraphrasing Gvasikov, "Dragons" are now called upon to fulfill a historical mission:

a) turn China "into a world power of the first order";

b) return of Taiwan to the fold of the Motherland;

c) After 2020, begin the transition to the Datun cycle, "great unity" (with the official name "community of peoples of one destiny").

The fulfillment of the mission of the full cosmic cycle of changes in the Celestial Empire (which began in the Han dynasty), according to the Confucian canon, requires the dragons to restore the connection between the people and the Great Tao lost during the period of "small prosperity." For this, Xi Jinping personally needs to solve the sacred task (the connection between the visible and invisible worlds), to receive a mandate for power, not from people, but from heaven. And with the "mandate of the heaven" to take on the burden of the Son of Heaven. This is the meaning of the period of the "new era" in the formula of the order of life, "Socialism with Chinese characteristics," written down in the Charter of the Communist Party of China.

The Chinese have a picture of the world, and it looks like this[27]: the center of the Universe, around which the sky revolves,[28] is the North Star. The starry sky of the violet color acts as the habitat of the Heavenly Emperor (Shang Di) and personifies the North Pole of the Universe. In the dogma of Christians, the Almighty Father is "the Creator of heaven and earth, visible to all and invisible." To the Chinese, the Creator of the World is impersonal – this is the Great Tao, about which nothing definitive can be said. "Tao gives birth to the One (the one). One gives birth to two (one divides). From two, Trinity is born. Trinity generates all things" (Tao Dejing).

That is, the Heavenly Emperor, the Most High, is not the Creator, but only the head of the hierarchy of order. To summarize: in the sky is the North Star, and under the heavenly sky on Earth is the Emperor (Huang-di) of the Middle Kingdom, around which the whole celestial world revolves. And therefore, history is made up of turns of different periods with the alignment of centrifugal (chaos), equilibrium (low prosperity), and centripetal (great unity) forces that people cannot change or control.

---

27  http://www.cits.net/china-travel-guide/chinese-mythology-how-the-heaven-and-the-earth-were-created.html
28  China's creation and origin myths cross-cultural explorations in oral and written traditions, Schipper, Mineke, Leiden publishing, 2011. https://library.villanova.edu/Find/Record/1342399/TOC

The Bible notes: "The sun rises and the sun sets; it hurries back to where it arose. Blowing southward, then turning northward, round and round the wind swirls, ever returning on its course." (Eccl. 1:6). The bottom line: Xi Jinping, in the circles of the Universe, is responsible for Heaven's destiny to begin globalization in Chinese.

Therefore, in the People's Republic of China important changes are taking place: writing the formula of a new era in the Charter of the Chinese Communist Party, amending the Constitution of the People's Republic of China under the indefinite rule of Xi and the leadership of the CCP as the essence of Chinese National Socialism: Polar star and cosmology of the world of the visible and invisible in the halo of the Almighty.

Politically, in China, conscience and justice don't exist, and neither does the recognition of the rights of others, (as in the West), but only an innate desire to "save face" before the clan is the motive of their behavior. In China, it is not the temptation and fear to cope with the management of a vast passive mass of people, but only a demonstration of power from heaven leads the masses to submissively obey the will of the ruler.

Not "energy capital" (the Chinese symbol of energy – the tiger) and neither the sophisticated insight (the square of mind and will – the snake), but the splendor of greatness and the punishing unrest of the dragon's power (the emperor's symbol is the dragon) in the hearts of ordinary people respond with a touching and reverent feeling of sincere fidelity, trust and obedience.

The dragon is a mythological animal[29] that, since the beginning of Chinese civilization, has been considered as the symbol of the Chinese people. For example, the red dragon symbolizes the indisputable power on earth. The red dragon of the new Gong dynasty (communist) will be the symbol of the modern era of socialism, with Chinese characteristics. Mao Zedong will be named the ancestor of the dynasty in his posthumous name, and Xi Jinping will be glorified in the name of the actual founder, but only with the acquisition of the "mandate of heaven."

British Freemasonry has long seen Xi in the image of the emperor of a new red dynasty. According to the Law of Changes (the East overcomes the Center), glorification can only be made by the mentors of the "Light from the East" (metapolitics) who distinguish the "Will of Heaven." The essence of the ritual of glorifying Xi as the patron saint of the family of peoples of non-Western civilizations.

---

29    *The Origin and Development of the Dragon in Ancient Chinese Mythology*, Matthew A. McIntosh, Brewminate online media, December 7, 2018

"The recognition by the ruler, who has risen under the symbol of the red dragon, of the urgent requirements of earthly progress exactly in accordance with the phase of the cycle – the influx or ebb of the energy of the Cosmos – ensures that there is no opposition to the strategic line of his policy. It is the relevance and timeliness of Xi's declared doctrine of the New Silk Road "from dragons to Teutons," proclaimed in 2013, that makes its mission consistent with the Law of the Universe.

"The perceived movement of stars around the North Star is circular, and the constellation of the Dragon deriving the energies of the Cosmos to the Earth in the order of the constellations along the "Way of Heaven" (the Age of Pisces, in 2014 was finally replaced by the Age of Aquarius).

"Man, of course, lives under the heavenly sky in the energies of the Cosmos, but on Earth, his life is determined by factors of geo-politics and geo-economics. Therefore, the geo-political project of land globalization under the name "One Belt, One Road" between China and Germany has both a purely economic basis and a sacred component for Russia, Mongolia and Kazakhstan, with the name "The *Tea* Horse *Road*" now generally referred to as the "Ancient *Tea* Horse *Road: China's* Ancient Trade *Road* to Tibet."(WanLi Ca Dao), where the Tao is not some kind of road map, but the Path of Heaven predetermined by fate. The political form of WanLi ChaDao is the Eurasian Union: The New Horde, repeated in a cycle (*novus ordo seclorum*). And the Scythian line, which Russia is called to lay, should become the sacral bond connecting the Dragons with the Teutons."[30]

Scythian line: China-Kazakhstan-Mongolia-Russia-Germany. The Scythian line is black and yellow, connecting the Aryan world of Shem (the spirit of the steppe) with the German-Saxon world of Japheth (reason).

It is quite obvious that Russia cannot perform the function of the "Earth's Core" – what Heartland is called in geo-politics. In order to close the Scythian line through itself and translate relations with China into the "mentor/patron" formula, tricolor Russia must be transformed. Transformation is possible within the framework of the Eurasian Union; here, the symbolism of power from heaven for the "Core of the Earth" in the form of figures and colors of the flag of a family of non-Western peoples is known:

a) on the transition in China from 2018 to civilizational thinking and universal motives for activities in the international arena;

b) about the change of fundamental attitudes and orientations;

30      Kings without a Crown in Red China, Vavilov, Nikolai, Konceptual Publishing, p. 119-131, ISBN: 978-5-907079-47-2

c) on the elimination of high costs for unnecessary opportunities;

d) on the destruction of corruption, vanity, and extortion;

e) on the development of the contours of the platform and shared economy.

# Diplomacy of Culture

Since 2013, the fate of mankind is at the turn of the global crisis of industrial society. A new hybrid war taking place in the form of World War III, the concept of the "cultural belt of the great tea road" in the framework of the officialdom of "Russian-Chinese strategic interaction" is becoming an essential aspect of the diplomacy of the culture of the new era.

If diplomacy has always been the art of subtle calculation, evasiveness, resourcefulness and clever conviction in achieving the goals of politics, then diplomacy of culture of the new era is a non-military way of solving the problems of the post-industrial war; when political goals are achieved through the traditional means of "forcing peace" of obstinate partners and overcoming global rivals with "soft power."

The old era of industrial society was characterized by such definitions as "mass production," "mass education," "mass armies," "mass information," "mass culture." That society is in a systemic crisis, the way out of which has acquired unprecedented features of a hybrid war. The new era of the future information society, according to the manifest signs of change, in the new world order, will lose its definition of "mass."

In the conditions created by the crisis, the clash between the civilizations of the Western world and the World of Islam and the unfolding battle of world projects to occupy the dominant peaks in the new world order, culture acquires the qualities of an accurate directed weapon to uphold the interests and impose the values of its globalization project. It becomes special forces of "soft power." According to the sinologist Piotr Gvasikov, the soft political pressure is conducted by organizations named after the cultural heroes of global projects, such as:

a) The project of the Chinese dream of creating around the PRC a "community of the unified fate of mankind" (Great Unity "Datun") is being promoted by the global network of "Confucius Institutes."

b) The values of the Christian civilization with the Latin root in Spanish are promoted by the Cervantes Institute network.

c) Cultural interaction with Germany in German abroad is carried out by the centers of the Goethe Institute.

d) The heirs of the Holy Roman Empire of the German nation are inspired by the Schiller Institute of Science and Culture.

e) The non-governmental organization of the Greater Eurasia project in Russia is called upon to become the Lermontov Institute of Culture Diplomacy.

Culture is what sets a person apart from nature (nature). New global political understanding as the doctrine of the Spirit of Time (intellectual tradition and style of thinking – (xx) as a concept of globalization in Russian focuses primarily on the internal content of culture as a unity of ethics, aesthetics, and logic of the heart, and not on external forms of manifestation in the set of arts (music, painting, sculpture, architecture, dance, cinema, literature, poetry, etc.).

a) Ethics is not what is good or bad, but what could be done, what is possible and what is not. Ethics is about conscience.

b) Aesthetics are feelings of what is beautiful and what is ugly.

c) The logic of the heart distinguishes truth from illusions and lies.

At the same time, the ethics of "five above" is taken from the Yasa, also known as a Code of Laws and Ordinances promulgated by Emperor Genghis Khan, when China, Russia and the peoples of the Great Steppe lived in a single state from sea to sea. The due in the code is expressed by the principles of "five above," where the worst crime punished by death is betrayal.

The spiritual takes precedence over the material.
Justice takes precedence over the law.
Service takes precedence over possession.
Power takes precedence over the property.
What belongs to all takes precedence over what belongs to one.

Genghis Khan's Great Horde was replicated and developed further by Stalin's Socialist Camp between 1926 and 1953. And today, within the framework of the project of the community of peoples of a united destiny, the theory of "socialism with the Chinese characteristics of the new era" by Xi Jinping continues.

To achieve the goals of globalization in Chinese, the "One Belt – One Road," the emphasis is on the economic interests of the countries and peoples included in this project. The accession of the Eurasian Economic

Union to the Chinese project "Belt and Road" is also a pure matter of interests, but not values.

The values that hold together the "hearts" of the peoples of non-Western civilizations of "Greater Eurasia" remain the principles of the "five above" ethics, the aesthetics of "socialist romanticism," and the logic of the heart. That is, for the completeness, integrity and adequacy of real politics to the natural course of change, the economic interests of countries and peoples should be imbued with cultural values.

## Cultural Codes of the Nations of United Destiny

Different civilizations are based on different cultural codes. Cultural codes are what is hidden inside external forms and therefore called in-formation. And this is by no means a collection of information (big data), but an ordered combination of characters – the alphabet – for recording, storing, and transmitting data (code words).

Therefore, wealth in the coming information society will be the possession of "keys to combination locks" of information. The essence is the ability to decode meanings, not the digitalization of anything and everything. The mouth of the "herd" of the peoples of the global world will be a figure, but to control the behavior of the "good shepherds" will be, not a figure, but a wave.

Cultural codes are associated with blood and soil (racial and national differences and different habitats: mountains, forests, steppe, sea). And blood and soil are human genotype and archetype. The rest of the culture tree of different nations grows on information encrypted with the cultural code.

The genotype is congenital (haplogroup), and the archetype (sample) is acquired by the collective unconscious from the environment. The cultural code of a person is recorded both in genes and in tradition. The genotype defines the potential (hidden opportunity), and the archetype creates a field (environment) for the realization of the energy of life. Changing the environment changes the arch-type of behavior, but the cultural code is preserved for generations.

Orthodoxy, with the dogma of the presence of God in the ethics of good and evil, is only one of the creeds. There are creeds where there is neither God, nor good and evil, nor sin. The Chinese have neither the hieroglyph "God" nor the hieroglyph "conscience" (instead of conscience in Confucianism, what is translated as "duty-justice").

Beliefs, and this is a combination of dogmatic definitions (revelations and rules) regarding the views, assessments, and figurative representations of the origin and development of nature and society, paint pictures of the world in the guidelines of the values of life. They are different. Images of the world (worldview) determine the goal setting of world projects. World projects are images of the potential future.

# The World is Controlled Via Signs and Symbols

Distinguished objects can act as symbols – that which connects the hearts of people. State symbols are the colors of the flag, the emblem, the music of the anthem. Symbols mobilize the will, raise the spirit. Therefore, they control the behavior of people more than words and laws.

We ourselves – our allies – our enemies. Against the backdrop of the American globalization project, relying on digital, artificial intelligence technologies leading to transhumanism, the New Horde project relies on wave management technologies leading beyond the "anthropological turn" of the middle of the 21st century when the "invisible world" becomes visible to all; where the doctrine of the New Silk Road from China to Europe advocates the economic and social methodology of addressing the challenges of globalization with the Chinese specificity. The Chinese globalization project called Datun-"Great Unity" of the countries and peoples of the world around China.

# Datun

Paraphrasing sinologist Gvasikov, the concept of Taoists regarding the next complete restoration began on the Path of Heaven (and the full cycle of changes: it started with the beginning of the reign of the first regular Chinese dynasty, Han, in 206 b.c. and ends in 2044, a period of 2250 years), called the Great Unity of the peoples of Datun.

"The idea of Datun as the goal of the Way of Heaven arose about 3,200 years ago when Wen-wang, "Enlightened King with Knowledge of Symbols," ruled in China. In a mystical insight, Wen-wang was the first to receive the great power of De (approximately 1148 b.c.), and he proclaimed himself to be the Son of Heaven; the ruler of the whole Earth, which is under Heaven.

"The Sage Dong Zhongshu (circa 179-104 b.c.) divided the wave of Chinese history into three long periods: "chaos of the warring kingdoms (JuLuan)," "small prosperity of the centralized state (XiaoKang)," "great unity of the peoples of the center and the periphery (Datun)," after which the Datun doctrine entered the canon of Confucianism. Datun is an era of peace and prosperity for all. "Celestial Kingdom belongs to everyone." And the nation of yellow people occupies a central place here.

"Mao Zedong pacified the last period of chaos by force and, in 1949, united the country under the name "the People's Republic." In January 1979, the architect of the Chinese miracle, Deng Xiaoping, proclaimed a plan to achieve China's small prosperity (xiaokang), designed for two generations of 20 years with completion in 2019. And in 1993, the Military Council of the CPC Central Committee adopted the secret doctrine of "Three North-Four Seas," according to which the fierce state giant of China by the middle of the 21$^{st}$ century (to the 100th anniversary of the PRC in 2049) would turn into a global leader with the highest total power.

"Xi Jinping had the historic task of realizing the "Chinese Dream,"[31] to peacefully revive the greatness of China, complete the construction of the Xiaokan in the country by 2019, and begin the transition to creating, by 2049, a united destiny of the Datun nations led by China."[32]

31      The Meaning of Xi Jinping's Chinese Dream, Winberg Chai and May-lee Chai, *American Journal of Chinese Studies,* Vol. 20, No. 2 (October 2013), pp. 95-97, American Association of Chinese Studies
32      Gvasikov, Piotr "Exploring the future in the context of globalism," Bookvenir publishing, p.200, 2017

# Chapter 5

# TRANSFORMATION OF GLOBAL PROCESSES

Political practice cannot be an abstract figment of the human imagination. At the heart of power, its intentions and decisions, one way or another, are ideas about how the world works and what place a political subject occupies in this world.

From a conceptual point of view, we perceive the picture of the world as the "Great Game" (the term coined by the prominent Freemason Rudyard Kipling), but not in chess (according to Brzezinski, when every political "grandmaster" conducts a session of simultaneous play on many boards between "whites" and "blacks"), but in a game of cards called Bridge (game of the elite)[1].

Bridge, is a card game played using a standard 52-card deck with each of the four players receiving 13 cards. If there are six players, then two jokers (black and red) are added to the deck, and the 54 card deck is divided evenly among the six participants, with each player receiving nine cards. Bridge is played by four or six players in two or three competing partnerships (two teams of three players or three teams of two players, never alone), with partners sitting opposite each other around a table.

Unlike chess, which the elite have successfully used as a cover story to convince the world that it is "the" game used by the powerbrokers to decide global politics, Bridge, the "Great card Game" is played in a clockwise circle, where representatives of existing world civilizations (global projects) are sitting at the card table of history, and behind them (behind the scenes) are global planners – carriers of a conceptual vision of the world. To sit at the "card game of history," players must be a fully developed Global Project (see chapter 2 for detailed explanation)

To be considered an independent "Global Project" you must have:

1. Conceptuality on a global scale. A planner who will set a goal, formulate a doctrine, develop strategies, and describe the opera-

---

1       The masters of the bridge game in the 20th century are/were: Queen Elizabeth II, British premieres Churchill and Thatcher; Mahatma Gandhi, American Presidents Eisenhower and Reagan; Chinese Miracle Architect Deng Xiaoping; transnational business tycoons Bill Gates and Warren Buffett.

tional construction of diverse forces for (mainly financial and informational) victory in WWIII of a new hybrid type.

2. Global financial structure.

3. Independent global intelligence apparatus (designed at the level of Illuminati/New Babylon, Opus Dei-Jesuits/Great Europe, Taoists/China, Sufi Tarikati/Islam, Bnai Brith/New Jerusalem, Templar Knights/Great Eurasia), which will reveal the conceptual foundations and a picture of the world of other global projects (regular intelligence does not deal with these issues).

The model is a card game in Bridge for six. The following projects sit at the card table of history:

1. Anglo-Saxons (project name New Babylon of American-style liberal-financier globalization/Finintern, capital New York);

2. Romano-Germanic Europe (project name Great Europe/"Black" International aristocracy, capital Vatican);

3. The Eternal Kingdom of Israel (project name New Jerusalem, the planners of the Solomon Plan, capital London);

4. World of Islam (project name New "Red" Caliphate of Political Red Islam, capital Istanbul);

5. China (project name Great Unity-Datun of the peoples of one destiny around, capital Pekin);

6. Russian world (project name Greater Eurasian Union, New Horde – the heirs of Genghis Khan and Stalin, capital Moscow).

The hidden confrontation between the Vatican (Christianity) and Finintern (Judaism/global network of the financial oligarchy with its major nodes in New York, London and Hong Kong) is the main contradiction of the entire biblical-Mediterranean civilization of the first two thousand years of the new era. This is a fight to determine the title of the "shepherd" who has the "mandate of Heaven" to shepherd the nations of the world as a "single herd," which, during the period of globalization, by the natural course of things, gathers "from many into one" (*E pluribus unum*, as we can read on the US $1 bill).

# Civilizational Codes of the 6 Global Projects

New Babylon – Skull & Bones (Illuminati). Conceptual base: hermeticism of ancient Egypt; victory weapon: NBIC-Convergence technologies/digital currency. Made possible through global banking-financier structures.

New Jerusalem – The Most Noble *Order* of the Garter, Bnai-Brith. Conceptual base: a *kingdom of priests* and a *holy* nation. 1,000 year reign of the Messiah. Symbol: British Monarchy (Kingdom of the House of David line). Objective: Illumination of the soul. To make it happen, non-liberal Russia plays a fundamental role.

Great Europe – The Legion of Honour. Conceptual base: the Vatican. Hidden element: Black International (Teutons). Visible element: Jesuits, Opus Dei. Heirs of the Holy Roman Empire of Germanic nations. Image of victory: Global Judeo-Cristian Theocracy.

Red Islamic Califate – Spiritual brotherhood. Mentor: Sufis via Islamic Ummah. Union via political Islam under the leadership of Turkey. Modus Operandi: Jihad and Holy war.

Datun China – Taoists via Dragon clans. Theology: Socialism with the Chinese specificity. Image of victory: a rebirth of the peoples of the unique dream. Symbol of victory: Red Dragon. Doctrine: One Belt, One Road from the Dragons to the Teutons.

Great Eurasia – Conceptual base: The Sovereign Military Hospitaller Order of Saint John of Jerusalem, of Rhodes and of Malta. Symbolic image: the Great Eurasian Steppe. Descendents of: Noah's eldest son, Shem. Image of victory: control of Eurasia from Mongolia to Altai, architects of the Great Horde.

The game is played clockwise in teams (projects) of two or three players within cycles of 12 years with each game covering a 4-year period. Each player represents one Global Project. The current cycle started with the beginning of the first wave of the global financial crisis in 2008 and will end by 2020.

The suits are[2]:

Diamonds-♦: Law and order, political system. Everything called "power."

Clubs-♣: Everything related to wealth, such as economy, financial interests.

Spades-♠: Society, everything related to social welfare.

Hearts-♥: Ideology, cultural values.

2    Gvasikov, Piotr "Exploring the future in the context of globalism," Bookvenir publishing, p.250-252, 2017

Each game starts with a project that finds itself in the dominant position at the moment the game is played. A Global Project that calls the game also decides the trump suit. Thus, the 2008-2012 game was ordered by New Babylon led by non-white US President Barak Hussein abu Obama II on the trump cards of the economy ♣. As a result of the collapse of the financial markets in 2008, New Babylon lost the game.

The following game covered the 2013-2016 period and was ordered by the World of Black Islam in the face of ISIS (the Islamic State of Iraq and the Levant), trump cards were declared hearts ♥ - Sharia law. Their partner was New Jerusalem (London). London post Brexit needed external markets to survive. With London shut out of the European markets, they were hoping to create an external market in the Greater Middle East using ISIS to clear the board. Russia's involvement in 2015 in the conflict in Syria (Red Joker trump card, unpredictability) saved Bashar Assad and changed the dynamics of the game. As a result, ISIS could not achieve the stated objective in the construction of the New Caliphate, and London couldn't realize their plan for a new economic pan-region.

China ordered the 2017-2020 game (with new maps of the post-industrial society, artificial intelligence, cyber weapons, digital economy, innovation, social networks, blockchain technology) from the perspective of the Third World War of the new hybrid type that began in 2013. The sign was given at the World Economic Forum in Davos in January, when Chairman Xi Jinping picked up the banner of globalism abandoned by Trump's United States, and announced the construction of the Global "One Destiny" Society (the historical name of the project is the Great Unity of Humanity "Datun"). Spades (♠) were declared as the trump cards for the game. China's partners in this game: World of Anglo-Saxons (New Babylon) and Romano-Germanic Europe (Black International, Vatican).

The unexpected version of the last game turned out to be when Moscow played as a partner with Great Europe/Black International on the trump cards of the social sphere (♠). Playing together, Moscow and Black International managed to take (five tricks) from London (New Jerusalem)/ New Babylon (New York), China (Datun), and the Red Caliphate (Istanbul). It is noteworthy that in the last trick, now the "black joker" of secret exotic technologies beats both the "stronger faith" card of Turkish state Islam and the new cards of the information society in the USA and China (digital economy and artificial intelligence).

An intelligence clue of the possibility of a Moscow/Great Europe-Black International alliance (in the political practice of autumn 2018) was Putin's visit to Austria in August 2018 to attend Austria's foreign minister, Karin Kneissl's wedding, where informal consultations took place between the guests.

How the political situation will develop from the autumn of 2018 to the end of 2020 will be shown in practice. However:

> a) For all three games, it is fundamentally important to note the supporting role of public authorities; as well as the powerlessness of the armed forces, special services and law enforcement agencies (♦) in the fight against the holy war of the soldiers of Allah (♥) and the opposition of the authorities to social institutions (♦).

> b) The aggravation of the situation in the world of those who ordered the game, London (planners) timed to the sacred date of the new Jewish year, September 9, 2018.

> c) One way or another, from September 2018, the WWIII of the new hybrid type entered the active phase of the strategy to crush the old world order and, above all, the currency world based on USD. True intentions of the Great Game are hidden behind the curtain.

The third game (the alliance of global projects in pairs or teams of three) turned out to be when Moscow played with China (Team 1) against London/Vatican (team 2) and Istanbul/New York (Team 3). It is noteworthy that London (Kabbalah) attacking and New York (liberalism) defending, who finds itself fighting for survival. With world liberalism on its death bed (end of Bretton Woods economic model), liberalism (global project new Babylon) is willing to give up its positions to Black International (in the face of Donald Trump) as long as they can negotiate the terms of surrender. In this position, Black International can run the table if Trump wins the 2020 Presidential election in the United States.

To advance their positions, it will become vital for Black International to reopen its old contacts within the Triple Alliance (Germany, Austro-Hungary, Vatican). The problem: until recently, Triple Alliance, was under the control of liberal Europe, and liberalism doesn't have the subjectivity of Black International. Subjectivity exists in Trump's USA, but Trump doesn't have the historical ties of the Triple Alliance.

New York (liberalism) does have the black joker (economy) as its "go to" card (collapse of the financial markets) and quite possible is willing to use it, or at least use it as a threat that leads to a negotiated surrender of the liberal-banking-financier positions.

Does liberalism have any other ways out? Can New York (liberalism) play on the same team with Istanbul? Not likely, as their economic model (Bretton Woods) is on its deathbed, and Turkey's primary goal is to find external markets to survive, something that New York can no longer provide them with.

There is one other option for the 2017-2020 period we need to examine. The six global players are divided into two teams of three projects each: Moscow/Istanbul/Vatican (Team 1) against London/Pekin/New York (Team 2).

Of note, only London (Kabbalah) and Beijing (Taoists) have a millenium project. Other projects are hundreds of years old. Also of note; historically, all US presidents since Carter until Obama have belonged to the liberal camp (New Babylon). If the liberal elite (New York) play their economic wild card of a market meltdown, the world will immediately find itself in a breakdown of established world order and regionalization of global markets.

The main problem of the liberal banking financier Deep State is the loss of control due to the lack of a reliable forecast. "Controlled chaos" (market meltdown) is a good option in a bad game: the legend of covering up the failure to calculate the consequences of decisions made and the inability of the elite to design and build the future. Be it as it may, there are four ways out of the crisis:

a) Continuation of the global crisis. Hybrid warfare. Slow reform.

b) A fierce struggle for the redistribution of resources.

c) The arrival of pragmatists-nationalists. Updating the economic structure. Autarchy.

d) Technological breakthrough. Transformation of the spiritual life. Strong Eurasian Union.

Trump (Great Europe/Black International) has a limited time-frame before the collapse of the global economy (end of first year of his second term) to hold international negotiations (something like a new "Yalta Agreement" and the new "Bretton Woods") to develop new regulations for international affairs and the world financial system.

However, this scenario has a caveat: Trump would need to immediately offer an alternative architecture for the world financial and economic system. What does Trump propose? 1. Regionalization of the world economy (the consequence of this also means that countries will disappear in favor of economic blocs, the disappearance of Westphalia as a model and turn to the post-industrial, post-technological economy); 2. Creation of regional currencies – dollar, ruble, yuan, rupee, peso, pound, etc. However, from a technical point of view, the creation of regional currencies poses a big problem because the markets today are global in principle, and the system of credit and insurance risks is not regionalized.

Regionalization of global markets will force the players to renegotiate their alliances. One such negotiation is taking place behind the scenes between the Rockefellers (bankers) and the Rothschilds (changers of physical goods, gold, diamonds, drugs, etc.). The liberal Rockefellers (who won both world wars against the Rothschilds) have lost the current war against the Rothschilds (London). As a result, in March 2016, after 146 years, the Rockefeller family exited the oil business by liquidating its investments in fossil fuel companies, including Exxon/Mobil.

This negotiated Rockefeller-Rothschild agreement is possible, but only with the presence of a third, strong player (in the form of a global project) that will act as a counterbalancing force – China. Why China and not any other player? The balance requires a strong third player and not a weak project. Any final agreement will put the liberal model into receivership, which will lead to international negotiations on a new economic model.

London has two options for the 2020 USA elections. Option 1: return the presidency to the liberal camp (Clinton or whoever is running the project for the liberals at the time) with a more than probable result of WWIII (chaos option with global collapse to write off $4 quadrillion-dollar debt via force major). Option 2: Trump's re-election with a forced surrender of positions of liberal financiers and reorganization of the world into regional economic blocks.

Most people interpret future regionalization as a world version of United Economic Europe. However, Trump's version goes deeper. The independent economy needs a market share to function. In the modern market, this quota stands between 300 and 500 million people. To reach a minimum quota, the world has to be reorganized financially into blocks, with each block using its regional currency. The following proposals are already on the table, although publicly, the subject is taboo:

# Economic Areas

Group 1: USA, Canada, New Zealand, Australia, and Northern Mexico. Total population base: 500 million people. Currency – USD.

Group 2: The Ural mountains divide Russia into a Western Russia (Russia-Iran-Turkey-former Soviet Turkic speaking republics and regions – Azerbaijan, Turkmenistan, Karachay-Balkar, Bashkir, Kazakh, Karakalpak, Kyrgyz, Uzbek, Altay, Tatar, Kumyk, Chuvash, Nogay, Khakas, Tyvan, Tofa, Sakha also Syria and the Balkans) and Eastern Russia (Russia-South Korea-Japan-Central Asia). Iran would join the group with Russia and Turkey and with Yemen, Bahrain, and the Shia part of Saudi Arabia. Saudi Arabia disappears as a country. Currency – Ruble.

Group 3: Rest of Mexico and Latin America. Currency – Peso.

Group 4: China. Or Japan with China if Japan cannot close the economic agreement with the Russia-South Korea cluster. China would simply absorb Japan because Japan is too small and too dependent on the natural resources of others. Currency – Yuan.

Group 5: India. Or Iran with India if Iran cannot close its deal with the Russia-Turkey economic cluster. Currency – Rupee.

Group 6: Western Europe (axis Paris-Berlin) with France's African colonies (resources + population).

Group 7: The UK with Arab countries (from Morocco to Saudi Arabia). This option was on the table as the most realistic solution to London's post-Brexit, (all that was required was for Clinton to win the presidency). No wonder, Arnold Toynbee, one of the most influential British historians, in the 1960s, said that Israel has a life span of no more than 75 years. Henry Kissinger and Rothschild warned the world in 2012 that Israel will disappear by 2022. However, with Trump's victory in 2016, the option was off the table.

# Chapter 6

# I Ching – Law of Change

The Law of Change is well-known to the Chinese. Since the antediluvian times (more than 4,000 years ago), the Chinese believe that the one (1) breaks up into two (2). A bundle of three forces (3) gives rise to changes in the cycle and the picture of the world breaks down into five elements (wood, fire, earth, metal, and water), the four cardinal points (Azure Dragon of the East, the Vermilion Bird of the South, the White Tiger of the West, and the Black Tortoise of the North) and the center.

At the same time, "the South overcomes the West," "the West overcomes the East," "the East overcomes the Center," "the Center overcomes the North," and "the North overcomes the South." Together the trajectories of overcoming form a "vortex of turbulence," where history looks like "the sum of waves of different periods," like tides and floods, like condensations and resorption, starting as a push (a shaft of ordered vibrations) and ending in the attenuation of multidirectional beats as a chaotic spot.

## 1. South Overcomes the West[1]

The South is occupied by the civilization of peoples speaking Semitic-Hamitic languages. In biblical tradition, these are the descendants of the sons of Patriarch Noah, who survived the Great Flood. The eldest of their sons, Shem, is the progenitor of the peoples of Asia, including the Semites: Assyrians, Chaldeans, Aramaeans (Genesis 10:22). And the youngest, Ham, is the progenitor of African peoples: Egyptians, Libyans, Canaanites (Genesis 10:6). Most Semitic Hamites in our time are Arabs and Jews. The descendants of the middle son Japheth populated Europe, forming the civilization of the West. In the fractal of the trinity of Being: Shem is spirit. Japheth is the soul (reflexes). Ham is the body (instincts).

Among the Semites are the roots of the secret, intended only for the initiates of the religious and mystical teachings of Kabbalah. Kabbalah, the secret knowledge of the "Chaldean sages," is the root from which all

---

1    Gvasikov, Piotr *Exploring the future in the context of globalism*, Bookvenir publishing, p.291, 2017

the esotericism of the biblical Mediterranean civilization of the South grew, and three world religions: Judaism, Christianity and Islam.

This confrontation in the terminology of classical geopolitics can be called the formation of African Europe, or otherwise the advancement of the Islamic world to the West. In 2007, the Muslim (primarily Turkish-Arab) overcoming of godless Europe manifested itself in refusing to mention the Christian foundations of European culture in what remained of the EU Constitution. An impotent ban on wearing hijab shawls by Muslim girls in French schools, followed by pogroms by the "new Moors" (immigrants from Algeria, Libya, Mauritania) of the suburbs of Paris. And most importantly, European connivance to secession from Serbia of its province of Kosovo, de facto captured by Albanian Muslims.

## 2. West Overcomes the East

This pair of opposites can be called the struggle of Atlanticism with Eurasianism, or otherwise of a United Europe with the Russian Federation. At the end of the 20th century, the united West defeated the East European Organization of the Warsaw Pact, and West Germany absorbed East Germany (1989). Under the pressure of Western liberalism, the Soviet Union broke up into the Commonwealth of Independent States (1991). In 2007, the process continued by the NATO alliance moving to the East and strengthening Western liberalism in Russia, launching Hybrid War against the tatters of the USSR.

The principal conditions were: 1) the Munich (February 2007) speech of Russian President Putin, which launched an information-psychological attack on Russia in the West as a "new evil empire"; 2) Plans for the West to deploy a missile defense system for the European theater of operations in the Czech Republic and Poland, which revived the threat of a disarming interception of missiles with nuclear charges on the trajectories of their launch from the East, and Russia's return from the Treaty on Conventional Armed Forces in Europe (CFE) regime; 3) Russian President Medvedev's speech which pledged loyalty to the West at the Davos forum and his subsequent nomination as a candidate for the presidency of the Russian Federation in 2008-2012.

## 3. North Overcomes the South

The North is the US Illuminati Freemasons with the "black magic" of transhumanism having embraced the wave: the North is conquering the South, relying on NBIC (nano-bio-info-cogno) convergence technology and artificial intelligence. Military attacks on Afghanistan (2001) and Iraq (2003) require a continuation of the attack on Iran (Bush's "axis of evil.") Following this logic, soon North Korea will defeat South Korea, just as North Vietnam conquered South Vietnam, and North Yemen defeated South Yemen.

## 4. East Overcomes the Center

According to the Law of Changes, only the East conquers the Center, while the East in the Chinese "heavenly" orientation is occupied by Russia. The Chinese proverb: "If you have a mind, then why use force," applies to Russia. Russia will not overcome China by force, but by its spiritual knowledge. We can assume that this spiritual knowledge will be the knowledge of "trinitarian harmony." Russians have a threefold type of knowledge, rooted in the genotype of the body and the archetype of the Soul. Weapons of metapolitics, instilling in the Chinese the prosperity of the Spirit of Truth lost in pragmatism within the framework of the project "Big Eurasia – The Third Horde," where Russia will take the place of a mentor, and China will be the patron saint of the family of peoples of non-Western civilizations.

## 5. Center Overcomes the North

The Center is occupied by the Middle Kingdom civilizations of yellow people (China, not the descendants of Adam but the Yellow Emperor/deity Huangdi, who came down from Heaven), which in our time prevails over the North (USA).

February 2007, when G.W. Bush congratulated Hu Jintao on the Chinese "New Year" (Spring Festival) over the telephone, the six-party talks on the Korean Peninsula's nuclear issue were not assessed by Bush, but by Hu Jintao, which makes Hu "senior" in the eyes of the Chinese, and Bush – "the younger." After a telephone conversation on February 15, 2007, US-Chinese relations moved from the status of "constructive cooperation" to the status of "strategic mutual trust." The new name indicates that the United States has reconciled with the role of China as a "first-order world power" and is no longer infringing on the interests of China in North-East Asia. The results of the strategic dialogue that began on December 14, 2006, in Beijing and continued up to the present day, indicate a difficult negotiation of a process for changing a global leader.

# Part II

# World Post-Crisis

# Chapter 7

# BRETTON WOODS AND THE
# 1970's OIL HOAX

T he postwar Bretton Woods System was an international treaty
agreement for regulating world trade and monetary and financial stability. The economic reality of the world as the 44 nations sat down to negotiate at Bretton Woods, was one in which the only
industrial power with ample industrial base, and the capacity to provide
urgently needed machinery and goods, as well as credit which would
be everywhere accepted as a solid currency, was the United States. The
core of the Bretton Woods System and the adopted IMF Articles of
Agreement of 1944 was the arrangement for fixed currency parities. Exchange rates were to be changed in relation to the dollar or gold, only
as a measure of last resort, and only after national policy measures had
been exhausted.

"Following the war, the value of the British pound, the French
franc, the Swedish kroner, the Italian lira, and, after 1948, the German mark, all were fixed at agreed, more or less permanent ratios
to the American dollar. Long-term investment and trade relations
could be undertaken on a stable currency background. Risk of dramatic currency losses was non-existent under Bretton Woods at
that time.

"In turn, the American dollar was fixed to a specific weight
of gold – a fine ounce of monetary gold was set to equal 35 US
dollars. The intent was to encourage member governments not to
cheapen their currencies by simply printing money and running
up deficits, a major problem preventing stability in many European countries in the postwar period. In addition, the guarantee of
fixed exchange was aimed to encourage the resumption of world
trade as soon as possible.

"The role of the dollar in the Bretton Woods system was unique,
for a good reason, in 1945. At that point, it was the only major currency which was backed by the world's strongest and most productive industrial economy, the largest trading nation, and one which

had ample gold to back the dollar. The US dollar was, in short, the only currency regarded to be "as good as gold."

"As the US Federal Reserve System held some 65% of the world monetary gold reserves after 1945, it also made sense to establish what was called a Gold Exchange Standard. Under the Bretton Woods Gold Exchange Standard, the dollar was considered an acceptable substitute for central bank reserves, i.e., as good as gold.

"An IMF member country's central bank was therefore allowed, under the Gold Exchange Standard rules, to issue currency in the defined ratio, against its reserves of dollars as well as its gold. The intent was that for European economies after the war, the process of non-inflationary credit creation would thereby be made far easier and encourage strong rates of needed industrial investment and reconstruction. The World Bank had been created as the vehicle to extend reconstruction dollar loans to the governments of Europe. The dollar would function for almost the next quarter-century, until the end of the 1960s, as the accepted substitute for gold.

"As a corollary, under the Bretton Woods gold-exchange system, with the dollar as the central reserve currency, unilateral dollar devaluation by the United States was ruled out. Only upward revaluation of other non-reserve currencies was allowed, as their economies recovered from depressed post-war conditions and began to build surplus currency balances. By the late 1960s, the rule prohibiting dollar devaluation was to become a central factor in the ultimate breakdown of the Bretton Woods system.

"The Vietnam War of the 1960s proved the ultimate undoing of the Bretton Woods system. With huge public deficits used to finance the cost of the unpopular war without imposing unpopular new taxes, year after year, foreign central banks built up large dollar accumulations, the so-called Eurodollar market."[1]

By the end of 1969, the US economy had fallen into a major recession. At the same time, the amount of dollars circulating in the world increased significantly in comparison with the amount of gold that backed it. For this reason, foreign states started to actively swap their dollars for gold, thus depleting US reserves. The reserves had contracted from 574 million ounces, at the end of WWII, to 261 million ounces by 1971.

By 1970, the Nixon administration and the Federal Reserve had eased monetary policy to lower interest rates and stimulate domestic growth. International currency speculators reacted immediately with a major attack on the dollar. By 1971, as a US recession worsened, and Nixon faced

---

1     "What the Bretton Woods system really was designed to do," William Engdahl, EIR, Volume 24, Number 33, August 15, 1997.

a hard re-election campaign, inflation and easy money from the Federal Reserve were stepped up under political pressure from the White House.

On August 15, 1971, President Nixon got rid of what remained of the gold standard. "It was one of the most important events in American history, alongside with the collapse of the stock market in 1929, the Kennedys' assassination and 9/11."[2]

Thereafter, the stage was set to leave the system of fixed exchange rates that gave an advantage to real productive development and investment, and after 1971 everything went in favor of the speculators.

> "When Nixon decoupled the dollar from FDR's gold reserve system, and got rid of the fixed-exchange rates, this was the first major step in the direction of the deregulation of the financial markets. This was then escalated – Glass-Steagall had been undermined when Alan Greenspan became the head of the Federal Reserve. When Glass-Steagall was officially repealed in 1999, this was the real starting point for the complete deregulation of the financial markets. Many countries implemented legislation which benefitted the speculators at the expense of the physical economy and to the detriment of the common good of the people."[3]
>
> "The original 1933 Glass-Steagall legislation was an important element of Franklin Roosevelt's New Deal, which also emphatically required a national credit institution (the Reconstruction Finance Corporation was put to use) and national credit. The leading features of Glass-Steagall were establishment of a wall of separation between commercial and investment banks and an insurance program to protect depositors, implemented by the FDIC. The repeal of Glass-Steagall in 1999 by the Gramm-Leach-Bliley Act, with the support of leaders of both U.S. political parties, opened the door for an orgy of speculative swindles, allowing commercial banks to buy and sell "instruments of financial innovation," such as "derivatives" and "swaps," which are, in reality, worthless pieces of paper, "bets" with no underlying value. With the repeal of Glass-Steagall, the U.S. government, including the FDIC, now stood behind all of these casino bets. The blowout of the Mortgage-Backed Securities bubble, which had been pumped up by speculative lending from deregulated financial institutions after Glass-Steagall was repealed, was the actual trigger for the Crash of 2008."[4]

---

2      "Trump Left Saudi Arabia Off His Immigration Ban... Here's the Shocking Reason Why," Nick Giambruno, Casey Research International Man, http://www.internationalman.com/articles/trump-left-saudi-arabia-off-his-immigration-ban-heres-the-shocking-reason
3      https://larouchepub.com/eiw/public/2018/eirv45n34-20180824/13-20_4534-hzl.pdf
4      https://larouchepub.com/eiw/public/2018/eirv45n39-20180928/24-31_4539.pdf

# Gold Window

At the time, Nixon said that the suspension of the god standard was only a temporary measure. Of course, he lied, because the situation has not changed over the last fifty years. He also said that this measure was required to protect Americans from international speculators – this statement was also not true. The main reason behind this step was the necessity to print money to finance uncontrollable government expenditures.

Nixon claimed that the suspension of the dollar-to-gold convertibility would help stabilize American currency. This statement was also false. Even considering the extremely doubtful government statistics, the US currency by that time had already lost 80% of its purchasing capacity since 1971.

The end of the Bretton Woods system (in fact, the default on the US liabilities to exchange dollars for gold) brought about the most serious geopolitical consequences. The major implication was the fact that foreign states lost the motivation to keep American dollars in their reserves and use them for selling balances in international trade.

After that, demand for the dollar was supposed to fall, together with the American currency's purchasing capacity. Something needed to be done. Washington invented a new agreement to give foreign states ample grounds to use the dollar as foreign currency reserves and so on. The new agreement, called a 'Petrodollar System,' retained the status of the dollar as a reserve currency.

# From Bretton Woods to PetroDollar

Economist Grant Williams explains:

"In the 1970s, Henry Kissinger and Richard Nixon struck a deal with the House of Saud – a deal which gave birth to the petrodollar system. The terms were simple: The Saudis agreed to "only" accept US Dollars in return for their oil and that they would reinvest their surplus dollars into US treasuries. In return, the US would provide arms and a security guarantee to the Saudis who, it has to be said, were living in a pretty rough neighborhood. As you can see, things went swimmingly. Saudi purchases of treasuries grew along with the oil price, and everyone was happy. The inverse correlation between the dollar and crude is just about as perfect as one could expect (until recently, that is).

"Beginning when Nixon slammed the gold window and picking up speed once the petrodollar system was ensconced, foreign buyers of US debt grew exponentially. Having the world's most vital commodity exclusively priced in US dollars meant everybody needed to hold large dollar reserves to pay for it and that meant a huge bid for treasuries."[5]

By 2015, there were treasuries to the value of around 6 years of total global oil supply in the hands of foreigners.

These agreements consolidated the purchasing power of the US currency, creating a bigger and more liquid market for the US dollar and US treasuries. The US also obtained a unique privilege to import goods, including oil, using their own currency, which they can simply print, unlike other countries that needed to buy it.

"In early 1973, the dollar was falling and the French, German, and Japanese economies were really beginning to boom."[6] In the beginning of 1973, the West German Deutschmark had already smashed the British pound, and by July-August was on its way to gaining hegemony over the ailing US dollar.

In May 1973, the Bilderberg Group met at an exclusive resort at Saltsjobaden, Sweden. "Certain elites connected with the money center banks in New York decided that it was time for a major shock to reverse the direction of the global economy, even at the cost of a recession in the American economy – that didn't concern them so much as long as they were in control of the money flows."[7]

The Egypt-Israeli war was used as a pretext for an oil embargo against the USA and other nations who supported Israel. The key point on the Bilderberg meeting agenda was the oil shock of 1973 – the 400% targeted increase in the price of OPEC oil in the near future. "The entire discussion was not how do we as some of the most powerful representatives of the world's industrial nations convince the Arab OPEC countries not to increase oil prices so dramatically. Instead, they talked about what do we do with all the petrodollars that will come inevitably to London and New York banks from the Arab OPEC oil revenues."[8]

All of that was aimed at continuing the systemic imperial process of looting the actual productive wealth of the major nations of the planet.

5    "Things That Make You Go Hmm... Like the Death of the Petrodollar, And What Comes After," Grant Williams, Things that make you go hmmmm, Vol.03 Issue 23, 11 December 2016. Zerohedge.com
6    "End of a golden age: Unprecedented growth marked the era from 1948 to 1973. Economists might study it forever, but it can never be repeated. Why?" Marc Levinson, AEON, February 22, 2017.
7    "A History of Rigged & Fraudulent Oil Prices (and What It Can Teach Us about Gold & Silver)," Lars Schall interview with F. William Engdahl, chaostheoren.de
8    Ibid

This oil hoax ultimately created an enormous volume of wealth transfer, nominally into the OPEC countries, the so-called petrodollars, but the money went to London and Wall Street to be managed. Thus, the financial oligarchy, in the major centers, used the oil-price hoax to establish absolute domination over the world's credit system, and to make sure it no longer went to civil and cultural development.

The oil price jump of 400 percent in 1973/74 saved the dollar as a financial entity, saved Wall Street, but not the real US economy by any means. The price shock halted growth in Europe; it smashed the industrialization of the developing countries in the Third World, which were enjoying a rapid growth dynamic by the early 1970's, and it tilted the power balance back in the direction of Wall Street and the dollar system.

Contrary to generally accepted opinion, "the oil market is controlled not by OPEC, but by the British Empire through its dominance over the giant oil companies which make up the international oil cartel. These companies, which control the transportation, processing, and distribution of petroleum products, control the physical side of the oil business, while the price is set through the financial markets. This arrangement allows the price to move independently of supply and demand, and has been of great benefit to the financiers who control the Empire."[9]

These petrodollars, combined with the proceeds of the British Empire's "Dope, Inc." drug-trade, were instrumental in restructuring Wall Street in the 1970s, paving the way for the junk bonds of the 1980s and the derivatives of the 1990s. The Deep State used the oil hoax to ...

> "fund operations to transform the United States from within, including the takeover of the US banking system and the cartelization – under the euphemism of mergers and acquisitions – of corporate America. Wall Street was transformed into a giant casino, where betting on financial instruments replaced investing, and the connection to reality was severed. At the same time, the petrodollars helped fund cultural warfare operations against the American people, to keep them blind to the damage being done, or even conning them into believing it was progress."[10]

There is an enormous financial rip-off that has been used by the Empire to run the assault in the takeover of the world. The effect of this assault is now becoming obvious. "The financial bubble has popped, and the great financial engine that was supposed to replace industry as the economic en-

9      "British Geopolitics and the Dollar, John Hoefle," EIR, May 16, 2008, pp 51-52.
10     Ibid

gine of the future has been shown to be as substantial as the emperor's new clothes. We are now left with a bankrupt banking system sitting atop a rusted hulk of an economy, dependent upon the 'world company' cartels for many of the necessities of life."[11] Progress and development were destroyed at the behest of monetary cartels in control of the world's economy.

# Credit System vs Monetary System

The world today is run by monetary systems, not by national credit systems. You do not want a monetary system to run the world. You want sovereign nation-states to have their own credit systems, which is a system of their own currency. Above all, you want productive, non-inflationary credit creation by the state, as is firmly stated in the US Constitution. This sound fiscal policy of credit creation by nation-states has been excluded by the Maastrich Treaty from even being considered as an economic and financial stratagem for Europe.

> A monetary system is a creation of the financial oligarchy that basically treats humanity like cattle. It is how the elite have operated for centuries. Oligarchies exist by controlling the "coin of the realm," they control its price and its availability, thereby controlling the people. They use their money control to manipulate our world. This is the system of Empire, the system that Alexander Hamilton challenged when the United States was created and the U.S. credit system invented. Hamilton said,
> "We are not going to ask you for money, we are a sovereign country, we create our own money. We will create credit and we will work in the economy in order to increase the productivity of our people. We will fund infrastructure projects, manufacturing projects, will fund things that increase labor productivity and make the economy more productive and therefore richer."

This is how real wealth is created: the production process. Instead of borrowing money from the oligarchs, you create your own money as a sovereign nation and use it to escape from the clutches of the oligarchy. And this is what allowed the United States to resist the continuous attempts of the British Empire to recover the US as an imperial protectorate. The difference between the monetary and credit systems is the principle on which the current oligarchic system is based.

Today, in Europe, this non-inflationary credit cannot be produced, because in Europe, the governments are subject to control by private banking

---

11      Ibid

interests. These institutions have the power to regulate (or deregulate) government and to dictate terms to government. The supposed "independence" of the European Central Bank is a decisive control mechanism for private financial interests, which in Europe have historically been installed as an authoritative instrument against economic policy of sovereign governments oriented towards the General Welfare of their populations. European banking is a remnant of a feudal society, in which private interests reigned, as typified by the ancient Venetian cartels that went into the shadows in the 14th century.

As far as the elite circles were concerned, the Bretton Woods system represented stability, and if you are going to throw the world into chaos, you have to get rid of those institutions of stability. How do you eliminate stability from the marketplace? First, you get rid of the fixed exchange rates and the currency exchanges, and then you co-opt the World Bank and the International Monetary Fund and turn them into agencies of the Empire, instead of what FDR intended – agencies of decolonization.

## The Essence of Bretton Woods

The unspoken essence of the Bretton Woods conference was not simply to ensure the expansion of the sphere of control of the dollar over half the world (and in 1991 to the whole world), but also to confirm that the right to legalize dollar emissions and, accordingly, earnings premiums belonged precisely to private entities, specifically transnational banks and affiliates. Until 1944 such structures simply could not exist: the dollar was the national currency of the United States, and American law forbade banks to create branches. Certainly, transnational banks existed in the world, but they did not work with dollars on their own.

After 1944, such structures appeared, and their activities were actively supported by the Bretton Woods institutions: IMF, World Bank and WTO (until 1991 – GATT). But the money printing itself, although carried out in favor of private institutions, was under national jurisdiction, the Fed, and acted under American law. Before the Bretton Woods Conference, when the scope of the dollar turnover was limited (it expanded, but slowly), and the dollar itself was tied to gold, emission mechanisms were used more to redistribute property, but after 1944, when a lot of dollars were needed and, especially, after August 15, 1971, when, as a result of another default, the dollar was untied from gold, the share premium of the financial sector rose sharply.

Numerically, this can be demonstrated by the share of profit that the financial sector in the United States redistributes in its favor: if before

World War II it did not exceed 5%, then a few years after Bretton Woods conference, it grew to 10%, by the beginning of the crisis of the 1970s it reached 25%, and by the beginning of the crisis of 2008 it exceeded 70%. In other words, for the longest time, the productive part of the physical economy "existed" on the remaining 30%.

Why did the governments of Western Europe, Japan, and China participate in such a scheme? What were they offered in exchange? Loans? But the volume of loans, even according to the Marshall Plan, in general, was limited, and growth began earlier. The answer is simple: The United States, whose share in the world economy in 1945 exceeded 50%, both in consumption and in production levels, opened its markets for these countries. As a result, the profit volume itself, in physical terms, was growing. And there was a feeling of financial stability. True, this stability is relative, since, for example, the entire growth of the US economy after 1981, (the beginning of "Reaganomics"), can be attributed to money printing. If we removed the trillions printed between 1981 and 2019, the real growth of the United States economy in this time frame is virtually zero percent. And a natural question arises: was there real growth at all, or simply a redistribution of the share premiums of banks? And then it becomes clear how the corporations obtained such insane profits.

Today, the US share in the global economy in consumption is significantly higher than in production (which is what Trump is trying to revert by the way), but dollar demand is the basis for the existence of all world currencies. That said, world capital is not reproducing, since interest rates have dropped too much. This was inevitable: the decrease in the cost of credit was used to refinance the growing debt. And today the world economy is facing a severe problem: it is no longer possible to issue US dollars because it will result in an inflation (Obama even stopped the corresponding programs in 2014), it is necessary to raise the rate to increase capital efficiency, but if the government decides to raise interest rates then it will be impossible to service the existing amount of debt.

Why did Obama stop emissions in 2014? And why did Trump restart it? First of all, there are two circuits in the economy, the real sector (the production of goods and services necessary for their use) and the financial sector. Moreover, the financial sector can be relatively large or smaller, it depends on the model of the economy, but it cannot be very small, since finance is needed to organize the division of labor, without which industrial economy can't exist.

Secondly, since the economy is adaptive, in general, it is possible to increase the financial sector in it relative to the real sector, and quite significantly. And although the transition itself can be painful, eventually, everything will settle down and will more or less function. But if you want to change the share of the financial sector again, problems will arise again, even if it will return the economy to a more "natural" state.

Why? The whole point of independent financial markets (the expansion of which increases the financial sector of the economy) can work only when assets from it can be transferred to the real sector. That is, something to buy from them. For example, a financial speculator buys a large stake in a company. Sooner or later, he sells part of it, but instead of purchasing new shares with the proceeds, he decided to purchase a brand-new expensive car. Thus, he has a real mechanism for evaluating stocks: how many shares can be sold to buy a particular car.

Therefore, as the share of financial markets expands, one way or another, income in the commodity markets must also be increased; otherwise, a gradual impoverishment of the population will take place. That is, a fall in total demand which will not be offset by elite demand, since it is generally much smaller.

In other words, if you begin to stimulate the demand of the population (for economic growth), then at the first stage of this process, maybe if you can find new assets to "bind" new money (for example, debts), there will be no inflation. The economy can adapt to excess money in other ways; for example, from 2009 to 2014, the credit multiplier in the US economy fell, so the expanded money supply remained virtually unchanged. But the multiplier cannot fall to zero, and new assets form new financial markets. And gradually additional flows from the financial sector to the real sector begin to form ... with subsequent price increases, of course.

It can be compensated by a new issuance aimed at maintaining private demand, but this will only accelerate the process. Real inflation begins. And an economy with a high level of division of labor and (as a consequence) complex technological chains cannot exist in conditions of high inflation, since it is impossible to predict the results of work for any long term.

If we look at today's global economy, we can see that it has practically exhausted the possibilities of "usage" of emissions. That is, the money printed goes directly to the financial markets, which leads to inflation. All the tools with which this inflation can be controlled have been used up over the last twenty-year period. And there are two options left: either you stop stimulating private demand so that it reaches an equilibrium state with consumer incomes (but this is a socio-political crisis). Or you continue to stimulate them stupidly, but with a sharp increase in inflation and a grave financial and economic crisis.

In other words, both the real sector and the financial sectors have problems (real sector needs money, and no one is willing to give it because it is totally unprofitable), and the financial sector (needs equity money, there is a liquidity crisis, and the Fed no longer gives it). True, the ECB and the Bank of Japan are still printing money, but it is clear that it is just a matter of time before they stop. Thus, you need to either resume printing money for banks (Clinton program in the USA), destroying the real sector with high inflation, or save the real sector by raising rates and stimulating demand through the budget (that is, issuing money which will never be repaid), but destroying banks who are holders of debt. This, in a nutshell, is Trump's program. At the end of the 1970s, with the model on its last legs, the financiers invented a new system.

## Reaganomics and Back to 1981

As Richard Cohen writes,

"Reagan's program as it was initially outlined virtually ceded control over the all-important area of monetary policy to the Federal Reserve Board and its Carter-selected Chairman, Paul A. Volcker. Critically, the program failed to advance reform of the world monetary system that would allow the US government to discipline London-controlled private and offshore markets and simultaneously failed to seize control of the direction of the nation's credit by allowing the Federal Reserve Board free rein."[12]

"Under the 'controlled disintegration' policies for the US and world economy, policies heralded in the late 1970s by a coordinated series of volumes published by the New York Council on Foreign Relations as the Project for the 1980s and publicly stated in 1979 by Paul Volcker, popular belief in and government encouragement of unlimited growth and progress were to be considered the enemy – in direct contradiction to Reagan's viewpoint.

"Controlled economic disintegration and the dismantling of the globe's advanced scientific-industrial concentrations were a major component of that report."[13] CFR, one of the oligarchy's central institutions in the United States, called this project, "the largest un-

12      "Reaganomics, Volcker, and the traps of 1981," by Richard Cohen, EIR, Volume 9, Number 1, January 5, 1982.
13      Ibid

dertaking in its history."[14] The 33-volume CFR report constituted blueprints, which the oligarchy used its power to institute during the second half of the 1970s and the 1980s. They imposed one of the most profound shifts in economic and nation-state policy during the XX century – the paradigm shift to a post-industrial economy.[15]

What does "controlled disintegration" mean? The world economy would be pushed into collapse – but not in a haphazard fashion. With the oligarchy controlling the disintegration process, it would be necessary to deliver economic shocks to carry this out: oil price hikes, credit cutoffs, interest rate instability, forcing the world economy to zero, and eventually negative, growth rates.

Simultaneously, there was the creation of the spot market in oil, of the euro bond markets, the derivatives market, and the expansion of the off-shore banking apparatus as well as the laundering of large quantities of drug money through some of the world's largest banks.

Starting the week of Oct. 6-12, 1979, Volcker began raising interest rates through raising the federal funds rate and increasing certain categories of reserve requirements for commercial banks. He kept pushing rates upward, until, by December 1980, the prime lending rate of US commercial banks reached 21.5%.

> "The effects of this policy were swift and devastating, especially because the Deep State had used two oil hoaxes during the 1970s, to send oil prices shooting upward. In the United States, industrial and agricultural production collapsed. Between 1979 and 1982, the production of the following critical US manufacturing industries fell by the following amounts on a per-capita basis: metal-cutting machine tools, down 45.5%; bulldozers, down 53.2%; automobiles, down 44.3%; and steel, down 49.4%."[16]

On top of that, beginning in 1981, the US economy has been growing with national debt biting at its heels. Without more debt, there would have been no growth at all. As both dollar printing and its legalization were performed by a financial institution, the share of the financial sector which stood for the redistribution of profit in the US (as I explained earlier) grew from 5% in 1939 to 10% in 1947 – just three years after the

---

14      "PROJECT 1980s: THE CFR'S PROGRAM FOR "CONTROLLED DISINTEGRATION," Angie Carlson, NewsWithViews.com, August 8, 2001.

15      "The Policy of Controlled Disintegration," Richard Freeman, EIR, October 15, 1999.

16      Project 80s: The CFR's program for "controlled disintegration," By Angie Carlson, News-With-Views.com, August 8, 2001.

Bretton Woods conference, to 20% by the onset of the crisis in the 1970s. In 2008, with the financial meltdown around the corner, its share reached as much as 70%.

What's important is this: beginning in 1981, the growth of global economy in one way or another was, in essence, driven by a redistribution of US dollars, printed by the Federal Reserve and passed through the Federal Reserve System – and that process is controlled by the IMF, WTO and other global Bretton Woods institutions.

The essence of Reaganomics was simple: given that the effect of expanding markets has been exhausted since the beginning of the 1970s, it was falsified through constant credit stimulation of demand. In other words, beginning in the early 1980s, the banking system allowed households to refinance their debts; that is, it became possible to repay old loans at the expense of new ones (this was part of the Reaganomics policy which allowed the government and US citizens to live beyond their means for decades).

Before it was adopted, the equilibrium macroeconomic parameters for American households looked like this: total debt – no more than 60-65% of annual income, savings – about 10% of real disposable income. By 2008, these parameters had changed as follows: average debt – above 130% of annual income, savings (minus) 5-7%. And in order to ensure that the demand did not fall, they began to lower the cost of the loan. In 1980, the discount rate of the US Federal Reserve was 19%, by December 2008, it had become virtually zero.

The collapse of the Soviet block in 1989-1991 guaranteed dollar expansion. However, the growth of the dollar system in the late 1980s and early 1990s did not have any effect, because instead of closing the debts created in the 1980s with assets received from the world socialism system (as suggested by the George H.W. Bush team), a different model was adopted under which Bill Clinton was elected president.

The essence of Clinton's model was that new debts were created for new assets (with the corresponding issue of the dollar, which was legalized through transnational banks). As a result, only in the USA the share of profit that the financial system took for itself grew from 25% in the 1970s to 70% by the beginning of the 2008 crisis. In 2008, the system of stimulating the economy through the growth of household debt was completely exhausted, and as a result, the share of financial sector profits fell to 40%. But then palliative methods were included (such as stimulating the outflow of capital from developing countries), and this share began to grow again. The trouble is that household debts were never reduced, while palliative measures have a very time-limited effect. In fact, the period of the last 10 years is analogous to the 1930s, when the deflationary shock that began (a sharp drop in the purchasing power of households) was not offset by emissions.

Since the debt did not go away, the deflationary shock was only postponed. And, as in the early 1930s, this will inevitably lead to the bankruptcy and collapse of the entire financial system. Thus, the financiers, in accordance with the greatly increased socio-political status, decided to save the financial system at the expense of the real economy. How was it done?

Beginning in the late 1960s into the 1970s and 1980s, the USA and the rest of the world was taken over by this rash of mergers, an ever-larger consolidation of industrial companies, of agricultural companies, of financial companies. They were slowly building these giant cartels to the point where we see now, today, giant cartels that control the resources of the world – effectively running the world.

By the early 1980s, the corporate raiders, financed by the dirty-money junk bond network, bought up significant chunks of corporate America and terrified the rest. The raiders' targets and those who feared they might become targets, turned to Wall Street's investment banks and law firms for "protection." As such, the leveraged buyout/junk bond operation functioned as a giant protection racket, destroying some as a way of collecting tribute from the rest. At the same time, dirty money poured into the real estate market, notably through the giant Canadian developers.... These firms built the skyscrapers, which were then filled up with service workers – bankers, lawyers, accountants, clerks, and other white-collar types...

The pouring of hot money into the real estate markets caused real estate prices to rise. The "wealth" created by these rising values provided more money to pump into the bubble.... The speculator went from being the enemy of society to the role-model.... The old-style productive industry became the realm of "losers," replaced by the hot new 'industries' of finance and information.

"The effect of all this deregulation and speculation has been the decimation of the physical economy of the United States. Over the last three decades, the productive capacity of the US economy has been cut in half, measured in terms of market baskets of goods on a per-capita, per-household, and per-square-kilometer basis."[17]

---

17      John Hoefle, "Southern Strategy, Inc: Where Wall Street Meets Tobacco Road," American

Today, bankers are running the corporations and their cartels. These cartels control the necessities of life, and they are now, virtually, more powerful than nations. This whole World Company project, in a sense, is a return to the old monopolistic days of the British East India Company with a modern computerized face. What should frighten people most is: the elite have actually done what they announced they would do, way back in 1968.

# Biderberg Conference 1968

In 1968, at the Bilderberg conference in Mont Tremblant, Canada, George Ball, a senior managing director for Lehman Brothers as well as the Undersecretary of State for Economic Affairs with JFK and President Lyndon B. Johnson, announced a project to build what he called the "World Company." The idea world globalists like to promote is that nation-states are outmoded and an archaic form of government, and that in a Malthusian world they can't be relied on to address the modern needs of society. "For Ball, the very structure of the nation-state, and the idea of the commonwealth, or of general welfare of a people, represented the main obstacle against any attempt of freely looting the planet, and represented the most important impediment to the creation of a neo-colonial world empire."[18]

In other words, according to Ball and others in the Bilderberg Group, the resources of any country do not belong to that country, but to the World Company Incorporated run by the Elite. And so, what is needed is a new form of government, one that will more freely distribute the world's resources. And that new form of government, they decided, is the corporate model. What George Ball called the World Company could then become a new government that would greatly surpass, in authority and power, any government on the planet. Doesn't that scare you?

Why was the plunge in incomes so sharp in the twenty-year period from the early 1970s to the early 1990s, and the loss of economic productivity so dramatic since the Kennedy Presidency? As economist Paul Gallagher explains,

> "London's Dollar One key parameter is that the dollar became decoupled from its sovereign function as credit for production, and was made the instrument for merely making money.
>
> The United States maintained essential control of its own issuance of currency and national credit, from the time President Frank-

Almanac, February 2001.
18      Pierre Beaudry, "Mennevee Document on the Synarchy Movement of Empires," Book IV.

147

lin Roosevelt replaced the British gold standard with a gold-reserve system in 1933, through the strong capital and exchange controls of the postwar Bretton Woods System initiated by Roosevelt's Administration. The idea of Roosevelt's Bretton Woods was that national capital and currency stayed at home for investment—the "non-exportable currency" explained in detail 70 years earlier by President Abraham Lincoln's economist Henry C. Carey.

International credit was to enable underdeveloped nations to purchase goods, machinery, and technology from developed ones. Governments restricted cross-border flows of financial capital to payments for trade; banks in member countries were not usually allowed to take deposits in foreign currencies unless the depositor proved that the deposits served for payment of trade. Economic growth was high and broad-based under this system.

The City of London banks, beginning with the one now called HSBC (formerly the Hong Kong and Shanghai Banking Corp.), set up British offshore centers of the so-called "eurodollar" market from just before 1960, directly violating the rules of the Bretton Woods System. British banks opened offshore dollar accounts, which paid significantly higher interest rates than did accounts in U.S. banks, and which made speculative loans and securities investments initially in Europe, particularly for corporate takeovers. The London banks did this initially, starting in 1955, in collaboration with banks in the Soviet Union, which wanted to move dollar accounts belonging to Soviet citizens or Soviet agencies out of the United States. But soon after, Wall Street banks jumped in. Before long, the City of London and Wall Street banks were directing the oil revenues of Middle Eastern countries and the Soviet Union into these "eurodollar-petrodollar" accounts as well. Already in 1958, $1 billion flowed from U.S. bank deposits into the eurodollar market.

By the mid-1960s, the flow had reached $60 billion, equal to almost 10% of U.S. GDP. This began London's "comeback" as what is today, again, the world's dominant and imperial financial center. It is the world leader in foreign exchange trading, cross-border bank lending, exchange listing of companies, and, by far, in financial derivatives issuance. The eurodollar accounts had the elevated interest rates and offshore speculative purposes of what has since been called a "carry trade."

Especially as European countries all made their currencies freely convertible into dollars by 1960, the eurodollar market progressively drew the U.S. money supply offshore and robbed the Treasury of control of the creation of its own currency. By 1980, approximately 80% of U.S. dollars were circulating, and effectively being created, outside the U.S. economy. The petrodollar, or "London dollar," effectively replaced the U.S. dollar. U.S. and other national "prime" interest rates were replaced in this process by the LIBOR (London Inter-bank Offered Rates), which became dominant, and are now known to have been systematically rigged by the British Banking Association, which set them daily.U.S. banking regulations disappeared.

A top Bank of England (BoE) official, James Keogh, said in 1963: "It doesn't matter to me whether Citibank is evading American regulations in London. I wouldn't particularly want to know." The BoE stated in a memo that year, as London offered unregulated and unnamed ("bearer") Eurobonds—perfect vehicles for tax evasion and financial crime—"However much we dislike hot money, we cannot be international bankers and refuse to accept money." And these offshore dollars, in the form of high-interest eurodollar loans syndicated by London and Wall Street banks, began to be used to replace American and European manufacturing and industrial production plants with substitutes in countries featuring lower, even much lower, wages. Kennedy vs. London and Wall Street. As this process progressed during the later 1960s and 1970s, inflation was triggered in the United States, and domestic interest rates were pulled up at the same time. The dollar-gold reserve fixing, which was central to the Bretton Woods System, was threatened with the breakdown.

The big Wall Street banks followed their accounts to the City of London, opening "offshore" arms there which evaded the Glass-Steagall Act's limits on securities speculation. The last President who tried to stop this massive speculative export of U.S. currency was John Kennedy. Kennedy planned, with aides, to restore enforcement of the currency and capital controls of the Bretton Woods Agreement.

Kennedy is quoted in Nomi Prins' *All the President's Bankers*: "It's an insane system to have all these dollars floating around [that] people can cash in for a very limited supply of gold." Prins reports that on July 18, 1962, Kennedy "announced a program... that included a 15% tax on purchases by Americans of foreign securities and a tax on loans made by American banks to foreign borrowers." He wanted to go further and reimpose currency and capital controls. Wall Street strongly opposed him, led by then-New York Governor Nelson Rockefeller. *LIFE* magazine on July 6, 1962 featured Rockefeller's open letter to Kennedy, opposing his proposed exchange controls and claiming that the entire financial and business community opposed him. Kennedy lost the battle. After JFK's death, Walter Wriston of Citibank wrote (again quoted by Prins]: "In 1963, the United States began a futile bout with capital controls. . . . In this period, New York banks began to finance projects in America with dollars deposited in European [i.e., London—ed.] banks."

President Nixon made the loss of U.S. management of the dollar into an uncontrollable flood. The turning point into this devolution was 1972, immediately after Nixon was bullied by the British and by his Office of Management and Budget Director/Treasury Secretary George P. Shultz into breaking Roosevelt's Bretton Woods System. The United States then let the dollar float speculatively against gold and other currencies. Nixon's and Shultz's actions triggered an explosion in the offshore markets for speculative U.S. dollar accounts: the eurodollar/petrodollar markets.

They also triggered an explosion of unregulated foreign exchange ("forex") trading to now $5 trillion daily, 98-99% of that trading independent of any trade in goods and services. Major London banks have recently acknowledged to regulators that forex values, too, have been unlawfully rigged. Since 2011, British financial institutions have been working to establish the City of London as an offshore financial center for investment and trading in China's currency, the renminbi. Beijing is well warned and has given priority instead to Frankfurt, for purposes of China's trade with Europe.

The 1970s U.S. economy was marked by steadily rising, and apparently uncontrollable inflation, and by a doubling of the number of officially unemployed Americans from 4 million to 8 million. The 1960s' sharp reduction of officially defined poverty was reversed, and the poverty rate rose from 12.5% in 1970 to 14% in 1980, its peak until the aftermath of the 2008 financial crash (it is now 15.9%). The decade was ended by Federal Reserve chairman Paul Volcker's brutal crushing of inflation by raising baseline interest rates to a usurious 21%, causing a deep and "double-dip" recession.

Employment recovered during the 1980s, but real household incomes and real hourly wages continued to drop. The stages of deep austerity would follow Nixon's breaking up the Bretton Woods system, were being carried out. Another extraordinary marker of what the destruction of Roosevelt's Bretton Woods meant, is the explosion of the amount of debt necessary to produce a given amount of GDP—under the circumstances of London's eurodollar/petrodollar system, floating exchange rates, and then globalized securitization of debt. The drop in real incomes and living standards leveled off in the late 1980s and was replaced by relative stagnation, until Bush, the 2008 crash, and Obama's "recovery" started another downhill slide. The leveling-off reflected the collapse of the Soviet Union, significantly strengthening the petrodollar. The United States was enabled to consume imports and run trade deficits in the hundreds of billions of dollars annually for decades. But the decline in productive employment did not stabilize; it has fallen by another 4 million, another 7% of the workforce, since 1990.

Fifty years later, the U.S. economy is in a permanent low-productivity, cheap-labor, part-time/temporary/self-employment morass, sometimes repugnantly called "the new normal." Low and declining real wages and household incomes now dominate the economic and social reality of the nation. Entire, once-productive sections of the economic platform of the continent have been destroyed—for example, the steel centers of Monterrey, Mexico and Pittsburgh, Pennsylvania. The North American rail grid is dysfunctional."[19]

That said, however, the system can only work in favour of the financial speculators if they control the emission of the U.S. dollar. But the difficulty was that the Bretton Woods reform was not completed in 1944 – the world currency-issuing center, the Federal Reserve of the United States, remained under the control of the US national elite, under their jurisdiction. And in 2011, an attempt was made to create a supranational emission center (the so-called "central bank of central banks"), which was supposed to set emission limits for all national central banks, including the Fed. This attempt was repulsed by the U.S. national administration under President Obama (Dominique Strauss-Kahn case), but it became clear that this was only the first round of the fight.

The second round took place in 2016 when financiers tried to lead their candidate (Hillary Clinton) to the White House. Today, we are witnessing the progress of the third round – namely, attempts to remove the feckless representative of the alternative elite group, Donald Trump, from the White House – on the cusp of the deflationary stage of the crisis.

What is Trump's game? He is trying to remove the emission mechanism from stimulating the U.S. economy. Since the additional issue of money no longer leads to the growth of the world economy (which is now manifested only in statistical figures), the USA no longer receives

19        https://larouchepub.com/eiw/public/2014/eirv41n47-20141128/04-13_4147.pdf

additional profit even from the export of capital, and the chronic deficit in the foreign trade balance creates big problems in the domestic market. Trump's idea is to reduce this deficit to zero and return production to the United States (and, as a result, jobs) exported from the country in the previous 40 years (going back to Reaganomics).

What is the problem with this idea? On paper, it looks adequate, as it dramatically reduces the role and influence of the financial system, both in the world economy and, accordingly, in politics, and on the scale of the United States itself. The trouble is, stimulate domestic demand through the financial system (structural crisis and the discrepancy between real incomes and household expenses) and the implementation of such a reform will automatically lead to a general decline in living standards (which is no longer determined by household incomes, but primarily by their living expenses).

Roughly speaking, today U.S. households spend 25% more money than they earn. And this stimulation occurs through the use of the financial system. If you write off their debts (or force them to pay), then real income will fall further from the current level, which already corresponds in purchasing power to the level of the end of the 1950s. And then what?

This, in fact, is the main theoretical error of those American economists who are preparing Trump's economic plans. They do not see a structural crisis and believe that if you simply write off household debts (with the collapse of the financial sector, of course) and ensure demand by increasing domestic production with the creation of appropriate jobs, then, in general, the situation with living standards in the United States will not be worse; however, the financial sector will lose its influence.

Again, if we take into account the structural problems of the U.S. economy, the upcoming recession will be one and a half times deeper than in the early 1930s (then structural imbalances were about 15%, now about 25%). And this, of course, will destroy the world's economic system. In fact, within the framework of the Trump plan, it is already being destroyed, but so far, the level of destruction is more or less controllable. In reality, the events will develop much more swiftly and much less controllably. Is this why the global financiers hate Trump? And how is this related to Trump's tug-of-war against the Federal Reserve?

## Trump vs. the Elite

First, Trump forced Fed leadership to cut rates. Forced, because all the institutions of the "Western" global project that are responsible for the theoretical foundations of financial policy (that is, at the current stage, for the support and maintenance of the Bretton Woods system) have been saying for many months that the rate needs to be raised!

True, they didn't say why. But, I will. The problem is that in recent years capital has not been reproducing, and thus, its profitability is negative. And for the Bretton Woods model (like any financial model) this is a disaster; it is impossible to allow such a situation to persist for a long time. Since the printing of money is finished (there is no way to manage it without the backing of the U.S. administrative authority; therefore, you need to be careful, otherwise you can run into different excesses, such as "Strauss-Kahn cases" or "Eliot Spitzer cases"), it remains to raise the rate above the level of "regular" annual losses.

And this is something that Trump opposes. Why he is against it is also understandable. Because the ensuing struggle is inevitable: after the collapse of the financial markets, emissions will still have to be made. And there are two options as far as what to do with the emissions: you either support the real sector of the economy, or you support the financial, parasitical speculators. There are questions, what are the views of Trump and Jerome Powell (head of the Fed) in this dilemma? And, by the way, to make sure that an alternative vision does not penetrate the power circles in the USA, the liberal media is up in arms against Trump. Trump's famous slogan, "Make America Great Again," could be correctly translated as follows: "Let's restore America's independence from international financiers!"

But back to the current events. A lower interest rate means that the financial lobby in the USA has lost! It could not regain the mechanism that ensures the reproduction of capital, which means that markets will collapse, and the power of this system will fall. Question: How quickly will other players understand this? Answer: They realized it almost immediately. This means they recognized that the financial lobby can no longer win under any circumstances and what is more, the restoration of the Bretton Woods model is a physical impossibility! Exactly what Putin said in June 2019!

What happened next? A few days after the rate cut in the United States, China devalued the yuan. This is fundamental destruction of the entire negotiating environment in which Xi interacted with Trump in recent months. Many said that they would unconditionally agree because it is mutually beneficial; they talked about win-win strategies, etc. Only this all makes no sense because the Bretton Woods model itself, in which all these machinations took place, has no future.

GLOBAL PROJECTS AT WAR: TECTONIC PROCESSES OF GLOBAL TRANSFORMATION

The reaction of financial markets followed immediately. What's important is this: China has abandoned hope for a strategic agreement. After the devaluation of the renminbi, even discussing long-term agreements with the United States is quite meaningless. The die is cast, the Rubicon is crossed, what else is there to do?

I repeat, it is impossibly foolish to destroy the old system without having a new economic model in place. Which, by the way, doesn't exist at present, since even discussing it was forbidden for the past several decades because the entire, global model was based on liberal principles. But an alternative system can be created. The question is how to implement it. To do this, it must, at a minimum, be legitimized. And this can only be done at an international conference, the very "new Yalta 2" or the "new Bretton Woods 2."

And the timetable can be quite clearly outlined. First of all, Trump has to win the elections in November 2020. After that, Presidents Trump, Putin, and Xi must begin preliminary work on the new Bretton Woods/ new Yalta conferences; secondly, exchange their views on how they see new, post-crisis models, and, finally, put in place technical teams charged with solving technical issues. As they decide (and it certainly won't take less than a year), the conferences will start somewhere in the years 2022-2023.

# Systemic Problems of the Modern Financial and Economic System

In 2017, global GDP, at purchasing power parity[20], was about $127 trillion, and its growth rate was no more than 2.6% per year. US GDP, according to their own official estimates, is about 21.35 trillion dollars. That is about 15% of world GDP,[21] and its growth rate is significantly lower than the global economy: about 2%, according to official figures – and around zero in reality.

In August 2018, the Institute of International Finance in Washington published a report, "showing that the total indebtedness of the world is now $247.2 trillion, representing an increase of 11.1% just for the last year. In other words, "we are sitting on a complete powder keg, and anything

---

20      Gross domestic product (GDP) or value of all final goods and services produced within a nation in a given year. A nation's GDP at purchasing power parity (PPP) exchange rates is the sum value of all goods and services produced in the country valued at prices prevailing in the United States in the year noted.
21      https://www.visualcapitalist.com/visualizing-the-composition-of-the-world-economy-by-gdp-ppp/

could trigger a collapse of the bubble, which if not remedied would then be the trigger of economic chaos with unforeseeable consequences."[22]

But the scale of the intragovernmental debt of the American economy (represented by the federal budget, the budgets of states and municipalities, corporations and households) is about $50 trillion, and it has been growing steadily at a rate of about 10% per year. And although 3/5 of this debt are the debts of some subjects of the American economy to other subjects, it is impossible to "offset" them in any way – since these debts have long been alienated from borrowers and are freely traded assets of the American financial system on the market. That is, the internal elements of any "debt chain" themselves become the "embryos" of new debt chains, which are provided only with their original assets, but not at all the assets that provide the primary chains from which they grow.

What does 10% of $50 trillion mean? It means $5 trillion. That is, the growth rate of debt is about a quarter of the country's GDP. If we take into account that about 70% of the US GDP is made up of services that cannot be reliable collateral for a debt, we get a wonderful picture: today, all American assets created during a fiscal year cannot provide new debts issued during the same time-frame. And at the pace they are growing, soon global assets will not be enough to ensure them (in the world GDP, services also make up a considerable share).

What this means is also understandable. The vast majority of new financial assets (and among them, there are significantly less reliable than direct debts) do not have any collateral. That is, none at all. This is pure speculative fiction, paper, or even electronic recording, which does not give its owner any real guarantees. Such a system cannot exist for a long time; its reliability is at the level of the Russian GKO pyramid in June 1998.

It is worth our time to review the period of the liquidity crisis in Russia in the late 1990s and compare it to the 2007 liquidity crisis that almost brought down the entire global financial system. Back in 1998, a $10 billion IMF loan front-loaded with a billion dollars in cash was given to President Boris Yeltsin. Immediately following the accord with the IMF, "the Russian Central Bank began to place funds, including much of the money Russia had been loaned by the IMF, into the accounts of its offshore subsidiaries Fimaco and Evrobank."[23] This money was then recycled back into the Russian financial markets to buy short-term Treasury bonds [GKOs].

22      https://larouchepub.com/eiw/public/2018/eirv45n34-20180824/13-20_4534-hzl.pdf
23      Pirani, Simon; Farrell, Ellis, The World Crisis of Capitalism and the post-Soviet States, conference Moscow 30 October – 1 November 1999.

This pump-priming inflated the GKO market, and western investors and financial institutions then caught the GKO mania, without understanding what was really going on; thereby both betting for and helping assure a Yeltsin victory at the polls. The Central Bank fixed the ruble exchange rate, interest rates rose, and the yields on the GKOs increased to insane levels. The 290-percent returns (on three-month paper at one point) on Russian GKOs were paid with U.S. taxpayers' money via IMF loans. It isn't difficult to surmise the investment's final destination. "By yielding that kind of non-market returns, the bond market ensured that all the country's resources and all that it was capable of attracting went to the support of the state."[24]

The August 2007 liquidity crisis in the European and American financial markets demonstrated this in full measure – it was caused solely by a crisis of trust between banks and other financial institutions to each other. This is natural – the Enron Corp, Fannie Mae and Freddie Mac, Lehman Brothers, AIG, and many others have shown very well how unreliable everything is in the modern world; however, since then the situation has not improved, to put it mildly.

There are two ways out of this predicament: the first is a forced stop of the debt pyramid with its gradual servicing and reduction; the second is its quick "reset," massive default, with the possible continuation of the creation of new debt obligations. The problem with the first option is that at the same purchasing power parity, the United States consumes about 40% of world GDP. And the difference with its own production – almost twice, is due precisely to the emission – both debts and money (for their turnover). And stopping this emission is an instant double decline in total U.S. consumption. Even in Russia in 1991-92, the drop was 40%.

There are questions: What is the elasticity in the primary commodity markets? How much will the oil price fall with a 20% drop in aggregate demand? What will happen to world production, in the context of an already excessive amount of capacity? Thus, no one dares to stop the emission of debt. But the second option is not much better – debt relief, mass defaults – this is, in fact, a repetition of the 1929-30 option, a deflationary shock, the same fall, only stretched over several years. Note that this option, unlike the first, can happen spontaneously, as it did in 1929. Actually, it almost happened in August 2007; and only large injections of liquidity and a decrease in the rate in the USA, which provoke inflation growth, "corrected" (temporarily) the situation.

24    Anne, Williamson, An Inconvenient History, WorldCity Essays, September 1999.

American economist John Hoefle explains this phenomenon in a few paragraphs.

> As the speculative bubble came to dominate the U.S. and world economies, feeding it became paramount. Among other things, this led to a sharp run-up in real estate values, to provide 'wealth' which could be turned into mortgage debt, and then into a wild assortment of securities to be used, with lots of leverage, to play in the derivatives markets. To keep the mortgage-debt flowing, as prices rose into the stratosphere, the bankers repeatedly loosened the requirements for home loans. This process, which was driven by the banks and the derivatives market, ultimately exploded. This was falsely portrayed as a 'subprime' crisis, but in reality, it was the death throes of the financial system itself.
>
> In mid-2007, the failure of two Bear Stearns hedge funds signaled the collapse of the global securities market as speculators realized the game was over and began to try to cash out. The demand for speculative paper quickly dried up, sending the nominal valuations plunging. The market, which had grown phenomenally through leverage, began to collapse in a reverse-leverage implosion. Speculators had borrowed trillions of dollars to place bets, gambling that they would win enough to pay back their loans and still turn a nice profit. This game worked for quite a while, but it quickly turned nasty when the market seized up. Suddenly, the speculators found themselves losing on their bets, leaving no profits to pay off their loans, and thus losing on both ends. Assets began vaporizing by the trillions, and worried lenders began demanding more collateral on margin calls, causing sales of assets that further depressed prices, in a vicious, reverse-leverage spiral.
>
> The 'solution' to this blowout adopted by the central banks, was to begin to flood the financial markets with liquidity, through a series of interest rate cuts and cash injections. Though they had sworn to impose discipline on the markets, the central banks quickly capitulated under the pressure of enormous losses, in a hyperinflationary panic. The injections quickly escalated from the billions, to the tens of billions, to the hundreds of billions, as they raced to plug the holes caused by the savage deflation of the valuations in the system. But no matter how much money they injected, the system kept collapsing. The money pumped into the bailout – money that serves no economically useful purpose – will only accelerate the process. This means that the faster the government pumps in the capital, the quicker the value of the dollar will collapse, and the faster the global economy will collapse.[25]

25    John Hoefle, "The End of the Line for the Anglo-Dutch System," EIR, March 28, 2008.

By 2008, the entire system imploded. In fact, the 2008 crisis was a twin of the prewar Great Depression that began with the U.S. stock market collapse in October 1929. The spring of 1930 saw a deflation shock. The crisis itself commenced in 1930. But, unlike the 1930 crisis, U.S. monetary authorities, mainly the Federal Reserve, for the first time openly started an issue of money not supported by any assets at all. But why did it not have any impact on inflation? It did not have any effect on inflation because the problem was caused by the changes in the structure of money supply. The credit multiplier dropped by a factor of four between 2008, when it stood at 18, and 2014, when it was slightly over 4. Hard money supply subsequently soared four times – from 0.8 trillion dollars to 3.3 trillion dollars. That means that Washington simply printed 2.5 trillion dollars with no inflationary impact. In 2014, Obama stopped the printing press. Why? Because a fall of the credit multiplier to less than 4 kick-starts a process called a "non-payment crisis."

What is terrifying, during the last ten years, over \$12 trillion in quantitative easing (Q.E.) money has been issued under the bailout policy, at the British Empire's direction and coordinated through the central banks of the United States, the European Union, Great Britain, and Japan.

> While industry and agriculture have been starved of credit, the reign of "quantitative easing" has actually done nothing to stabilize financial markets. The central banks of Europe, Japan and America are now them-selves choking on a total of approximately \$14.5 trillion equivalent (at face value) of bank, government and corporate financial paper that they have purchased since 2008. This deployment of "helicopter money" has only increased financial indebtedness, while also producing a dramatic growth of the S&P 500 Index from its low in early 2009 – this, itself, a sign of increasing financial instability, as "Ponzi scheme" financial betting replaces long-term productive investment.[26]

Do you remember the 2009 bank bailout? What was the real reason the bankrupt banking sector was bailed out? Were Wall Street and the US Government honestly thinking of "saving America" as they said? Hidden from the public, there was a far more sinister reason for the massively fraudulent bailout. Under the guise of saving the economy, the bankers transferred vast amounts of debts from private hands, from the banks and other powerful interests, to the books of the government, but because the economy is collapsing, this debt is absolutely unpayable. Let me repeat it.

---

[26]   https://larouchepub.com/eiw/public/2018/eirv45n39-20180928/24-31_4539.pdf

There is no way that this debt can ever be paid, so the effect of the bailout will be to, eventually, bankrupt governments.

# The Federal Reserve

The essence of the modern paradigm is that it is built on private control of a monopoly emission center. The basis of the modern financial system is investment banks – owners of the US Federal Reserve. Their privileged status developed over the decades at the end of the 19th and the beginning of the 20th century and was institutionalized in two stages: in 1913, with the creation of the US Federal Reserve System, and in 1944, following the results of the Bretton Woods Agreements. While linked to the Federal Government of the United States, much of the Federal Reserve essentially operates just as a private corporation would.

> At the very top of the Federal Reserve System is the Board of Governors, with the Federal Open Market Committee (FOMC) – a 12 member committee of top-level officials from the Federal Reserve, one of the most powerful and influential arbiters of financial policy decisions in the USA as well as Federal Advisory Committee (FAC) directly below them as advisers. The majority of the FOMC is made up of the Board of Governors and has complete control over all open market operations. The Board of Governors and FOMC oversees 12 Federal Reserve district banks. These district banks have no direct ties to the government.[27]

The entire IMF/World Bank system (created under the Bretton Woods Agreements) works so that no one except the Fed can issue money. The dollar was the core of the Bretton Woods system, and it was to become the foundation for a new worldwide system. It was dollar investments and dollar-denominated loans that were meant to be a tool to govern economically-occupied territories at some point in the future. This was euphemistically called "the Washington Consensus."

Thus, the Washington Consensus is nothing but a rulebook for those who were building the new economic model in Russia and other countries of the defeated socialist bloc. The idea, was to ensure complete and unconditional transition of those countries towards the Western financial and economic system, which by that time had acquired a dominant position in the world. Therefore, there were several basic binding principles, and no alternative option was allowed whatsoever.

---

27    The Solari Report, Part 1, 2019 Volume I, 2018 Annual Wrap Up, pp. 82-83

First and foremost, only the dollar was to drive growth. The countries coming into the orbit of the Bretton Woods system could have no internal sources of growth not tied to the dollar. Therefore, any investment or credit must be based on dollars, which the country had to get any way it could. That's how the infamous "Currency Board" system emerged. The idea behind it is that a country is allowed to have only as much national currency as could be exchanged for real nternational currency, primarily the dollar.

Second, foreign investments were to be given top priority. They were supposed to be the sole source of growth, and, at the same time, to guarantee that the added value formed within the country could be easily transferred abroad. There should have been no financial flows that would be confined within Russia (the same was true for any other country that took up the dollar system in the late 1980s or early 1990s). Attracting foreign investments became the primary goal of any national government.

It should be noted that national bank systems, private in principle, could also create money – through the issue of loans. Virtually, it undermines the dollar's monopoly, and that is why the Washington Consensus rulebook reads that foreign investments can be allowed only if the inflation level is low, and to achieve it, the money supply has to be limited. In practice, it leads to severe restrictions on issuing loans to the real economy sector and a decrease in the credit multiplier (i.e., banking system efficiency ratio). The third point naturally stems from the first two and is explicitly stated in the IMF.

Charter, and reflected in all Bretton Woods principles: any possible restrictions on the circulation of the U.S. dollar and cross-border trade shall be banned. For the record, the General Agreement on Tariffs and Trade (GATT) and the WTO were created upon the decision taken at the Bretton Woods Conference in 1944.

Thus, it shouldn't surprise anyone that the Central Banks use all available national currencies for currency speculations. The profitability of such operations by far exceeds that of investments, and that is the reason the remaining options to invest at home are virtually blocked. It is absolutely impossible to compete with foreign manufacturers who can get far less expensive loans, because Western countries do not limit the operation of their own banking systems; on the contrary, they actively stimulate it.

Another key element of the Washington Consensus is the elimination of "centers of power" of the national economy, which could use its lobby capabilities to overturn the ban on national currency loans imposed by the champions of the Washington Consensus.

But the destruction of the debt system destroys both the economic and financial basis of this model. The first – because the emission of debts stimulates aggregate demand, a sharp drop in which (at least 20%) the modern world economy will not survive. As for the financial system, it will be forced to largely abandon the dollar – which makes it unregulated within existing institutions.

## Historical Perspective

The system I am describing, is not very old: usury, the basis of the modern banking system, was publicly allowed in Europe only in the 16th century, and the system of private central banks was established only in the 19th century. Before that, the Old Testament value model, which strongly condemned usury, had been operating in Europe for more than 1,500 years. Yes, of course, usury existed, but society as a whole condemned it, only Jews were allowed to publicly practice it (they could always be robbed and debts erased at any convenient time), and it could not be the basis of the economy. Even the trading republics of Italy (Venice, Genoa) and the Hanseatic League used loan interest only in the framework of co-operative trade operations; rather, as an insurance premium, the production in them was quite traditional, workshop.

But in the 16th century, there was an economic catastrophe on a pan-European scale – the importation by Spain of colossal amounts of gold from the New World destroyed the monetary system in Europe, built on traditional gold supplies. This hit especially hard in the north of the continent, with its already lower yields, and the question became the physical survival of millions of people in a vast territory. In particular, it was necessary to find reserves for the restructuring of the local economic system and come up with a new economic system that ensured the survival of the population.

The resource was found – the gargantuan wealth accumulated by the Roman Catholic Church's 1,000 year-old monopoly on Christianity – and a good reason to take it. One of the many "heresies" that have arisen and faded over the centuries, received a powerful tool for development and the Reformation began.

True, Martin Luther's initial theses still contained a ban on usury – but then, as part of the development of new economic practice, it was pretty quickly smudged over and forgotten. As a result of the use of loan interest, another economic phenomenon appeared – technological progress. The industrial society of expanded reproduction and accumulation of capital,

161

having emerged in the West in the throes of the Netherlands (1566-1648) and English (1640-1660) bourgeoise revolutions, went through three stages of a progressive increase in wealth. On the "lineal progress" these stages are marked by a measured step of improving energy and production technologies.

1. Manufacture on manual textile machines - Dutch stage: 18th century. The first technological paradigm.

2. Factory mass production, where a worker became an appendage of a steam engine – the British stage: the 19th century, the second, coal and the third, the electric engine, technological paradigm.

3. Conveyor production, the internal combustion engine, and microelectronics. American stage: 20th century, fourth, oil and fifth, computers, technological structures.

Note that the problems of modern civilization are, in many ways, objective in nature. Technological progress requires strengthening the division of labor, and thus, in turn, expanding the scale of the market for the sale of goods. What does this mean?

As far back as the 18th and the beginning of the 19th century, Europe had a mass of really independent states in a technological sense. And by the beginning of the 20th century, the market volume, which was necessary to control a truly sovereign nation, was somewhere around 50 million consumers. At that moment in Europe, only five or six truly self-sufficient states existed. The Russian Empire, German, Austria-Hungary, France, Great Britain, and, with a decided limp, Spain. All other countries were not independent in the sense that, to provide their citizens with average and adequate world consumption leaders, they would inevitably have to join, as satellite or "junior" partners, associations led by one of the listed countries.

By the middle of the 20th century, the volume of markets that a country needed to control in order to ensure a self-sufficient and developing economy reached around 500 million people. At that moment, only two nation-states could be truly independent, and leaders of large inter-country associations. The USSR (representing the socialist block and economic model) and the USA (capitalist block). China and India at that time could not be taken into account – they were not consumer markets in the modern sense of the word, their economy was still mostly agrarian.

However, they caught on pretty fast, and the global economy continued to develop. By the 1970s, the volume of markets necessary for the healthy development of a self-sufficient economy reached the order of a billion people, and it became clear to modern elites that, in the world (while maintaining the traditional paradigm of world development, in other words, technological progress), there was room for only one independent state (economic model).

The people who headed the Politburo of the Communist Party of the Soviet Union Central Committee in the 1970s faced the question of whether it was wise to speed up the destruction of the "Western" economy and the USA after the default of 1971 (the rejection of its gold content) and the catastrophic "oil crisis" of 1973. Moreover, the question was posed explicitly. And the answer to it was reduced to two much more straightforward, and most importantly, technological problems. One of them concerned the ability of the USSR to directly control territories that were part of the US-influence zone at that time and in which, after the collapse of the "sovereign," uncontrolled, in many ways, destructive and dangerous processes for the whole world would inevitably begin.

The second concerned the readiness of the USSR to face China, which by that time had already begun its own technological revolution. The answers to both of these questions turned out to be negative – the country's leaders came to the conclusion that the USSR was not able to directly control almost half of the world, sliding towards totalitarianism, rampant terrorism and anarchy – and at the same time limit the growing possibilities of China. As a result, the USSR subsequently entered into negotiations with the United States and began the process, which later became known as "détente," of sharply increasing the volume of oil sold to world capitalist markets. In other words, a technological answer was given to an inherently political question.

Since, as already noted earlier, the death of one of the superpowers (that is, the transition to the only independent state in the world) was predetermined by the objective development of the global economic paradigm, the United States faced the same issue 10 years later, and solved it in a completely different way. The United States made a purely political decision, first to finish destroying the USSR, and then deal with emerging issues of the post-communist block. Which, as we see today, turned out to be exactly the same, the solutions of which the leaders of the Soviet Union could not find.

As a matter of fact, from my personal point of view, the United States could not (and will not be able) to resolve the issues raised – which will soon become apparent to everyone. The collapse of the USSR forced the

United States to take over its former sphere of influence, and today America is clearly not able to cope with this job. The sharp increase in terrorism, (which, incidentally, was created and developed by the superpowers themselves as part of their confrontation with each other), and the loss of control over it, is connected precisely with the destruction of the world parity system negotiated by FDR, Churchill, and Stalin, at Yalta in 1945.

However, this is not the main point. Taking advantage of the resources of the crumbling USSR, the USA made another technological breakthrough and faced the need to finance the next. Which will require for its payback not 5, but about 10 billion consumers. Consumers that physically do not yet exist on the planet Earth.

Many of the financial problems of the modern capitalist system are caused precisely by the fact that, in the absence of new consumers, the US leadership has begun (explicitly or implicitly) to increase the capacity of consumers to increase demand – which, in many ways, caused the debt crisis mentioned above. But the essence of the problem does not change as a result of this: the paradigm of blind technological progress has exhausted itself, has reached its limits. And, to survive as a species, we absolutely need to look for a new standard.

## The Value Basis of the New System

There are serious reasons, some of which I mentioned earlier, to believe that the ills of the modern world financial system come from the private nature of control over money circulation and, as a result, the issue of money by a modern single measure of value – the American dollar. And two questions arise. First: whether we can altogether refuse the loan interest, and if not, how it can be controlled.

The answer to the first question is negative: modern humanity cannot live outside the framework of a technological society, if only because modern food production is highly industrialized. The cessation of the corresponding processes will inevitably lead to a significant reduction in the population of Earth, a situation which it is simply impossible to allow, voluntarily. And the industry today, most likely, will not function without loan interest.

But control over loan interest existed. Actually, in Islam, it was banned almost categorically, and it is possible that due to this, the Islamic world was not able to build sustainable technological states (there is one exception – Iran – but this is a special case). In Roman Catholic countries, the lending rate was controlled by societal bias, in Orthodox countries (and under socialism) – by the State. Technological development under socialism was also based on loan interest, and state redistribution made it possible to achieve unprecedented economic growth rates (in the USSR and in China) based on a two-contour economic model (Asiatic) of production which I will explain in detail in chapter 3 of this section.

Thus, we have the following picture: the new financial and economic paradigm cannot wholly abandon loan interest but must be built on its much stricter control by the whole society. The emphasis should be placed on socialist ideas for this reason: today, traditional Christian culture loses significantly to Islam, or rather the Islamic global project, in key issues of economic morality. And stopping it, within the framework of Christian ideas, will be quite difficult, since all Christian denominations have demonstrated their weakness and (by and large) criminal tolerance, of the "Western" global project, built, not on the primacy of justice, but on the primacy of profit. In the conditions of the economic crisis, the demand for effective justice will quickly grow – which will further increase the pace of expansion of the Islamic project.

But its victory will almost inevitably lead to the rapid degradation of modern technological society in Western countries and Russia. And the consequences, as we have already noted, will become extremely unpleasant – right up to the mass starvation of hundreds of millions of people. And the only program that, not only theoretically, but also practically, demonstrated its ability to assimilate Islam, is socialism. Of course, no one says that this should be the very scheme that was implemented in the USSR, especially in its post-Stalinist version. In conclusion, the current global financial and economic paradigm is not just in a state of crisis – it is on the verge of collapse, which cannot be prevented.

# Chapter 8

# USA vs. China

Before discussing the trade war and its global after-effects, I'll start with the relationship between Xi and Trump. As I explained in the first section of the book, the United States and China have been in a conspiracy relationship for several decades, which led to the creation of a mutually beneficial framework associated with the Bretton Woods financial model. Its essence lies in the fact that the Fed prints dollars for which industrial capacities are created in China, which, in turn, creates cheap goods, which are then exported and sold in the United States.

As a result, everyone benefits (China receives part of the profit, and US citizens get cheap goods, which allowed them to increase their standard of living significantly), and it is entirely unclear why this mutually beneficial arrangement should be interrupted. But there are two problems to consider.

The first is that the printing of dollars no longer provides economic growth. At the same time, inflation and financial bubbles have not disappeared. And this dramatically increases the overall tension in the markets. The second is, since the primary beneficiaries of the Bretton Woods scheme are transnational banks that are losing the political struggle in the USA today. Trump cannot afford to support this scheme, given that he and his enemies are waging an all-out war for survival; neither can he stop its destruction, even though in a medium-term this will lead to problems associated with a decline in the standard of living of the population.

Xi could probably wait and see what happens, but the liberal financiers are opponents of Xi, just as they are of Trump; and, most importantly, China's President understands that the Bretton Woods model cannot be saved anyway. And for this reason, Xi is ready to support Trump on the political level, even at the cost of accelerating the destruction of the Bretton Woods model on which the Chinese economy is based today.

The trick here is that the entire economic establishment of China and the United States are a part of the scheme. And its destruction seriously affects almost all economic entities of not only China and the USA but of the entire globe. Therefore, it is extremely difficult for Xi and Trump to agree (financially, economically, or politically): they are under tremendous pressure at home. At the same time, a new economic model is yet to be defined, which means that a Trump-Xi conspiracy should be a set of purely tactical moments/movements to be played out after Trump's re-election in November 2020, which makes any comprehensive negotiations extremely difficult. Now, let's step back and examine the USA-China trade war in greater detail.

## Trump vs. China Trade War

Trump has refused a trade deal with China. Outwardly, this is simply a step in the negotiations, emphasized by the hope of reaching an agreement sometime down the line; in fact, it is a principled position. After all, in the fall of 2018, Trump had already unleashed a trade war against China. And the President was immediately sabotaged by Jerome Powell, Chair of the Federal Reserve, who, by raising the interest rate, made money more expensive and thereby discounted Trump's initial victory.

What was Powell's thinking behind this decision? The United States prospers by issuing a world reserve currency and reducing the deficit in foreign trade with China reduces, with other things being equal, the outflow of US dollars. If the US dollars remain in the country, they threaten inflation, and in order to neutralize this inflation, it is necessary to increase the interest rate, thus reducing competitiveness.

The problem is that for many years now, China has been actively stimulating domestic consumption (that is, the standard of living of its population) through emission programs. China does this through the development of its infrastructure projects. Such projects cannot but pose a threat to high inflation, and to overcome it, you need to take certain proactive steps.

For example, to combat inflation, China used the withdrawal of capital in the form of dollars, which were formed due to the enormous surplus in the foreign trade balance (mainly due to trade with the United States). But at the same time, China was still actively increasing its presence in other markets and was actively striving for the EU market (the "new" silk road). The trouble is that, on the one hand, the USA is closing its markets to China's products, and, on the other hand, the money will not be available in Western Europe either.

Again, despite howls and protests, Xi and Trump are working together, given that the Bretton Woods system itself is on its deathbed, and the beneficiaries of the Bretton Woods system are sworn enemies of both Trump and Xi (as well as Putin).

Xi is well aware that the standard of living of the Chinese population will fall, since incentives will have to be reduced, and foreign markets will collapse (in the case of the USA, pretty quickly). Yes, he has a political excuse (national interests and trade war with the USA), but still, he can not reduce the standard of living of the population too quickly. Especially in the new China.

And this means that you need to look for other mechanisms to support emission programs. And here comes the wonderful experience of the United States, which witnessed extraordinary economic growth between 1947 and 1971, due to the expansion of the use of U.S. dollars. The USA was able to print money without causing any inflation, given that the sphere of dollar turnover was continually expanding. And there is no reason for China not to use this experience for its benefit. Moreover, no short-term alternatives are available.

The picture is completely transparent and a win-win. The renminbi zone (in Southeast Asia) has not yet been formed, but as soon as it happens, the renminbi will have a tremendous opportunity to squeeze out the dollar, which today is the world's leading trading and reserve currency. And for the next 20 years, China will be able to calmly print the yuan (which will then be taken outside China's economy, but not in the form of dollars, as it is now) but as yuan itself. This will allow China to solve at the expense of this issuance of money the problem of stimulating the falling private demand at home. And, at the same time, to continue China's technological development towards sixth and seventh technological paradigms.

I do not see other options for China; more precisely, all others will lead to a quick collapse of the economy. Today, the scale of internal stimulation of the Chinese economy roughly corresponds to a similar stimulation of demand in the USA. It amounts to about 2 trillion in the dollar equivalent per year. The question is, why are these two trillion not causing inflation? The reason is simple.

Stimulating domestic demand goes through a surplus in foreign trade. 400-500 billion dollars of international trade surplus per year multiplied by a credit multiplier of about 5, gives us 2 trillion in the dollar equivalent of domestic demand. And such an issue does not produce high inflation, since excess money is converted into dollars and withdrawn from the country. This system used to give the balance to reserves, now the withdrawal sometimes starts to exceed the income, but here you can just keep balances.

For China, this decrease in the surplus in trade with the United States is not just a big problem, but an economic disaster, because if the surplus in foreign trade decreases, China needs to either reduce the emission stimulation of the domestic economy (this is not only a sharp decrease in growth rates, but also conflicts with the regions, because the investment occurs through regional authorities), or put up with a sharp increase in inflation. Both of these factors – in the conditions of intensification of intra-elite conflicts – are unacceptable. True, the Chinese are ready to "tighten their belts," but in the absence of an answer to the question: "Why should they do it?" This is precisely Xi's problem – he does not have a conceptual description of the future and thus doesn't have a good answer to give his people. And taking into account the specific thinking of the Chinese, Xi's position is weakening as the crisis deepens.

At the same time, there is a very specific time period, the middle of Trump's second term, when this conflict must inevitably be resolved. Trump wants to be friends with Xi, they have common enemies (Xi has liberal Komsomol members, clans that united around Hu Jintao and among Trump's enemies are the transnational bankers), but the problem is that China's development model since the late 1970s (Deng Xiaoping – Carter secret agreement) was adopted as part of a conspiracy with the US leadership, which at the time was controlled by the financiers. In other words, Trump has a cognitive dissonance: to defeat the internal enemy (and compromises are impossible here), he is forced to fight his strategic ally against this enemy. How Trump will cope with this is a separate issue, but he cannot stop the destruction of the model that provides China with a surplus. Moreover, he will step up his efforts. What's the solution? The need to develop an alternative mechanism that takes into account the interests of the United States in the framework of Trump's logic and China's in the interests of Xi. In other words, an alternative economic post-Bretton Woods model.

By the way, in the notorious question of friendship or enmity with China, Trump perfectly understands that it is impossible to quarrel Russia with China today. And he offers a very worthy option, in which China and Russia become equal regional leaders. After which, of course, these two countries will cease to be allies in the matter of confronting the United States.

In such a situation, Xi Jinping must solve at least two fundamental tasks. First, he must somehow persuade Putin to cooperate. In what does this cooperation consist? Namely, the need to fulfill three conditions: It is necessary to create an image of the future (to raise the spirit of creation).

It is essential to "correct names" (discard obsolete schemes). It is essential to strengthen the ritual (to bet on the unconscious).

This is difficult because it is not clear what Putin can offer in return. Cooperation with Russia is either sabotaged by Russia's pro-Western liberal government (and here, of course, Putin is to blame, but what to do in such a situation is another story); or this conflict turns into Chinese encroachment of Russia's territories in Siberia, something that Putin cannot possibly like nor allow as it compromises Russia's sovereignty and future survival as a country. And if Xi does not solve this problem, then it may turn out that in the near future, China will find itself surrounded by enemies of China and allies of the United States.

The second task is to develop mechanisms for alternative economic growth, which should replace the liberal model of the 1980s-2000s period. There will no longer be money printing (to stimulate the economy), and the economy will have to be rebuilt in any case, but how to do it? Modern economic science in China is purely liberal (in contrast to governance), it cannot give birth to any alternative concepts (and, honestly, what have the Chinese invented within this area over the last 2,000 years?).

Thus, more or less, the only solution for China is to embark with Russia not economically (this is the next stage), but rather towards conceptual cooperation; using China's resources and Russia's alternative economic theory to create, not just academic centers that should develop appropriate methodology and models, but schools and universities where future managers of Russia and China would be educated. And, if the scenario of new conferences like Yalta 2 and Bretton Woods 2 is realized (it seems to me that this is almost inevitable), then this is a guarantee that Russia and China will adequately oppose the positions of the United States.

At the same time, the "new Yalta" should include the leaders of the victorious powers (the defeated financial globalism will not be allowed to participate), and they should control a significant part of the world. The US-China option of dividing the world into two (bilateral) does not work. Like the former anglo-Saxon/USA-England alliance. And therefore, today there are three or four participants in the conference: the USA, Russia, China and, separately, India, if only because it has one and a half-billion people. On paper, Germany can be included as Europe's biggest economy, but only in theory; in practice today it cannot present its own concepts of world governance, it is deeply secondary, and the basic rules for it are written by liberal (financial) puppeteers deeply hostile to Trump and the whole logic of the "new Yalta."

One of the alternatives, as I described in first part of the book, is the regionalization of global economy. The territorial division in this situation becomes a natural outlet: as private demand decreases, it again becomes profitable to reduce the maximum number of technological (currency) zones, and their subsequent growth (more precisely, a return to self-sufficiency, after globalization specialization) is possible only by stimulating demand through emissions of regional (zonal) currencies. The rejection of such a policy leads to critical social problems associated with the impoverishment of the middle class.

Furthermore, all discussions about "extra-territorialization" will also disappear after the crisis. The scale of production and, accordingly, the size of the global output of useless objects (consumerism) will dramatically decrease. And the decline in population levels, because in the face of falling standards of living, hunger will become the norm and, as a result, numerous epidemics will take center stage. With antibiotics, the role of natural selection in society fell sharply (a large number of individuals who would have died had it not been for the medicines, survived), and, in an upcoming global crisis, this cross-section of the population will almost certainly perish.

In context, the end of the Bretton Woods model (and thus liberalism based on a model of infinite growth on a finite planet ) for the first time, officially was made public by none other than Russian President Vladimir Putin in an exclusive interview with *The Financial Times*. According to President Putin, the underlying problem is the lack of a driver of global growth. World trade has ceased to fulfill this role, but a new mechanism has not appeared. This factor, as well as the loss of a dominant position (over 30 years, the share of G7 countries in global GDP by purchasing power parity decreased from 46% to 30%), forced the country – the leader of the Western world – to switch to the language of trade wars, sanctions and raiding to eliminate competitors from nonmarket ways.

The President of the Russian Federation identified two inertial scenarios for the development of events. The degeneration of the universalist model of globalization into a caricature with an attempt to extend US jurisdiction to the whole world or fragmentation of the global economic space, (and not only) trade wars, endless conflicts and fights without rules: a free-for-all.

As an alternative to these two scenarios, Vladimir Putin called for a "new world" treaty with a wide range of participants and recognition of the unconditional right of each country to its development path. The most resonant part of the speech was a criticism of the Bretton Woods financial system, which is used today as an instrument of pressure by the United States on the rest of the world.

Putin's "Munich Speech" in 2007 was a political warning to the unipolar, globalized world. His speech at the St. Petersburg International Economic Forum (SPIEF) economically put everything in its place. One: The reason for the crisis is the loss by G7 countries of their leading positions (global lack of competitiveness). Two: The mechanism of the crisis is the inability and unpreparedness of Western countries (primarily the United States) to revise the rules for distributing the effects of economic growth.

The Russian President called the filling of international institutions with new meanings and reaching agreements the only alternative to fragmenting the global economy. And since such agreements are impossible, it is necessary to prepare for a "civilized violence" (economic fights without concrete rules). After all, *si vis pacem, para bellum* (if you want peace, prepare for war). And a global war is a distinct possibility.

If we look at the debt bubble, global debt is at least $270 trillion. But when the debt bubble pops, other liabilities like the $1.5 quadrillion of derivatives will pop as well. When the debt bubble pops, virtually all that fiat money becomes worthless. No one can repay it, and no one is willing to buy it. Remember, globals wars (as opposed to small, regional conflicts) write off global debts and responsibilities. Rob Kirby writes:

> When the Fed adds liquidity [aka fresh fiat money], they purchase debt – either temporarily [repo] or a permanent basis by outright purchases [expanding their balance sheet]. Fresh fiat money is the oil that greases the wheels of our debt-based money system. When the Fed purchases debt, they are signaling concern that the wheels of our money system are ceasing up. Why does this happen?
>
> Any fiat money system with compound interest is fundamentally flawed in its very design because virtually all new money is "lent" into existence. So, when $1 million in new money is loaned into existence [by issuing debt], the interest due at maturity is *not*. The implications of the interest due not being created when the principal loan amount is created – mathematics dictates that, for the debt to be serviced, money supply *must* continually grow [or debt be purged], or the system collapses.[1]

As billionaire investor, Egon von Greyerz explains,

> Central banks are panicking, and Q.E. is back with a vengeance. The Fed is injecting a total of $200 billion monthly if you add up Repos and Pomos (permanent open market operations). The ECB has started with €20 billion a month, but that is likely to increase

---

1    The ABC's of Fiat Money, Rob Kirby, https://www.kirbyanalytics.com/, December 10, 2019.

since Lagarde most certainly also will do "whatever is takes" as Draghi stated. These are massive amounts and a clear indication that these two central banks are seeing real problems in the system.

The whole financial system is just a massive paper tiger but the world hasn't realised it yet. In effect, there are no true markets, no true prices and no solid counterparty standing behind any transaction. A small minority has rigged the system in their favor, and this is the way players like it, investment banks make massive profits every day. These investment banks make gambling bets that are exponentially greater than the risk they can cover when all goes wrong. They are totally aware that they are too big to fail.

The world experienced the "too big to fail" syndrome during the LTCM collapse (Long Term Capital Management) in 1998 as well as during the 2008 collapse. Both these times, the financial system was minutes from a total breakdown but the investment banks had to be saved at an enormous cost. With central bank printing and guaranteeing at least $25 trillion, the system was saved temporarily. But it wasn't actually saved. All that happened was that a smaller problem became an exponentially bigger problem. And this is where we are today. The 2006-9 Great Financial Crisis was never resolved, just deferred. So the proverbial can was kicked down the road again, but the next time it will be too big to kick.

Just to understand the size of markets, let's for example consider the Forex market. Daily turnover in the Forex Casino is in excess of $5 trillion. That means $1.5 quadrillion a year is traded in foreign exchange. That's 19x annual global GDP of $80 trillion. But since global trade is only $20 trillion, global forex trading is 75x the amount of goods that involves foreign exchange. So the majority of the $1.5 quadrillion forex trading is pure speculation leading to the currency price being set in a casino with no relevance to the underlying goods traded. Thus, the price has very little correlation to the products or services traded.[2]

Again, remember, one of the most effective means to ensure peace is always to be armed and ready to defend oneself.

2     Gold Price is not the Price of gold, Egon von Greyerz, November 14, 2019 https://gold-switzerland.com/gold-price-is-not-the-price-of-gold/

# Chapter 9

# Soviet Two-Contour Economic Model

Historically, Russia has invaluable experience in building a productive economy. Whatever critics of the Soviet economic model may say, today it is becoming clear that it turned out to be more "competitive" for Russia, in the modern language, than the so-called Western "market economies."

The first period – industrialization, was carried out under the conditions of a "mobilization economy": in terms of the total volume of gross domestic product and industrial production in the mid-1930s, the USSR came out on top in Europe and second in the world, losing only to the USA and significantly surpassing Germany, Great Britain and France. During three five-year periods, 364 new cities were built in the country, nine thousand large corporations were built and put into operation – a colossal figure – two corporations per day.

For the years 1951-1960, the Soviet gross domestic product grew 2.5 times, with industrial output growing more than three times and agricultural production increasing by 60%. If in 1950 the level of industrial production of the USSR was 25% in relation to the United States, then in 1960 it was already 50%.

The thirty-year period of USSR history (from the beginning of the 1930s to the beginning of the 1960s) can be called the Soviet "economic miracle." This miracle was even more impressive if we consider that the Soviet Union suffered the heaviest casualties of World War II against Nazi Germany, with most of the Western Soviet Union destroyed and over 26 million Soviet citizens killed.

Today, 99.99% of all information related to the "economic" category is devoted to the "market economy." The remaining 0.01% of the information is related to the Soviet model. But at the same time, reports, articles and books offer no detailed description of this model; everything is limited to pointless criticism and the traditional conclusion: it is "an administrative-command economy." There are no clear definitions of a "command economy," except that it is the opposite of a "market economy." The essence of the Soviet model (1930-1960) comes down to this:

1. public ownership of the means of production

2. the decisive role of the state in the economy

3. centralized management

4. directive planning

5. single national economic complex

6. maximum self-sufficiency (especially during the period when the socialist camp has not yet appeared)

7. focus primarily on natural (physical) indicators (cost plays an auxiliary role), limited nature of commodity-money relations

8. accelerated development of a group of industries "A" (production of means of production/capital goods) vs. a group of industries "B" (production of consumer goods)

9. combination of material and moral incentives for labor

10. the inadmissibility of unearned income and the concentration of excess material wealth in the hands of individual citizens

11. providing the vital needs of all members of society and the steady improvement of living standards, the social nature of appropriation, etc.

Particular attention should be paid to the planned nature of the economy. After all, critics of the Soviet model, using the derogatory phrase "administrative-command system," primarily mean economic planning. Which is the opposite of the so-called "free market" with its magic invisible hand – an economy focused on profit and private enrichment.

In the Soviet model, it was a question of directive planning, in which the plan has the status of law and is subject to mandatory execution. This, in comparison to the so-called indicative planning, which was used in the countries of Western Europe and Japan after the Second World War and which has the character of recommendations and orientations for economic entities. By the way, directive planning is not unique to the "Stalinist economy." It exists today in large corporations. But more on that, later.

Therefore, even if the critics of the Soviet model fell in love with the expression "administrative-command system," they should also zealously criticize the world's largest transnational corporations, such as IBM, British Petroleum, Google, Microsoft or Siemens.

It is well known (including from the works of the classics of Marxism) that the most important contradiction of capitalism is that between the social character of production and the private form of appropriation. So, the most important principle of the Soviet economy was the social nature of appropriation, which attempted to remove the contradiction that existed under capitalism.

The principle of distribution according to work, is supplemented by the principle of public appropriation. Specifically, the point is that the surplus product created by common labor is evenly distributed among all members of society through the mechanism of lowering retail prices for consumer goods and services and through the replenishment of public consumption funds.

Focusing primarily on natural (physical) indicators, when planning and evaluating the results of economic activity, is another key principle. Cost indicators, firstly, were somewhat arbitrary (especially in the production sphere, and not in retail trade). Secondly, they played a supporting role. Moreover, profit was not the most important indicator. The main criterion for efficiency was not an increase in monetary profit, but a decrease in the cost of production (cheap labor).

The Soviet model can be likened to a vast corporation called the "Soviet Union," which consisted of separate workshops and production sites that worked to create one final product.

The final product was not considered a financial result (profit), but a set of specific goods and services that satisfy social and personal needs. The indicators of the social product (and its elements) in value terms only serve as a guideline when implementing annual and five-year plans, evaluating the results of the implementation of these plans.

Due to the division of labor, specialization, and well-coordinated cooperation, rather than competition, the maximum production efficiency of the entire corporation is achieved. Such competition will only disorganize the work of the entire corporation and create unjustified costs. Instead of competition, we have cooperation in the framework of a common cause and a common good. Separate workshops and sections produce raw materials, energy, semi-finished products, and components, from which, ultimately, a product to be used by the many is formed. Then this common product is distributed among all participants in its production.

All this enormous production, exchange, and distribution were managed by the governing and coordinating bodies of the "corporation USSR." In other words, by the government ministries and departments of the ministries. As the structure of the national economy of the USSR became more complicated, the number of these ministries increased con-

177

tinuously. Within each union ministry, there were also units called head-quarters and various local, territorial institutions (primarily ministries in the union republics). Such bodies played the coordinating and controlling role as the USSR State Planning Commission, the USSR Ministry of Finance, the USSR State Bank (Central Bank) and some others. They also had their territorial network, including departments with similar names at the level of Union republics.

By the way, a similar organizational and management scheme exists in the largest Western corporations (especially transnational ones) associated with the real sector of the economy. There are no market relations within them; there are conditional calculations based on "transfer" (intra-corporate) prices.

## Western Model vs. Stalinist Model

What is the key difference between the Western capitalist model and the Stalinist socialist model? Corporations are privately-owned, their activity is primarily focused on financial results (profit), and the financial result is not distributed among employees, but is privatized by the corporation owners. Today, this organizational structure and management of the corporation is a shambling thing of the past. Why? In a profit-obsessed economy managed by the financial sector, real production activity is becoming uncompetitive and even unprofitable. There is a reversal of activities of corporations traditionally associated with production, in the direction of working in the financial markets. In these financially oriented corporations, everything is arranged differently.

The little-understood Stalinist economy aimed to:

- ensure overcoming the age-old economic backwardness of the country and become, along with the United States, the leading economic power in the world;

- create a single national industrial complex, which allowed the Soviet Union to become independent of the world market;

- defeat the most powerful enemy in the Second World War – Nazi Germany and the countries of the Hitler coalition;

- ensure a steady increase in the well-being of the people based on a consistent reduction in the cost of production;

- show the whole world the inefficiency of the so-called "market" (capitalist) economy and reorient many countries on the path of the so-called "non-capitalist development path;"

- ensure the military security of the country by creating nuclear weapons.

Stalin managed to increase the labor activity of Soviet people significantly, and the methods of coercion played a subordinate role here. The "supra-economic" goal was to protect the country from external aggression. But after the death of Stalin, who bequeathed the "nuclear shield" to the Soviet people, the sensation of an external threat began to recede into the background. Economic tasks arising from the "basic economic law of socialism" I have mentioned earlier had come to the fore. But here is the paradox: people do not consolidate economic goals, do not mobilize, do not reveal their creative potential, but, on the contrary, disconnect, relax, and deprive themselves of creativity. The latter is replaced, at best, by so-called "entrepreneurship." For commercial purposes, the Stalinist economy cannot work, it is doomed to die and be replaced with variants of the "market economy" model, which is exactly what happened with the eventual collapse of the Soviet Union under its last president, Gorbachev.

Until 1985, that is, before perestroika, the USSR occupied the second place in the world and the first in Europe in industrial production. In 1975, the share of the USSR in world industrial production was 20% (for comparison: in 1999, the United States was 20.4%, the European Union, 19.8%); the Soviet GDP was 10% of the world. In that same 1975, the national income of the USSR amounted to 60-65% of the national income of the United States. Israeli intelligence gave even higher numbers – according to Israeli analysts, the standard of living in the USSR, including paid and free services, as well as the so-called inevaluable humanitarian factors (crime rate, social security), was 70-75% of the US. From 1970 to 1975, the share of industries that most determine the effectiveness of the national economy (mechanical engineering, electric power, chemical, and petrochemical industries) increased from 31% to 36%; then, slippage began, but the level reached by 1975 was high.

At the same time, over the indicated period, the output of mechanical engineering products increased 1.8 times, including computer technology – 4 times; instruments, automation, and spare parts for them – 1.9 times. In 1975, with a population of 9.4% of the global CMEA (the Council for Mutual Economic Assistance), it accounted for more than 30% of world industrial production and more than 25% of world income; The USSR produced 60% of the CMEA industrial output.

To this should be added the successes of Soviet agriculture in the 1985-1990 period and especially 1991: growth was 9.8% compared to 5.8% in the previous five-year period. Per capita, food consumption in 1990-1991 reached its maximum in the country's history of the 20th century: bread – 119 kg, meat – 75 kg, fish – 20 kg, milk and dairy products – 386 liters, eggs – 97 pieces. 1990 and '91 were marked by an exceptionally large yield and an increase in livestock numbers. Yet, the shelves in the shops were empty; the deficit was created deliberately to finally alienate the population of cities against socialism and provoke unrest. Agricultural products were purchased from Canadian farmers at 5-6 times the price instead of buying them at a fraction of cost from Soviet farmers.

As I explain in my book, *The Shadow Masters*, "with the passage of time, the degree of corporate theft, the outrageousness of the cruelty, and the absurdity of the lies we are being fed as part of a daily news diet can only increase as financial resources dwindle and desperation becomes the norm." In the post-Cold War world, Russia's role has been fundamental, for whosoever gains Russia's resources holds the key to global supremacy. Thus, destabilizing the Russian state became the goal of the global elite after the collapse of the Soviet Union in December 1991.

In other words, the Soviet Union, possessing the world's largest mineral wealth, a vast reservoir of gold and gemstones, the world's largest oil reserves, untold quantities of nickel, platinum, and palladium, and more timber than the Amazon, not to mention an immense stockpile of Soviet-era weapons – was to be asset-stripped. The strategy was intended to topple the country into anarchy, to the point Russia could not oppose US military operations designed to secure control of the oil and gas reserves in Central Asia. The plan developed, as echoed by former National Security Adviser under President Carter, Zbigniew Brzezinski, in his 1997 book, *The Grand Chessboard: American Primacy and Its Geostrategic Imperatives,* became a part of the most spectacular criminal coup ever devised.

In the period leading up to its collapse, floods of movable wealth left the USSR. Truckloads of Soviet roubles motored down autobahns. Many were used in complex swap operations in which billions of narco-dollars were laundered on behalf of the Calabrian Mafia, Ndrangheta. Numerous prime western banks such as the US Treasury, using the Harvard Endowment, Bank of New York, Goldman Sachs, Massachusetts banking giants Fleet Financial and Bank of Boston, looted up to $500 billion. Also participating was the CIA, whose chief goal was to destroy the Soviet currency. Ndrangheta, one of the most feared criminal organizations in the world, is financially interlocked in its drug-running business with Colombian and Mexican criminal cartels. Since the dismemberment of the Soviet Union, the Russian Mafia has joined Calabrian operations, providing an eastern root to the already lucrative cocaine and heroin business.

In one operation, 280 billion roubles – with a market value of hundreds of billions of dollars at the official commercial rate of exchange – were being auctioned to leading figures in the world of organized crime. In January 1991, shady Russian dealers were offering "140 billion clean, clear, good, legal, bundled, counted, verified, packed and stamped Russian roubles" for an estimated $7.7 billion from a dubious Liechtenstein-based company, but the transaction was foiled by a KGB sting operation. Six months later, another transaction with a market value of 140 billion roubles netted $4.5 billion, demonstrating how quickly the currency had been devaluing. The entire Russian government apparatus was gripped with panic as cash was draining out of Moscow at an astronomical rate.

At the time, no one could understand why Colombian cartels, the Mafia and the world's other criminal fraternities were lining up to purchase with hard cash (albeit at a fraction of the official rate, sometimes for as low as eight cents on the dollar) vast quantities of what was in effect little more than colored paper. These were hard-nosed criminals with keen business minds honed by decades of greed and power, and not known for squandering their wealth.

In a murky cloak-and-dagger operation, Western intelligence services worked with black market profiteers, leading banking houses, the Italian Cosa Nostra, the American Mafia and the Russian Thieves' World, former KGB officers, veterans of the Afghan war, and unemployed military officers to expedite illegal alliances on a colossal scale meant to destabilize, and eventually to destroy, the USSR. On the one hand, you had criminals preparing to launder their dirty narcotics revenue, while on the other, opportunists expected to garner a hefty profit when the rouble became repatriated. They bought bargain basement-priced commodities with devalued currency as "inward investments" and financed "crooked" joint venture companies mushrooming in the meantime. In 1990 and 1991, the rouble proved to be the currency of choice.

Fearful of plunder, then-Prime Minister Valentin Pavlov announced in his February 12, 1991 interview in a Russian daily newspaper, *Trud*, that the government had uncovered a "plot by Western banks in Switzerland, Canada and Austria to flood the country with billions of rouble bank notes." Such a move would create instant hyperinflation and, in turn, destabilize the Soviet Union financially. Pavlov saw this plot as a quiet and bloodless annexation of the Soviet Union's economy, to eventually topple the government.

According to British investigator David Guyatt,

> It became clear that the massive quantities of exported roubles weren't just colored paper. Wasting no time, the now rouble-rich Mafia set about plundering Russia's abundant natural treasures: platinum, gemstones, oil, lumber, strategic raw materials, non-ferrous metals such as cobalt, copper, bronze, titanium, and even caterpillar tractors and other high value equipment—all went under the hidden hammer. Almost worthless on the international market, they were repatriated through some of the 260 Mafia-controlled banks that sprang-up around the country.[1]

Robert Friedman, in the January 1996 cover story, "Money Plane," for the *New Yorker* magazine explained how the process worked:

> Russian assets, such as oil, are stolen by underworld figures or corrupt plant managers and sold on the spot market in Rotterdam. The proceeds are wired through front companies on the Continent and deposited in London banks. Gangsters place an order for, say, $40 million in US currency through a bank in Moscow. The bank wires their bank of choice, placing a purchase order for the cash. The bank of choice buys the currency from the New York Federal Reserve. Simultaneously, a bank of choice receives a wire transfer for the same account from the London bank. Bank of choice pockets a commission and flies the cash from New York to Moscow. It is then used by mobsters to buy narcotics or villas; or run political campaigns.[2]

A Wall Street brokerage or investment bank may also go "offshore" to legally borrow once-laundered drug money to finance a corporate merger or leveraged buyout (LBO). Why do this? If you were a major investment banker or securities firm and could arrange to borrow laundered drug money at, say, five percent rather than the ten your bank wants, and you are in a cutthroat competition to buy a company, would you be willing to lower your cost of capital in this way? It is hardly surprising that such practices are becoming "business as usual."

That was 1991. Today, 8% of the global money supply exists in physical form, whereas the rest is digital "cash."[3] In Russia the ratio is approxi-

1    David Guyatt, "Gangster's Paradise," DeepBlackLies.co.uk, 2004.
2    Robert Friedman, "The Money Plane," *New Yorker* magazine, January 22, 1996.
3    https://www.newsbtc.com/2017/04/17/around-8-money-supply-exists-cash-rest-just-

mately 70 to 30. Cash is a banknote issued by a central bank. Digital cash is records on paper, and today almost exclusively electronic money, also called deposit money. Commercial banks issue them in the form of loans that are placed in bank accounts (deposits). In this case, cash can go into noncash form, and noncash money – into cash. That is, in the modern monetary (market) system, the two circuits are interconnected.

Now let's try to compare this system with the Soviet system from the 1930s-1960s, at which the maximum growth of the industrial economy was reached. To begin with, post-revolution Soviet Russia lacked two main resources for industrialization – labor and energy. There were a lot of potential workers – 80% of the population lived in the countryside.[4] To industrialize the economy, the government had to free these workers, that is, to raise labor productivity and efficiency in agriculture. At the beginning of the first five-year plan, most of the surplus product received from agriculture was used to finance industrial development.

If, in the early 1920s, investment from agriculture amounted to almost 80%, by the end of 1932, this figure dropped to 18%; and a year later, it fell almost to zero. Moreover, by 1937, total industrial production increased by a factor of 4 compared with 1928. In other words, investments from agriculture fell to zero, while industrial production increased several times.

Farm collectivization solved this problem; the villages were rid of "excess" people, while agricultural production in the USSR, thanks to industrialization, not only did not fall, but significantly increased. This was precisely the goal of collectivization, and not at all "to break the backbone of the freedom-loving Russian peasant," as capitalist propagandists would like us to believe.

Things were much more complicated with the energy sector, but success was evident here as well: in 1932, electricity production increased almost seven times compared with 1913, from 2 to 13.5 billion kwh. This was a complex undertaking because in the framework of the fourth techno-paradigm, the critical technologies were precisely the production of electric motors and electric generators, internal combustion engines and jet engines. Critical technologies are those technologies that provide the industrial power that assures them a qualitative advantage over others. Therefore, critical technologies are not for sale. Electric motors and jets are sold, but their production technologies are not. For those who don't agree – try purchasing a license to manufacture an iPhone. It cannot be done.

faith-based-currency/
4      Growth of world's urban and rural population 1920-2000, UN population study 44, p.49.

The Dneprostroi Dam (DneproGES) built, in 1932 to stimulate industrialization, was one of the largest early Soviet undertakings. Over 200 engineers and scientists, led by Gleb Krzhizhanovsky, took part in its development. Generating about 560,000 kilowatts, the station became the largest Soviet power plant at the time and the third-largest in the world. The General Electric Company manufactured the first five giant power generators. "Engineers were invited from abroad, many well-known companies, such as Siemens-Schuckertwerke AG and General Electric, were involved in the work and carried out deliveries of modern equipment, a significant part of the equipment models produced in those years at Soviet factories, were copies or modifications of foreign analogs (for example, a Fordson tractor assembled at the Stalingrad Tractor Plant)."[5]

> In February 1930, between Amtorg and Albert Kahn, Inc., a firm of American architect Albert Kahn, an agreement was signed, according to which Kahn's firm became the chief consultant of the Soviet government on industrial construction and received a package of orders for the construction of industrial enterprises worth $2 billion (about $250 billion in prices of our time). This company has provided construction of more than 500 industrial facilities in the Soviet Union.[6]

During the second five-year plan, four more generators of similar power that were produced by Elektrosila in Leningrad were installed.[7] The American newspaper *New York Evening Post* wrote that the construction of the Dnieper station is a triumph of technology that every country could be proud of.

The growth of the physical volume of the gross industrial output of the Soviet Union in the years of the first and 2nd five-year plans (1928–1937) was mind-boggling with cast iron, steel, rolled ferrous metals, coal, electricity, cement, metal-cutting machines increasing its output by an average of 400%.[8] Its transformative capacity was described by the National Security Council of the United States as a "proven ability to carry backward countries speedily through the crisis of modernization and industrialization."[9] Impressive growth rates during the first three five-year

5       https://web.archive.org/web/20140222060552/http://www.sem40.ru/evroplanet/destiny/22778/

6       https://archi.ru/lib/publication.html?id=1850569787&fl=5&sl=2

7       https://web.archive.org/web/20081028221209/http://www.history.org.ua/Zbirnyk/11/1.pdf

8       Индустриализация СССР 1929 - 1932 гг. Документы и материалы. М.: Наука, 1970

9       Bradley, Mark Philip (2010). "Decolonization, the global South, and the Cold War, 1919–1962." In Melvyn P. Leffler and Odd Arne Westad, eds., *The Cambridge History of the Cold War, Volume*

plans (1928-1940) are particularly notable given that this period is nearly congruent with the Great Depression.[10] "During this period, the Soviet Union saw rapid industrial growth while other regions were suffering from crisis."[11]

The question is, how were such massive projects financed when Western capitalists refused to provide vital funds? The transformation of the Soviet Union from a predominantly agrarian state into a leading industrial power required extraordinary financial investments. The Soviet government, desperate for growth, was ready to accept any conditions, up to the recognition of czarist debt in exchange for much-needed investments. Still, the capitalists rejected the Soviet pleas. The total share of all foreign investments in the industrialization of the USSR was about 4%.

The government tried selling bonds, but in 1928-1929 they provided only 0.8 billion rubles out of 7.7 billion expenses. In 1932, the Soviet government spent 27.5 billion rubles for the needs of industrialization, of which only 4 billion rubles were withdrawn from the population voluntarily, through the forced sale of bonds. In total, in the first two five-year plans, "domestic investments" provided about 23% of all investments. Where did the other 73% of the costs of industrialization come from?

We will leave the fairytales about common and political prisoners in labor camps (GULAGs) forced to do unpaid labor[12] to the liberal fablers. A slave can break a large rock with a crack-hammer for free, but he will not build a four-engined plane and harvest wheat that can grow in circumpolar regions such as the Arctic unless he's working for a higher ideal.

# Cash and Noncash Rubles

The question of rapid industrialization was a key element of the Soviet economic model. In early Central Planning Committee discussions, one idea was to use England as an example, the so-called "industrial revolution." Early English industrialization occurred in a relatively short period time, about half a century. True, "by the mid-18th century Britain was the world's leading commercial nation,[13] controlling a global trading empire with colonies in North America and the Caribbean, and with ma-

1: Origins (pp. 464–485). Cambridge: Cambridge University Press. ISBN 978-0-521-83719-4

10      Allen, Robert C. (2003). *Farm to Factory: A Reinterpretation of the Soviet Industrial Revolution*. Princeton, NJ: Princeton University Press

11      https://en.wikipedia.org/wiki/Economy_of_the_Soviet_Union#CITEREFAllen2003

12      Gulag prisoners, when they were released, received monetary payments which consisted of money earned minus the cost of food, uniforms, accommodation.

13      Reisman, George (1998). *Capitalism: A complete understanding of the nature and value of human economic life*. Jameson Books. p. 127. ISBN 978-0-915463-73-2

jor military and political hegemony on the Indian subcontinent."[14] But in the case of England, the source of the industrial revolution was the initial accumulation of capital in the form of ruthless robbery of the colonies. The Soviet Union simply did not have such an option available to it.

Therefore, it was decided not to "tie" industrialization to the savings of the population and the profits of industries producing consumer goods. Rather, to rely on non-cash money that is not related to the sphere of consumption of goods and services by the population. Non-cash money in the USSR was intended primarily to create and develop industries to produce the means of production (capital goods).

That is, machines, equipment, vehicles, metal cutting, weaving, woodworking, and other machinery; as well as raw materials, energy, building materials, components and semi-finished products. The production of means of production (capital goods) was called a group of industries – "A." There was also a group of industries "B" – the production of consumer goods (food, light, furniture, pharmaceutical, household appliances, etc.).

The main thing was that the products of the group of industries "A" did not have the status of goods. Why? Because in the case of purchase/sale of products of a group of industries, "A," products could be turned into capital. That is, as a means of obtaining unearned income, or profit. This is a key moment of economic transformations of that time. We usually focus on the technical and economic side of the transformation (the creation of industrial enterprises), but less often think about their socio-economic side. But it is very important, its essence is the complete eradication of capitalism, the exploitation of man by man, obtaining unearned income, profit.

But if there is no product, then it is logical to assume that there is no money. In the Western capitalist economy, yes. But we are talking about non-cash money of the "economy of Stalin." The fact of the matter is that the expression "cashless" money, in this case, should be put in quotation marks. In all sectors of the economy (not only group of industries "A," but also group of industries "B") distributional rather than market relationships were established. We are talking about the very distributional relations, which today are derogatorily called the "command economy." But this distribution was not a manifestation of voluntarism, it was carried out based on five-year and annual plans for the development of the national economy.

Plans were developed based on intersectoral balances. The principal departments involved in organizing the distribution of resources were

---

14    https://en.wikipedia.org/wiki/Industrial_Revolution#cite_note-4

Gosplan (The State Planning Committee), the Ministry of Finance, Gossnab (State Supplies of the USSR), and the State Bank of the USSR. In the "Economic Problems of Socialism in the USSR" (1952), Stalin formulated the essence of that economy. And then, in his speeches and articles, he explained in more detail why the means of production cannot be a commodity. The government distributes them only among the nation's enterprises.

They are not even sold to collective farms that had a different form of ownership (tractors and agricultural machines were not transferred directly to collective farms, but to state machine-tractor stations – [MTS], state enterprise for ownership and maintenance of agricultural machinery). That is, the state as a single and sole owner of the means of production, after transferring them to one or another enterprise, in no way loses the ownership of the means of production. And the directors of enterprises that received means of production from the state are only authorized representatives responsible for the safety of the means of production and their use in accordance with the plans for the development of the national economy.

These are striking examples of the "command economy," because the distribution of resources between units is based on decisions emanating from a management center (government). Accounting for the movement of funds within a corporation is based on the so-called "transfer" prices, which may have little to do with market prices.

Everything is set to maximize the "integral" result. The fundamental difference between the "corporation of the USSR" and the ordinary capitalist corporation is that the former was dedicated to the realization of higher objectives (social, military, scientific, technical, cultural), and the latter aims primarily to maximize profits for its owner or group of shareholders. Just as the loss of at least one of the corporation's divisions from the administrative-command vertical line can cause considerable damage to the entire corporation, so in the "USSR corporation" the appearance of any centers of "commodity-money relations" could lead to unpredictable consequences. Such was the strict, and somewhere even tough logic of the "Stalinist economy." Perhaps the only exception to these strict rules was related to foreign trade. If the products of the industries of group "A" were exported, then it became a product that had a market price. But this element of "commodity-money relations" was reliably isolated from the entire economy thanks to the state monopoly of foreign trade and the state-currency monopoly.

Thus, non-cash money did not have such a classic function as a medium of exchange. They could not even be called a measure of value (the first "classical" function of money). They were a kind of conventional unit, with the help of which the planning of the distribution of all types of resources in the economy, the accounting and control of their use, and the discipline of contractual relations between enterprises were maintained. For example, violation of product supply agreements by one enterprise to another could lead to the fact that the second enterprise did not accept (approve) the payment requirements of the first. As a result, the first did not receive non-cash funds in its bank account. And this, during the time of Stalin, was considered a severe state of emergency. This was a fairly clear mechanism of distribution relations.

After the credit reform of 1930-1931, the sole issuer of non-cash money was the State Bank of the USSR. Several government-chosen banks were involved in long-term lending to enterprises. Their resource base was formed mainly due to the state budget. The State Bank of the USSR, during the credit reform of 1930-1931, acquired the status of a monopolist in the field of short-term lending; it also became a single settlement center, which served enterprises, the state budget, and special state banks. All "horizontal" accounting between enterprises, bypassing the State Bank, were prohibited. First of all, a commercial loan, which was widely used during New Economic Policy, was banned. Credit resources, which came in the form of non-cash funds to the accounts of enterprises, had as their source the funds of the state budget and those temporarily free funds that the enterprises placed on the accounts of the State Bank. If these two sources were not enough, then the State Bank resorted to issuing an additional mass of money.

For the years 1931-1935, an increase in non-cash money supply as a result of the issuance by the State Bank (Soviet Central Bank) amounted to 5.2 billion rubles; its volume increased 2.25 times. In 1938, shortly before the war, credit investments of the USSR State Bank in the national economy as of January 1 of that year amounted to 40.7 billion rubles. These investments amount to 14.5 billion rubles. (35.3%) were covered by borrowed funds from households in bank accounts for the amount of 12.8 billion rubles. (31.2%) – by the State budget, and 13.6 billion rubles were covered by emissions. It turns out that 1/3 of all credit investments were made by the State Bank. Given that the State Bank was a division of the People's Commissariat of Finance, an additional issuance of money can be considered as a means of covering the State budget deficit.

The question remains whether this issuance was "covered" or "not covered." New loans from the State Bank were issued for specific projects, the return on which was expected in future periods. A certain analogy can be found in the current scheme of the so-called "project financing" (a loan secured not by property, but by a project that can provide cash income in the future); in a market economy, such a scheme is considered extremely risky. In the Stalinist economy more than once there were failures in the delivery of projects and the repayment of loans. But such failures did not lead to defaults of either the enterprise or the state. They were quickly covered by maneuvering with the financial resources of the state. The non-cash issue of the State Bank was carried out on the basis of the country's credit plan, which was linked to the general national economic program of the country and the state budget.

I would like to draw attention to the fact that solid barriers were put up between the cashless contour (non-cash rubles) and the cash contour (cash rubles) of money circulation. Enterprises were allowed to transfer into cash only those amounts that were necessary to pay wages, travel expenses, and a small amount of discretionary funds. Over the many years (decades) of the existence of a double-contour (circuit) monetary system, cases of illegal "cashing" in the USSR were few and far between.

Thus, the working principles of the Soviet financial system were so camouflaged by ideological constructions that they are unreasonable to this day to Western financiers and economists. The great leap in the economy led to a complete change in its structure and the creation of an appropriate financial system. This leap gave a direction of development in which the economy does not develop in accordance with the growth of personal consumption, but rather, consumption grows after the growth of the economy.

The financial system created in the USSR had no analogs in history. It entered into such a striking contrast with all the experience accumulated by economic science at that time that it took a whole ideological, not scientific, justification for its implementation.

# Part III

# Latin America as the Key Node in the New Global Order

# Chapter 10

# LATIN AMERICAN ECONOMIC INTEGRATION

As the world financial system disintegrates in a hyperinflationary blowout, the planet today is teetering on the brink of widespread starvation. The world needs to increase food production between 25 percent and 70 percent to meet projected 2050 food demand,[1] with national self-sufficiency in production in every sovereign nation-state. According to Rabobank economic research analysis, "Latin America is an important net exporter of agricultural commodities to the world, accounting for an estimated 16% of global food and agriculture exports, while representing just 4% of global food and agriculture imports."[2] Indeed, Latin America is the key global near-future player.

> Global demand for agricultural commodities is rising as a result of the growing global population and rising real incomes. The world´s population is projected to reach 9 billion people by 2050, and the demand for food is forecast to be 60% higher than it is today. Although part of the need for greater output can be met by raising productivity, the new land will nevertheless be required for agriculture in the future. The distribution of unexploited agricultural land around the world is extremely uneven, with the Latin American region standing out as having considerable future potential.[3]

The report explains,

> ... in the case of Latin America, basic grain production can be nearly *tripled* in a decade, if vast new areas of rich agricultural land in South America's interior are opened up to development by the construction of a continental network of high-speed rail lines. This network would be an integral part of the 65,000-kilometer World Land-Bridge, whose Eurasian components in the form of China's One Belt, One Road initiative is well on its way to completion.[4]

---

1       https://www.futurity.org/food-production-2050-1368582-2/
2       https://economics.rabobank.com/publications/2015/september/latin-america-agricul-tural-perspectives/
3       Ibid
4       *How To Triple Food Production By Developing High-Speed Rail*, Dennis Small, August 15, 2008, p.27

The Land-Bridge plan for the economic development of the entire planet is an integrated system of "the most crucial projects in transportation, water management, power generation, resource development, agricultural production, and city building – can be the cornerstone of a new international system of common benefit among nations for mutual cooperation and progress, a new system which is already emerging with the historic agreements for a new international economic order among the BRICS nations and others."[5]

In 2017, *Popular Mechanics* magazine asked a fascinating question in one of its feature articles: "Could we build a road around the entire world?"[6] The article raised two major issues: One of them is the Bering Strait, the freezing sea between the tip of Russia and Alaska. Another problem is the Darién Gap, a lawless swampland between Panama and Columbia teeming with paramilitary troops, drug lords, deadly snakes, and anti-government guerrillas that make building a road there nearly impossible. Or so they say.

*Executive Intelligence Review,* in collaboration with famous American rail engineer Hal Cooper, proposed routes for the South American portion of the World Land-Bridge, including both the small number of existing rail lines, as well as new tracks to be built. According to their research, "these will be high-speed, standard-gauge rail lines that will be double-tracked for most of the route. They will have to be entirely electrified, and/or magnetic levitation lines, which will, in turn, require a major increase in the availability of power – which can only come from the large-scale development of nuclear energy."[7]

With the global economic collapse, a foregone conclusion in our scenario, and no alternative model in sight, at least until well into Trump's second term, the Darien Gap railroad has suddenly become a central, live issue on the international stage. As the story goes,

> ... the Gap's legend as a black zone is steeped in bloodshed and tragedy. After Spanish conquistadors discovered the region in 1501, they consolidated their first mainland colony in the Americas by slaughtering tens of thousands of natives, often by turning ravenous dogs loose on villages. The Spanish conquered the Amazon and the Andes but eventually gave up on taming the Gap,

5     https://larouchepac.com/world-landbridge, LaRouche Pac, The New Silk Road
6     https://www.popularmechanics.com/technology/infrastructure/a28051/road-around-the-entire-world/
7     *How To Triple Food Production By Developing High-Speed Rail,* Dennis Small, August 15, 2008, p.27

which became a bastion for pirates and runaway slaves. In 1699, more than 2,000 Scottish colonists perished from malaria and starvation, and in 1854 nine explorers died from disease and exposure on a U.S. Navy survey expedition, scuttling plans for a grand canal project through the isthmus. In more recent times, efforts to build a road link have foundered because of fears that foot-and-mouth disease could spread and devastate the U.S. beef industry, and because of resistance from the Kuna and Embera-Wounaan Indians who inhabit the rainforest.[8]

They say that it is technically impossible to build a highway or railway there, because "the jungle will swallow it up." If Latin America is to prosper in the age of post-Bretton Woods economic collapse, the problems can and must be overcome.

On the technical side: If the Biosphere, left to its own devices, has denied the Great American Desert (which stretches through western Canada, the United States, and northern Mexico) enough water to sustain life to the degree required, it has dumped excessive amounts of water in the Darien region. The area is one of the wettest places on Earth, with very heavy rainfall, over 300 days a year, producing annual precipitation of more than 5,000 mm (5 meters) per year—about 20 times more than the Great American Desert! As a result, the area is a swampy jungle, and any highway built in the ordinary fashion sinks into the mud with each rainy season.[9]

The Emberá Indians build their roads and homes up on stilts or on top of tree trunks, which then float when the solid land turns into marsh. But a more sophisticated approach will be required if the Darien Gap project, which would link up rail routes stretching through North and Central America, with South American corridors extending down to Argentina's Tierra del Fuego, is to become a key node in the future maglev rail lines which will be built there, including the use of elevated roadways and railways, among other technical advances.

"Doing this involves crossing a 60-mile stretch of dense jungle along the which has never even had a highway built through it, let alone a railroad – despite the fact that detailed plans for the construction of a Pan American Railway, including the Darien Gap, were drawn up as far back as the administration of U.S. President William McKinley (1897-1901)."[10]

8      https://www.outsideonline.com/2098801/skull-stake-darien-gap#close
9      NAWAPA: Bridging The Darien Gap, Dennis Small, August 20, 2010, p.29, EIR.
10    *How To Triple Food Production By Developing High-Speed Rail,* Dennis Small, August 15, 2008, p.27

The Pan-American Highway network "is a remarkable feat of engineering that runs about 19,000 miles from Prudhoe Bay, Alaska, to Ushuaia, Argentina, with just one break in the pavement: the Darién Gap. It can't be bypassed on land. It's roughly 100 miles wide, stretching all the way from the Caribbean Sea to the Pacific Ocean. It has long defied the advance of colonists, road builders, and would-be developers."[11]

The Darien Gap has been extensively studied by the highly qualified American rail engineer Hal Cooper. Cooper presents two distinct, viable routes for the project. "The Darien Gap railway connector would be approximately 85 to 95 miles (136 to 152 km) long, and could go by either a central lowland route, parallel to the uncompleted Pan American Highway or by an elevated hill and mountain route to the east of the Pan American highway," Cooper proposes. The former route would run

> ... through thick tropical rain forests in parallel to the Chucunaque and Tuira Rivers where heavy rainfall, thick jungles, insects and snakes, plus frequent flooding, would be major problems over much of the year.... The alternative eastern mountain route would go over the Serranía del Darién Mountains to the Atlantic drainage side over relatively gentle grades through rolling hills with maximum elevations of 1,500 to 2,000 feet (455 to 610 meters) through heavy tropical forests. A significant challenge would be involved no matter what routes were chosen.
>
> The western lowlands route would be shorter in length, but would go through flood-prone areas with heavy rainfall, and would have to be built through a national park. The eastern highland route would be longer, but would be able to avoid much of the flood-prone areas, and would probably not need any tunnels, and would not have to be built on an elevated courseway.[12]

Based on Cooper's work,

> ... once the rail line has crossed the Darien Gap into Colombia, it will branch into three major North-South continental corridors, which run the length of South America. The *Western Corridor* will run south from Bogotá through Ecuador, Peru, Bolivia, Paraguay, and into Argentina. This route will run along the eastern foothills of the Andes Mountains, laying the basis for opening up the entire undeveloped interior of the continent, which runs from the Andes to the Atlantic coast.

11      https://www.outsideonline.com/2098801/skull-stake-darien-gap#close
12      Further considerations by Cooper can be found in an interview with EIR, Jan. 30, 2009
http://www.larouchepub.com/eiw/public/ 2009/2009_1-9/2009_1-9/2009-4/pdf/49-55_3604.pdf

A second major route, the *Central Corridor* will run southeast from Bogotá, to Leticia, and from there will cut across the Amazon jungle to Pôrto Velho, Cuiabá, and São Paulo in Brazil. A third, *Eastern Corridor* will hug the Atlantic coast and run from Colombia to Venezuela, Guyana, Surinam, French Guiana, Brazil, Uruguay, and Ecuador.

To the North, an east-west route along the Colombia-Panama border should be joined to another great infrastructure project on the Colombian side of the border, which would run north-south: the *Atrato-Truandó Canal.* This canal, some 50 miles (80 km) in length, would use two semi-navigable rivers in the region—the Atrato and the Truandó—to create a sea-level canal between the Atlantic and Pacific Oceans, through which ships larger than 65,000 tons—the current limit on the Panama Canal—would be able to travel.

In this way, what is today perhaps the most inhospitable region of the Biosphere in the Western Hemisphere, would be turned into a unique world crossroads for north-south and east-west transport and commerce.

Various East-West corridors will also be built from the Western Corridor to cross the Andes and reach the Pacific coast. One of the more promising is Saramirisa in Peru, where the Andes reach their lowest elevation, 2,500 meters (8,200 feet) above sea level. Other cross-Andes spurs will link Argentina and Bolivia up with a Coastal Corridor running the length of Chile. These are essential to transform an integrated South America into a two-ocean economic power—much in the same way that Abraham Lincoln's transcontinental rail project achieved that objective for the United States in the second half of the 19th Century.[13]

# Food from the Plains and the Cerrado

Abraham Lincoln was the real architect of the unprecedented global colossus of Industrial America. It was Lincoln who signed the bill authorizing the transcontinental railroad.

> ... And it was Lincoln's railroads that also allowed for the transformation of the U.S. Great Plains states west of the Mississippi River, into the agricultural powerhouse that they became. That same principle applies, 160 years later, to the heartland of South America. There are two principal areas of under-utilized cultivatable land

---

13    Hal Cooper addressed the Second Panel of the Schiller Institute Conference on April 13, 2017

in South America where a vast increase in food production can be readily achieved: the Colombian-Venezuelan Plains, and Brazil's Cerrado. The Amazon jungle lies between them.

This includes the highly fertile Colombian-Venezuelan plains region, a continuous stretch of some 50 million hectares (212,000 square miles) in the Orinoco River basin, where adequate rail and water management infrastructure would allow the production of some 60 million tons of grain per year. There is significant annual rainfall – in fact, too much in certain seasons – and there are major rivers, which cross the region, including the Meta and the Guaviare. The land, once treated with lime (between 3 and 5 tons per hectare) to address the problem of acidity, is well suited for extensive agriculture. Today, it is vastly underpopulated, underdeveloped, and largely controlled by London-promoted drug-trafficking armies. For example, the Colombian portion of the region (about 60% of the total for the two countries), constitutes 27% of Colombia's national territory but has only 3% of its total population – some 1.5 million inhabitants. There are few roads in the region and no railroads.[14]

To effectively combat narco-terrorism, the continent must find a way to "produce sufficient food, generate an exportable surplus, and to physically integrate the various geographic regions by rail and water corridors. Together, the Colombian and Venezuelan plains represent some 50 million hectares, of which 15 million could be cultivated with relative ease. Back in 2008, Presidents Hugo Chávez of Venezuela and Alvaro Uribe of Colombia agreed that through navigation of the Orinoco Basin rivers – in particular, the Orinoco and the Meta rivers – and with railway corridors, it will be possible to transport grain grown on the Colombian and Venezuelan plains, in the amount of at least 60 million tons a year. Thus, the goal to double worldwide food production and eliminate hunger from the face of the Earth could be achieved in this region.

> President Uribe accepted Venezuelan President Chávez's proposal to integrate their two nations through a Colombian-Venezuelan rail line. This would consist of two main trunk lines, one would come down from Panama and run along the Caribbean coastline from Cartagena in Colombia to the city of Maracaibo in Venezuela. Another would originate in Venezuela, passing through the border city of Arauca, and crossing the Colombian provinces of Arauca,

---

Casanare (Yopal), Meta (Villavicencio), Guaviare, Caquetá (Florencia), and Putumayo, and from there into Ecuador.

The then Brazilian President Luiz Inácio Lula announced that his country would invest in the rehabilitation and expansion of the Carare railroad, making Brazil's dream of a route to the Pacific Ocean into reality, by connecting to the river transport system of the Amazon and Putumayo rivers, through a corridor that would reach the Pacific via the Colombian port of Tumaco.[15]

# Intermodal Transport

President Uribe has insisted that the large amount of food that could be produced in the Colombia-Venezuela Plains could be transported using rail corridors and the water corridors of the Orinoco and Meta rivers. This would mean taking advantage of the vast agricultural potential of the Orinoco Basin region, which today is wasted because enormous expanses of land are used for extensive cattle-raising. Instead, meat production should take the form of intensive ranching within fenced areas.

In addition to navigation of the Meta and Orinoco rivers, the rail corridor should extend from the foothills of the Andes, through Villavicencio, and connecting San José del Guaviare, Puerto Inírida, Puerto Carreño and Yopal, as well as the corresponding cities and ports on the Venezuelan side. Thus, there would be an efficient intermodal transportation network for goods and passengers, year-round, combining rail, water, and highway links.

These development and transport corridors, as well as the region's energy integration (electricity networks, gas and oil pipelines, and so on) should extend both northwest to Central America and Mexico, as well as to the south, as far as Argentina.[16]

In other words, the time has come to finally adopt the recommendations which David Lilienthal, made back in 1954 to the President of the Republic of Colombia, Gen. Gustavo Rojas Pinilla: Get a great plan of infrastructure projects underway.

Lilienthal had served as director of the Tennessee Valley Authority, the greatest hydraulic and related public works project carried out by Franklin Delano Roosevelt's government, which did away with the floods that, year after year, had devastated the seven states

15       "Reaping the Food Potential of The Colombia-Venezuela Plains," Maximiliano Londoño Penilla, President, Lyndon LaRouche Association, Colombia, EIR, August 15, 2008, p.33
16       Ibid

through which the Tennessee River flows. FDR built more than 45,000 infrastructure projects: dams, levees, tunnels, highways, railroads, aqueducts, hospitals, hydroelectric plants, irrigation districts, and so on. Among these were 43 important hydroelectric projects and dams, as well as more than 450 small and medium-sized dams. In this way, FDR not only defeated the Great Depression of the 1930s but also put an end to many "natural disasters," like the floods that had been a curse to the crops and inhabitants along the riverbanks.

Invited to Colombia by Gen. Rojas Pinilla, Lilienthal proposed the use of the coffee bonanza (from the high coffee prices of the time), along with the creation of a public finance corporation able to issue bonds, to help finance the construction of great infrastructure projects. Lilienthal described these as "a kind of Second Liberation," after the first accomplished by Simón Bolivar.[17]

In a memorandum for General Rojas, Lilienthal proposed, among other things, that the Cauca and Sinú river valleys be made the axis of a pilot project for all Latin America, where the achievements of the TVA could be replicated.

Otto Lilienthal observed:

General Bolivar won a victory over colonial oppression and thereby opened the door to political independence and freedom. The time may well be close at hand, indeed it may be here, for another epochal series of events in Colombian life – and through her, for all of South America, a kind of Second Liberation.

The weapons of this Liberator will not be swords and cannon, nor will the price of this victory be exacted in the blood of Colombians, spilled for one's homeland on the field of battle. The arms of Liberation this time will be new highways and railroads, electrification, dams for irrigation and flood control and power, new schools and universities and hospitals, new and improved methods of raising coffee, sugar, cattle, rice. It may be said that the fruits of victory over ignorance and disease, over floodwaters, and soil erosion, and poor crops, can be as glorious as those won in the battles fought by Bolivar and his fellow patriots. The Colombians who lead their countrymen toward this 20th-Century Liberation will surely be as highly honored and as long-remembered as those who, following Bolivar more than 100 years ago, offered their lives to win their country's independence.

---

17    Adopt Lilienthal's Infrastructure Plan! Maximiliano Londoño Penilla, EIR, April 15, 2008, p. 37

Lilienthal established the mission as the transformation of Colombia into an agricultural and industrial power, endowed with the most modern infrastructure, and he explained with absolute clarity that, in this way, the unification of all Colombians would finally be achieved.

Let us heed him:

> Such a great forward surge in the physical development of a nation's resources as once can realistically envisage for Colombia in the next quarter-century carries with it more than physical benefits alone. The very foundation of such a program can, in and of itself, serve as a center about which the whole people can unite and stand together, despite their economic or political differences. With so much constructive and creative work to be done, and so much improvement for everyone at stake, such a program may help to bring the entire nation together on the essentials of certain concrete tasks that need doing.

If a future President of Colombia would adopt the infrastructure program which Lilienthal proposed, then the basis for a lasting peace can be laid upon the foundation of stable and well-paid jobs for all Colombians of working age. This is the war, which has to be won, the war against hunger and unemployment. And in the process, we would defeat the floods and their horrible consequences.

# Cerrado Region of Brazil

In addition, new infrastructure and a rail network would lay the groundwork for also opening up Brazil's highly fertile *Cerrado* region, which could produce some 210 million tons of grain per year.

> The Cerrado has many faces: arid tablelands, open grasslands, palm-dotted marshes. But what most people see is its *campo sujo*, or "dirty fields" – a dry and unruly expanse dotted with low, twisted shrubs. Unlike the Amazon and the Atlantic Forest, the cerrado is not one of the biomes accorded "national heritage" status in Brazil's constitution. The Cerrado's 770,000 square miles of acidic, aluminum-rich soils were long written off as worthless. Then, in the 1970s, researchers at Embrapa, the government's agricultural research agency, figured out how to "correct" those soils with prodigious doses of lime and fertilizer.[18]

---

18      The Slow Death of Ecology's Birthplace, Jonathan Mingle, Undark Magazine, December 16, 2016

A scientific article on cyanobacteria from the Brazilian extreme environment describes Cerrado as a

> ... vast dry and hot savanna ecoregion, which constitutes 24% of Brazil's total land area of 846 million hectares. Three main river systems drain the region: the Araguaia-Tocantins (into the Amazon basin), the Paraná (southward to the Río de la Plata basin), and the San Francisco (to the Atlantic Ocean). Like the Colombia-Venezuela Plains, with the right fertilizer and lime applications to the soils, the region's agro-climatic potential is vast. The temperature regime for much of the Cerrado will permit two, and sometimes three crops a year.[19]

According to scientific studies, approximately "50 million hectares out of the Cerrado's total of 205 million can be put under crop cultivation. This will produce about 210 million tons of grain per year. Similarly, in the Colombian-Venezuelan Plains, grain can be grown on some 15 million of its 50 million hectares, producing about 60 million tons."[20]

Grain needs water. According to joint research from Leibniz-Institute of Freshwater Ecology and Institute of Biology at Freie Universität, both in Berlin, Germany, as well as Department of Civil, Environmental and Mechanical Engineering at Trento University in Italy and Center for Applied Geosciences at the Eberhard Karls Universität Tübingen, Germany,

> ... future Water Transfer MegaProjects will play a significant role in the water-food-energy nexus, and this approach, therefore, could facilitate the resolution of some of the approval processes regarding realization of projects and their expected dimensions. The Aquatacama Project, which will transfer around $1.5 \text{ km}^3 \text{ a}^{-1}$ over a distance of 2,500 km from the south to the north of Chile, is expected to double its area of agricultural land and food production.[21]
>
> Large-scale projects proposed in North America as NAWAPA (The North American Water and Power Alliance), PLHI-NO (Plan Hidráulico del Noroeste, or Northwest Hydraulic Plan), and PLHI-GON (Plan Hidráulico del Golfo Norte, or Northern Gulf Hydraulic Plan) will jointly form a single water transfer network, boosting food production in Mexico. The area of irrigated land in Mexico will increase by 75% and grain production will be doubled[22]

19    Diego B. Genuário, Itamar S. Melo, in Microbial Diversity in the Genomic Era, 2019

20    Chapter 16 - Cyanobacteria From Brazilian Extreme Environments: Toward Functional Exploitation, Academic Press, pp.265-284

21    Dourojeanni, A., Jadue, N., León, G., Osborne, K., and Serra, D. (2013). Aquatacama Project: Preliminary Socio-Economic Analysis. Fundacion Chile. Available online at: http://www.acquatacama.cl/sites/default/files/AQUATACAMA%20REPORT%20FINAL%20-%20F.%20Chile.pdf

22    Front. Environ. Sci., 12 December 2018 | https://doi.org/10.3389/fenvs.2018.00150, Alek-

Even if we factor in: a) replacing current imports (40 million tons) with regional production; b) bringing food consumption levels up to the point where hunger is eliminated for the 40-50% of the population today suffering from hunger (another 60 million tons); and c) providing for a 3% yearly population growth over the decade that it will take to bring these major projects on line (90 million additional tons); the total required grain production of 350 million tons by 2018 will be more than matched by the 450 million tons that will be produced. Regional food self-sufficiency is unquestionably an achievable goal.

But, to achieve this, it is absolutely necessary to build high-speed rail corridors to bring capital inputs into the agricultural regions, to transport the product to market, and to provide the overall infrastructural backbone for the industrial development of the interior of the continent.

South America must do today, what the United States did in the 19<sup>th</sup> century at the behest of Abraham Lincoln. The outlook required is that of the Peruvian patriot Manuel Pardo, who, as President from 1872-1876, in alliance with Lincoln's networks in the United States, launched a major national railway project, which included crossing the Andes. Their enemies sarcastically dubbed it "the Train to the Moon." But Pardo already knew, in 1860, the enormous role to be played by railroad infrastructure:

> Join the three central lines by means of the fourth, and decide if, in ten years, a revolution will not have occurred in Peru, a revolution at once both physical and moral, because the locomotive – which, like magic, changes the face of the country through which it passes – also civilizes. And that is perhaps its main advantage: populations are put into contact. It does more than civilize; it educates. All the primary schools of Peru could not teach in a century, what the locomotive could teach them in ten years.

# Financing these Projects

There are many ways that these projects could be financed.

First, a Financial Reconstruction Corporation (or some great national infrastructure fund) must be established, authorized to issue bonds. This was the model used by [U.S. President Dwight] Eisenhower to finance the construction of the United States' great highway system. In addition to this concept of a Capital Budget, a portion of Latin American nations' foreign reserves could be channeled into that fund for financing infrastructure. This is precisely

sandra Shumilova, Klement Tockner, Michele Thieme, Christiane Zarfl.

the idea behind the Bank of the South: to create a financial instrument, part of whose reserves would be designated for financing great projects, rather than permitting our money to sit in foreign banks, which use the funds but don't lend them to us when we need them.[23]

The Bank of the South is, potentially, one that reflects programmatic proposals – the New Bretton Woods and the Eurasian Land-Bridge – conceived of as the seed-crystal of a new international financial architecture, free of the dictates of private financier interests whose system is now crumbling.

> This conception is based on a specific republican historical tradition of cooperation among the sovereign nation-states of the Americas, as John Quincy Adams envisioned. Bank of the South is not merely a regional operation but the beginning of a new international financial architecture—which is what it must be if it is to succeed. In reality, it is only as a regional component of a new international monetary system, that the Bank has any chance of success.[24]

In the early years of the U.S. Republic, the first Treasury Secretary, Alexander Hamilton, issued money that was used as credit for financing the development of manufactures (industrialization), mechanization of agriculture, and promotion of great infrastructure works. Hamilton said,

> We are not going to ask you for money, we are a sovereign country, we create our own money. We will create credit and we will work in the economy to increase the productivity of our people. We will fund infrastructure projects, manufacturing projects, will fund things that increase labor productivity and make the economy more productive and therefore richer.[25]

This is how real wealth is created: the production process. Instead of borrowing money from the oligarchs, you create your own money as a sovereign nation and use it to escape the clutches of the oligarchy. And this is what allowed the United States to resist the continuous attempts of the British Empire to recover the U.S. as its imperial protectorate. The difference between the monetary and credit system is the principle on which the current oligarchic system is based.

---

23    Colombian LaRouche Movement: Vote for Great Projects, Maglev, Maximiliano Londoño, October 26, 2007, EIR, p41
24    Which Bank of the South Will Prevail? Cynthia R. Rush, EIR, December 21, 2007
25    TransEvolution: The Coming Age of Human Deconstruction, Daniel Estulin, Trineday Press, 2014, p.35. ISBN 978-1-937584-77-1

The "American System" meant using the government's ability to generate credit and other means to create national wealth through technological progress. "It was abhorred by the British enemies of the American Revolution, who sought to destroy it from the time it was first conceived by George Washington's treasury secretary, Alexander Hamilton, and articulated in Hamilton's 1791 Report on Manufactures."[26]

Hamilton redefined the meaning of debt within a functional nation-state economy. "Hamilton suggested that the United States look at debt not as a problem, but as an asset. He proposed to fund the debt through a gradual schedule of dependable tax resources, assume state debts as a measure of good policy, and generate new revenue through western land sales and taxes."[27]

As the power of the productive economy grew, particularly in industry, so, reciprocally, did the Bank's value of capital and the general value of the public debt. All of this would be an increased capability of lending for commerce, and increasing the means of payment in the economy available for trade.

> After the National Bank's charter was allowed to lapse in 1811 under Jeffersonian influences, Hamilton's credit system was revived by Nicholas Biddle, Mathew Carey, and President John Quincy Adams with the Second Bank of the United States, particularly during 1823-36 period. Under Hamilton and Biddle, who was chairman of the Second Bank, the system was managed to increase the number of transactions occurring on credit rather than liquidating wealth for the present. Transactions were settled by the future resources generated, which gave a credit to the initial borrower. Credits and debts were coordinated according to the cycles of production to defray the time of payment, till each party had sufficient credit to balance their debts. This allowed productive surpluses to be absorbed into future growth and productive investment.
>
> The Bank directly intervened into the economy, not by upholding inflated securities, but by assisting the productive economy or the needed infrastructure projects with capital, in order to maintain the surplus productive capacity. The protection for manufacturing and support for internal improvements that Hamilton had called for did not come about until the 1820s, under President John Quincy Adams. The major canals, new railroads, and new industries were made possible by federal credit and direct loans and

26      "Lincoln's 'American System' policy was a far cry from Reaganomics," by Nicholas F. Benton, EIR Volume 14, Number 6, February 6, 1987
27      How Alexander Hamilton tackled the National Debt, smithsonian.com, April 19, 2017

other indirect functions of the Bank. Adams used the nation's stock in the Bank for financing large projects, and under Biddle's direction, the Second Bank of the United States loaned and subscribed directly for nearly 50% of all the capital raised to construct the largest canals, which made possible the transport of anthracite coal for the iron industry.

Under the regulation of the credit system under Biddle, the currency bore a proper relation to the real business and exchanges of the country. As more agricultural land was developed, as more manufacturing facilities became established, and as more transportation networks for produce and coal for manufacturing facilities were completed, the amount of bank credit that could safely be put into circulation through loans and discounts increased in proportion.[28]

# Lincoln's System of Public Credit

As Paul Gallagher and Michael Kirsch explain,

New York banks and the British East India Company opposed the Second Bank of the United States and the internal improvements and domestic manufactures it facilitated. Those interests were politically successful in taking down the U.S. credit system by means of the Jackson and Van Buren administrations. However, Abraham Lincoln, a longtime supporter, and advocate of the system of national credit of John Quincy Adams and Alexander Hamilton, revived this system when he began his Presidency.

The first step that Lincoln took was the passage of a strong tariff, the second Morrill Tariff, in the summer of 1861. Hamilton had established that protection of manufacturing is essential for a sound banking and credit system, not only because it generated revenue (customs duties) to fund and support national credit, but also because the specie that was kept on reserve could not be maintained when the country ran a negative trade balance, because imports had to be paid in specie. Lincoln's next measure, the policy and issue of "greenbacks," then created the medium to revive and accelerate the machine of domestic production and commerce.

At the end of 1861, after buying (at a very high-interest rate) an initial round of U.S. Treasury bonds to get the Union mobilized for the Civil War, New York bankers blocked with British and French lenders to stop all revenue streams to the Treasury. These banks suspended payments of gold owed to those who had made deposits in their banks, ceased their purchase or acceptance of government bonds, and blocked foreign loans. The government responded by taking control of the currency, and issued its own U.S. Treasury notes – "greenbacks" – as a circulating medium of payment necessary for commerce and war. The Legal Tender Act, February 25, 1862, read, "To authorize the issue of United States Notes and for the redemption or funding thereof, and for funding the floating debt of the United States." Despite widespread doubts in Congress, even in Lincoln's Republican Party, the greenback credit-issue policy was as successful as the Hamiltonian national bank policy on which it was based.[29]

In their in-depth report, *The New Silk Road Becomes the World Land-Bridge*, the authors explain that

The Lincoln Administration increased government spending by 300% by creating $460 million in greenbacks during the Civil War. This legal tender was used, in the first instance, by the Treasury to pay soldiers, contractors, teamsters, manufacturers of weapons and uniforms, farmers, etc. Greenbacks could be used by investors (along with state banks' notes) to purchase bonds sold by the Treasury. From October 1862 to January 1864 the Treasury Department oversaw the selling of more than $500 million in bonds to individual citizens, enough to finance the greenbacks that it issued. And the greenbacks were used to pay the war taxes on imports, industry, and high (more than $800 per year) incomes. The bonds sold were largely part of the next action taken by the Lincoln Administration, the National Currency and Banking Acts of 1863 and 1864, which, united with the greenbacks measure, and a national funding system, built a system of national banks on the same principle of Hamilton's Bank of the United States. State banks were rechartered as national banks on the basis of the requirement to purchase United States stocks to hold as securities for their circulating notes. The U.S. bonds purchased by the banks were deposited in the Treasury, and the newly chartered national banks received greenbacks in return, upon which to lend.

Just as the Bank of the United States and its branches had had a large portion of its capital stock in the form of public debt, under Lincoln's Presidency greenbacks and banknotes now circulated on the basis of the public debt, which the nationally regulated private banks purchased and held in the Treasury. The United States bonds, upon which the greenbacks were issued to national banks for lending, were 20-year annuity bonds, paying a dependable in-

29    Ibid

terest, but which were not tradable and were callable only by the government prior to their maturity. As with Hamilton, it was the strict regulation of the terms of the public debt by the government that made the credit, which circulated upon that debt a reliable medium for growth.

The greenbacks were safely leveraged on the basis of the 20-year bonds, which were held as security, and which themselves were funded by tariffs and taxes. Import duties far exceeded the interest to be paid out on the bonds, in specie.

Lincoln's economic advisor Henry Carey, described the greenbacks as a "non-exportable" and reliable internal source of credit, which was debt-free for its domestic users. With the greenback circulation instead contracted to $330 million by the end of 1867, American businessmen, farmers, and artisans became more dependent on greater amounts of debt, and the United States' general industrial expansion again became dependent for credit on European banking centers and on the use of gold. When the United States "resumed specie currency" in 1879, Americans kept their greenbacks and turned almost none in for gold certificates, proving Carey right that their quantity was much too small to meet the demand for circulating credit. Three decades later, in the debt crisis and panic of 1907, President Theodore Roosevelt considered expanding greenback circulation with a large new issue; he hesitated, however, and let Wall Street bankers take the initiative from him with the 1908 Aldrich Act, allowing private banks to issue "U.S." currency and leading to the Federal Reserve System five years later. The U.S. Treasury has not issued national credit since.[30]

# Franklin Roosevelt's RFC

When Franklin D. Roosevelt entered the White House in March 1933, "the banking system was near total collapse, and unemployment had reached 25%."[31] The Reconstruction Finance Corporation Act was signed into law on January 22, 1932, creating the Reconstruction Finance Corporation (RFC) and providing for "emergency financing facilities in response to the Great Depression and mass unemployment."[32] Wall Street shenanigans did not determine prices. Rather,

---

30    The New Silk Road becomes the new Land Bridge, EIR News Service, Helga Zepp-LaRouche, Michael O. Billington, p.27, section II, ISBN: 978-0-943235-24-0
31    "The Great Depression," Herbert Hoover Presidential Library and Museum, National Archives and Records Administration (accessed May 22, 2019).
32    Reconstruction Finance Corporation Act," Pub. L. No. 72-2, 47 Stat. 5 (1932). For the full text of the act, see http://legisworks.org/sal/47/stats/STATUTE-47-Pg5.pdf

... the credit of the RFC offset the economic cycles of the private financial sector. The RFC operated separately from the authorizations and appropriations of the Federal budget, borrowing from the U.S. Treasury according to limits set by Congress. All loans made through the RFC, as loans, and not appropriations, were repaid, not only with a financial profit to the Treasury, but more importantly, with a productivity increase for the nation as a whole not measurable in dollars, not to mention the profit savings in human and productive capital that would have been lost had the loans not been made.

Under Franklin Roosevelt, the RFC was the embodiment of directed credit and operated almost exactly as the Banks of the United States had under Nicholas Biddle and Alexander Hamilton, increasing the overall indirect and direct long-term credit in the economy, itself directly lending to the economy on non-restrictive terms. The striking differences were that it was not the chief depository institution for United States tax revenues and thus could not lend them out as a source of credit to banks, industries, and other corporations, as had the Bank of the United States. It also did not receive private subscriptions to its capital stock. The RFC was acting in an environment which included the structure of the Federal Reserve Banks, and therefore was not as efficient as the Bank of the United States, which was acting as the chief institution and the key mover in the banking system. President Roosevelt's 1934 proposal to create national credit banks for industry, directly within the Federal Reserve System, and which would act as depositories for U.S. tax revenues, was blocked in the Congress.[33]

# International Credit Agreements for Development

The emergence of two new multilateral infrastructure-specific development banks, the Asian Infrastructure Investment Bank (AIIB) headed by China and backed by a founding shareholder membership of 57 countries and the New Development Bank (NDB) is operated on an equal basis between the BRICS countries has opened up an opportunity for creating convergence. "The existing global governance architecture could be sustained only through the inclusion of emerging economies, as advanced economies need to engage with the new institutions set up by their emerging counterparts."[34]

33      The New Silk Road becomes the new Land Bridge, EIR News Service, Helga Zepp-LaRouche, Michael O. Billington, p.29, section II, ISBN: 978-0-943235-24-0
34      Rise of Asian Infrastructure Investment Bank and New Development Bank reinforces need for World Bank/IMF reform, Syed Munir Khasru, SCMP, October 19, 2015

According to *The New Silk Road becomes the new Land Bridge* feasibility study, "the critical infrastructure projects require cooperation among several nations, including credit cooperation among the major economic powers providing the bulk of capital goods and industrial products for these projects – but not supranational direction. The United States and European economic powers led by Germany easily can, and need to, participate in expanding these banks toward the trillions of dollars-equivalent in new infrastructure credits actually required immediately. But they must give up their "green" hostility to the most productive scientific advances and technologies, to do so.

The example of the Bering Strait Tunnel crossing and high-speed rail linkage of Eurasia and North America, now seen as increasingly urgent by China and Russia in particular, or the large-scale water-management breakthrough necessary to stop desertification of western North America, illustrate the general principle. The agreements among the countries involved in joint funds or agencies to carry out these great projects, require clear rules on issuing credits over the long term and at low rates of interest. Moreover, these nations remain sovereigns with their own national credit systems, so that the long-term credits are required in several currencies with relatively stable parities over the long term, together with currency-swap arrangements among central banks. A current negative example of this requirement is the serious disruption of trade and development projects in Kazakhstan due to the abrupt drop of the Russian ruble's value in 2014 under increasing sanctions.

Benjamin Franklin and Alexander Hamilton, and later Mathew and Henry Carey, explicitly insisted on protection as a feature of national banking, to prevent the newly invested capital of the bank from being rapidly dissipated. For example, without regulations to protect manufacturing and thereby reduce imports, which require payment in real money (then specie, today dollars), the strain on the national bank and its branches for such payment will break the system.[35]

India's Prime Minister Narendra Modi stated, "The expansion of the NDB membership will strengthen the bank's role as a global development finance institution and further contribute to the mobilization of resources for infrastructure and sustainable development projects."[36] India's Ministry of Finance confirmed on September 3, 2019 "The mandate of the

35    The New Silk Road becomes the new Land Bridge, EIR News Service, Helga Zepp-LaRouche, Michael O. Billington, p.29, section II, ISBN: 978-0-943235-24-0
36    BRICS Summit: PM Modi calls for early opening of New Development Bank's regional office in India, The Economic Times, November 14, 2019

Bank is to mobilize resources for infrastructure and sustainable development projects in BRICS and other emerging economies and developing countries, complementing the existing efforts of multilateral and regional financial institutions for global growth and development."[37]

For infrastructure and sustainable development projects via New Development Bank (NDB) to become real,

> ... it must issue credits in their own currencies to capitalize a NDB, created by treaty, with several trillion dollars equivalent in capital, so that it becomes the ultimate funder and initiator of investments in the great projects. One or more sovereign wealth funds of other nations may also invest capital in the IDB, but the credit issued to it by the cooperating economic powers must define how it is capitalized – by 20 to 30-year debenture investments of an "annuity" type, paying a dividend but callable only by the Bank itself should it decide to reduce its capital for any reason or to accept other investors. This is the same principle on which national credit banks, able to invest in the NDB, will be created by the United States or other investing nations, insofar as their credit for investment is not created on the basis of trade surpluses and foreign reserves.

> In making equally long-term loans for the development of projects in individual nations, the IDB will book a credit with the national development bank of the nation involved, which will use that as the basis to issue credit in its own currency to authorities and enterprises carrying out the work. By design of the national development banks in the borrowing nations, and by capital controls, this currency too must be "non-exportable" except for trade.

> The borrowing nations must establish not only capital controls, but more importantly exchange controls, to ensure that no NDB credits are diverted to flight capital or "carry trade" securities investments, and that their use for development projects preempts any attempted use for repayment of other sovereign debts of countries receiving credits.

> Furthermore, it is necessary to the effectiveness of the NDB's development credit issuance that over-in-debted nations with sovereign debts which have been imposed on them illegitimately, in whole or in part, be able to place the illegitimate debt in moratorium, replacing it with much longer term debt if agreements cannot be made to write down, or write off, such debt. Otherwise, the borrowing nations' fiscal burden of foreign debt repayment will harm their ability to participate in the NDB's credit issuance for vital

---

37     https://pib.gov.in/newsite/PrintRelease.aspx?relid=192988

great infrastructure projects. This NDB can be a means of debt re-organization for over-indebted nations or groups of nations requir-ing NDB credit for great infrastructure development platforms.

Where national and regional authorities receive loans from the NDB in order to carry out the actual creation of great infrastruc-ture projects and/or scientific and technological developments, which will generate highly productive economic activity as well as revenues for them, they will repay these NDB credits in the same way—by creating national credit banks, both to generate addition-al internal development credit and to invest in the NDB them-selves, using their own national currencies.[38]

The question is, how can we describe this process, as a proposal to the nations of Latin America for debt reorganization and development, as being identical in its requirements for debtor nations and for the (then) creditor nation, the United States? The International Monetary Fund pro-posals based on "control of the public finances, wide-ranging economic reforms along with institutional reform where necessary,"[39] are a recipe for abject poverty and dismantling of a nation-state. However, we don't need to heed their advice. The economic policy paper of *The New Silk Road becomes the new Land Bridge* offers several solutions:

1. In no republic must any other issues of credit be permitted, ... excepting (a) Deferred-payment credit between buyers and sellers of goods and services; (b) banking loans against combined lawful currency and bullion on deposit in a lawful manner; (c) loan of issues of credit created via issues of national currency – notes of the Treasury of the national government.

2. Loan of government-created credit (currency notes) must be di-rected to those forms of investment which promote technological progress in realizing the fullest potentials for applying otherwise idled capital-goods, otherwise idled goods-producing capacities, and otherwise idled productive labor, to produce goods or to devel-op the basic economic infrastructure needed for maintenance and development of production and physical distribution of goods ...

3. In each republic, there must be a state-owned national bank, which rejects in its lawfully permitted functions, those pri-

38      The New Silk Road becomes the new Land Bridge, EIR News Service, Helga Zepp-LaRouche, Michael O. Billington, p.29, section II, ISBN: 978-0-943235-24-0.
39      The Difference is in the Debt: Crisis Resolution in Latin America, Anne O. Krueger, First Deputy Managing Director, IMF, Latin America Conference on Sector Reform, Stanford Center for International Development, November 14, 2003.

vate-banking features of central banking associated with the Bank of England and the misguided practices of the U.S.A.'s Federal Reserve System ...

4. No lending institution shall exist within the nation except as they are subject to standards of practice and auditing by the Treasury of the government and auditors of the national bank. No foreign financial institution shall be permitted to do business within the republic unless its international operations meet lawful requirements for standards of reserves and proper banking practices under the laws of the republic, as this shall be periodically determined by proper audit ('transparency' of foreign lending institutions).

5. The Treasury and national bank, as a partnership, have continual authority to administer capital controls and exchange controls, and to assist this function by means of licensing of individual import and export licenses, and to regulate negotiations of loans taken from foreign sources...

6. Sovereign valuation of the foreign exchange value of a nation's currency must be established ... The first approximation of the value of a nation's currency is the purchasing power of that currency within the internal economy of that nation. What are the prices of domestically produced goods and services, relative to the prices of the same quality of goods and services in other nations?

As the authors of the report explain,

Because trade will increase among the nations participating in the treaty agreements for the building of these great projects, both those issuing credit through the NDB and those receiving loans, the national banks of the participating nations will necessarily create currency swaps large enough for increasing trade payments in each others' currencies. These currency swaps for increases in trade can provide the basis for agreements on stable ranges for exchange rates between and among currencies.

The responsibility and purpose of the International Development Bank is to guarantee that development credits issued by nations go exclusively into the development of the new infrastructure platforms and technological developments most important to increase the productivity of national economies and of the labor forces of the human species.[40]

---

40      Ibid

# Extending the New Silk Road

Given that we are dealing with a global rebalancing of the economy, it would only make sense to involve some of the financially viable nations of the Gulf Cooperation Council (Saudi Arabia, the United Arab Emirates, Kuwait, Bahrain, Qatar and Oman) along with other potentially large economies such as Egypt and Turkey in the creation of the South-west Asia/Africa Regional Infrastructure Bank. Key objective of the initiative: create credit to cooperate in new infrastructure projects with the new international development banks led by the Asian Infrastructure Investment Bank (AIIB).

> Proposals were made by the United States more than 20 years ago for a $100 billion regional development bank to be formed in Southwest Asia, and that can be taken as a baseline level for the Bank's equity and borrowed capital combined. The Bank should be managed by a combination of bankers with experience in construction and engineering financing, business leaders from the productive sectors of the economies, and scientific and engineering experts of governments from the broad region. Their task will be to identify the new infrastructure platforms that are most important for the productivity and growth of the region, and to work out both financing and timetables for projects, as well as future growth in economic activity and revenue the new infrastructure platforms are likely to bring about.
>
> The nations forming the regional development bank should provide a basic share of its equity capital, at least 20% of the total stock, in the form of new full-faith-and-credit bonds issued by their Treasuries, and back those bonds by dedicated future tax revenues which are to make the payments on the bonds to the Bank. The Bank will have other revenues directly and indirectly related to the infrastructure projects it invests in and the economic expansion around these projects; but the "sinking fund" for the Bank's stock dividend payments should be identified in advance and be inde-pendent of future expansion, to ensure the soundness of the Bank's liabilities.
>
> The founding nations will offer stock in the Bank directly to their citizens and to their private banks in order to subscribe the other 80% of the equity capital. This will include banks or citizens who already hold bonds issued by their governments, subscribing those bonds to the Bank in exchange for its stock—which will increase the future payments of the governments to the Bank.

The Bank should be authorized to issue bonds to the public as well, including internationally, to reach its targeted capitalization with the help of borrowed capital. But the goal should be to meet the original capitalization entirely by stock subscriptions of the governments, citizens, and private banks of the countries forming the Bank. The Bank's stock should carry a dividend, which is higher than the (currently extraordinarily low) interest rates on developed countries' sovereign debt and the bonds of large international corporations. It should be preferred stock with a relatively long term before redemption.

The Bank will issue loans exclusively to agencies assigned to carry out important infrastructure developments, whether those be local government agencies or agencies created for the project. It will conduct discounting activities with private banks only as those banks make loans to contractors and service providers on the projects, and only as necessary for those loans to flow. It will also buy and/or syndicate infrastructure bonds issued by regional governments and local governments for approved projects.[41]

# Cooperation with International Development Banks

As economist Paul Gallagher notes,

The recent important emergence of new international development banks for non-austerity-conditioned, infrastructure-specific lending – the BRICS, New Development Bank and the Asian Infrastructure Investment Bank (AIIB) initiated by China – open up potentials for credit agreements not seen since the 1944 Bretton Woods Conference." The critical infrastructure projects proposed can't be successful unless we achieve mission-critical credit cooperation among the major economic powers providing the bulk of capital goods and industrial products for these projects—but not supranational direction.

A Southwest Asia/Africa Regional Infrastructure Bank will be able to develop credit agreements for major projects in cooperation, for example, with the Export-Import Bank of China at low, government-to-government interest rates, if that country's companies are involved in providing capital goods and logistics; and could develop similar agreements with the AIIB, New Development Bank, or the Silk Road Fund. Such credit partnerships will minimize the need of the Bank to borrow capital by issuing bonds on international capital markets at higher rates.

41    Extending the New Silk Road to West Asia and Africa, Schiller Institute strategic report by Paul Gallagher, Hussein Askary, Chapter 4, November 2017

Were the United States and Japan to join both the AIIB and the Belt and Road Initiative (which already suggests the connection of high-speed rail corridors across the Bering Strait and their development across North and South America), an international combination of powerful development banks would be capable of acting as an International Development Bank with capital in the trillions.

A Southwest Asia/Africa Regional Infrastructure Bank will be able to act as an arm of this combination of international development banks, and the mediator between them and national banks of the nations of Southwest Asia and Africa.

Agreements among the countries involved, on joint funds or agencies to carry out great projects, will require agreement on issuing credits over the long term and at low rates of interest. Moreover, the nations involved must remain sovereigns with their own national credit systems, so that the long-term credits are required in several currencies with relatively stable parities over the long term, together with currency-swap arrangements among central banks.[42]

Currency swaps and other financial arrangements would allow for the implementation of Global Land-Bridge projects and an extensive transportation network, which provides for economic growth and development. For example,

> ... the idea of a railroad running from Alaska to Patagonia goes back at least to the first Conference of American States in 1899. Some consideration was given to this proposal as witnessed by the map proposed in 1904 by Charles M. Pepper, United States and Pan-American Railway Commissioner.[43] Instead, in 1923, during the fifth Conference of American States, a decision was made to build a Pan-American Highway, which today is almost complete, except for the Darien Gap, which is about 90 km in a straight line between Yaviza in Panama and El 40 (also called Lomas Aisladas), near Chigorodó in Colombia. When, and if, the Darien Gap is closed, the 26,000 km backbone of the Pan-American Highway will be complete. The current project to close the Darién Gap is a road that divides in half the Darien National Park in Panama, which was declared a World Heritage Site in 1981 and a Biosphere Reserve in 1982.
>
> The Pan-American highway will parallel the Tuira River, up to Palo de Letras, where it will cross the Serranía del Darién, which in

---

42      Ibid

43      C.M. Pepper, "The Pan-American Railway," Bulletin of the American Geographical Society, Vol. 36, No. 8 (1904), pp. 466-470.

this zone is the border between Panama and Colombia. The road descends into the Katios National Park in Colombia, which was inscribed on the list of World Heritage Sites in 1994.[44] The length of the project in Colombia is 41 km from Palo de Letras to Cacarica on the Atrato River (30 km), and then to El 40 (11 km). In the lowlands, there are many swamps associated with the Atrato River. Both in Panama and in Colombia, there are groups in favor and against the construction of the missing portion of the Pan-American Highway. Proponents stress political integration and economic and commercial benefits. In contrast, opponents stress negative impacts – deforestation, perturbation of habitats – on the two national parks, which harbor a large genetic and biological wealth, and negative cultural effects on the indigenous inhabitants in the national parks, mainly Emberas. An alternative to complete the Pan-American Highway is to build a Land-Bridge without entering the Darien and the Katíos National Parks. This novel alternative is called here the Balboa Route-2007.[45]

According to Engineering Society of Antioquia,

The Balboa Route-2007 may branch from the existing Pan-American Highway, say at the little town of Palmira in Panama, and go northwest across the Panamanian central plain to reach the Caribbean coast. In this stretch, the road bridges the Chucunaque River near the mouth of Mortí River, follows the Mortí River canyon upstream until a summit pass on the Serranía del Daríen, and descends to the coastal plain (alternatively, the Serranía may be crossed by a tunnel).

On the Caribbean side, the road is in Kuna-Yala Province, and runs southeast, parallel to the Caribbean coast. After passing Carreto Bay, the road reaches the Panama-Colombia border in the vicinity of Tiburón Cape, which is the only zone of the international border outside the Darien National Park. The road will turn south in Colombia along the western shore of the Gulf of Urabá, until reaching the Atrato swamps at Unguía. The proposed route turns east, bridges the Atrato River, and joins an existing road leading to Carepa in the vicinity of Caño Carepita.

The Balboa Route-2007 is longer than the current proposal to close the Darien Gap, but it has two significant advantages: It is outside ecologically preserved areas, both in Panama and Colombia; and it brings needed infrastructure to regions currently under-

44      www.unep-wcmc.org/
45      "Two Large Engineering Projects for the Social and Economic Development of the Atrato Region in Colombia," Héctor A. Múnera, EIR, October 26, 2007, p.45

going economic development. In Panama, the road may open to tourism this section of the Caribbean coast, which today is mostly populated by the Kunas, so that there will be a need to negotiate with the government of Kuna-Yala Province. In Colombia, the proposed route will serve the towns of Zapzurro and Capurganá, which presently are open to ecological tourism, but cannot be reached by land. There exist already stretches of dirt roads between Acandí and Triganá, and between Tanela and Unguía in the Department of Chocó, and from Caño Carepita to Carepa in a banana- producing region of the Department of Antioquia. The proposed route will complete and improve these roads.[46]

It is beyond doubt, that the potential for economic development in the Americas is enormous, both in terms of the provided natural resource base and the natural man-made resources created as part of infrastructure projects, many of which have been on drawing boards for a decade, waiting only for policy approval.

## North America: Rail Grid, Water Project

What are some of the Priority Projects for the Americas? According to Sovereign States of the Americas: Great Infrastructure Projects report,

The great Amazon River – the world's longest, most abundant, and most navigable over its length. In this context, the priority rail routes – are not simply proposed speedy travel routes from point-to-point, with connections to Eurasia/ Africa (Bering Straits crossing), and new inter-oceanic routes (a new canal through Central America – a new sea-level canal at the Darien Gap, or in the adjacent Colombia region); rather, these routes indicate corridors of development, whose pattern arises from topography, key mineral and other physical resources, and also historical settlement patterns (where populations are already concentrated), and where proposed new development zones should be. The rail route/corridors indicate intended locations of new concentrations of energy, water, agricultural and industrial activity, and also, centers for health care, cultural, and educational activity. This is how the 19th-Century trans-continental rail development worked in North America, crossing the U.S. plains and mountains of the West, sowing new towns, advancing farming and industry.

46    J.E. Botaggisio, "Alternatives for an Inter-Oceanic Canal in Chocó," talk to the Engineering Society of Antioquia (Sociedad Antioqueña de Ingenieros), Feb. 20, 2007

218

First, build the intercontinental lines planned for decades: the United States/Canada/Alaska line – already mapped out by the Army Corps of Engineers in the 1940s! Second, build the Pan-American rail connection southward linking Central America and South America with the North, likewise planned for decades. Third, upgrade the existing rail grid in Mexico, the United States, and Canada, which had been developed as of mid-20th Century, then taken down drastically during the last 40 "post-industrial" years. The priority routes for high-speed are shown. Note in particular how Mexico City is interlinked with the entire northward grid, and to the south.[47]

# Great Water Projects

An in-depth July 31, 2015 *Foreign Policy Magazine* report (a mouth piece for the U.S. establishment), underlined Mexico's "struggles with aging infrastructure, strapped resources, and poor access," while pitching "privatization as the cure to Mexico's water woes."[48]

The current trend is indeed, worrysome. Mexico has too much water, and also too little. The Southeast is virtually floating on water, and the North and Center of the country are bone dry. According to the Congressional Research Special Report on U.S.-Mexican Water Sharing, addressed through The International Boundary and Water Commission, the United States and Mexico share the waters of the Colorado River and Rio Grande pursuant to binational agreements. Under the 1944 Water Treaty, the United States is required to provide Mexico with 1.5 million acre-feet (AF) of Colorado River water annually. This figure represents about 10% of the river's average flow. The Rio Grande is governed by two separate agreements. Deliveries to Mexico in the northwestern portion of the shared basin (near El Paso/Ciudad Juárez) occur under a 1906 convention. In contrast, deliveries for the southeastern portion (which is below Fort Quitman, TX) are laid out in the 1944 Water Treaty.[49]

Pursuant to the U.S.-Mexican Transboundary Aquifer Assessment Act,[50] aquifers were identified as priorities for study under the legislation.

47    Sovereign States of the Americas: Great Infrastructure Projects, Sept 26, 2003, EIR Chapter 5: Priority Projects For the Americas
48    The War for Mexico's Water, David Adler, *Foreign Policy Magazine*, July 31, 2015 https://foreignpolicy.com/2015/07/31/the-war-for-privatization-mexicos-water/
49    U.S.-MexicanWater Sharing: Background and Recent Developments, Congressional Research Report, March 2, 2017, Congressional Research Service7-5700www.crs.govR43312
50    P.L. 109-448, 42 U.S.C. §1962 note

The act authorized the Secretary of the Interior, through the U.S. Geological Survey, to collaborate with the states of Arizona, New Mexico, and Texas through their Water Resources Research Institutes and with the International Boundary and Water Commission, stakeholders, and Mexican counterparts to provide information and a scientific foundation for state and local officials to address pressing challenges along the U.S.-Mexican border. Ground-water pumping has lowered the water table, depleted aquifers, and reduced the base flow of many streams, thus decreasing the quantity of water available to support critical riparian habitats. Excessive groundwater pumping in some major urban centers, such as in the El Paso/Juárez metropolitan region, has caused land subsidence that has damaged homes and essential urban infrastructure. In addition to the effects of ground- and surface-water depletion, degradation of water quality has reduced habitat suitability for the region's diverse biota.[51]

In terms of its water resource base,

North America is cut by an isoline of 500 mm of average annual rainfall (running north-south through the High Plains), defining the eastward lands as humid (more than 500 mm), and westward as drylands (well under 500 mm), to the point of desert. The Great American Desert thus covers a vast part of the states of northern Mexico and the Western U.S. (apart from the Pacific coastal region). The landforms in the various sub-areas of the Great American Desert vary from mountainous to rolling, to flat terrain.

How do we bring new water supplies into these desert lands?

The 1950s-60s North American Water and Power Alliance (NAWAPA) plan proposed diverting some of the plentiful northern continental waters southward. In Mexico, likewise, some of the ample run-off of the Southern and Western Sierra Madre can be diverted northward. In addition, nuclear-powered seawater desalination, on coastal sites, can provide additional supplies, as well as desalting inland brackish water. Specific proposed designs for this from Hal Cooper, a U.S. engineer, and key routes in eastern Mexico, proposed by Manuel Frías Alcaraz, a Mexican engineer.[52]

In other words, what is needed is U.S.-Mexican relations based on cooperation around great infrastructure development projects. Exem-

51    https://www.congress.gov/congressional-report/109th-congress/senate-report/17
52    Sovereign States of the Americas: Great Infrastructure Projects, Sept 26, 2003, EIR Chapter 5: Priority Projects For the Americas

plary are Mexico's PLHI-NO (Plan Hidráulico del Noroeste, or North-west Hydraulic Plan) and PLHIGON (Plan Hidráulico del Golfo Norte, or Northern Gulf Hydraulic Plan), as well as the aforementioned giant NAWAPA (North American Water and Power Alliance): Projects to be built in stages over a 30-year period. These are the results, according to the Executive Intelligence Review Economics feasibility study.[53]

**Water**: It will increase Mexico's freshwater withdrawals by nearly 70%, from today's 89 cubic kilometers (km3) per year,[54] to 140 km3, for use in industry, households, and agriculture.

**Irrigated Land**: It will add about 5 million hectares of new irrigated land to the 6.5 million that currently exist in Mexico – a 75% increase.

**Food**: It will increase food production dramatically: Grains, for example, will eventually rise by as much as 20 million tons per year, nearly doubling today's production of 25 million tons. This will vastly improve the nutrition of the existing population, help feed Mexicans born in the coming years, and also those who will be returning from the United States.

**Employment**: Perhaps a million Mexicans will be employed directly in the construction of the PLHINO and the PHLIGON projects at their height – including dams, tunnels, canals, and pumping stations.

> So, Mexico may have an average rainfall of 773 millimeters per year (which compares favorably with the 742 mm for the U.S.), and an average 4,573 cubic meters (m3) per capita per year of available water. But human beings don't live in mathematical averages: They live in real, geographical-economic space. In Mexico, the essential features of that space are defined by two large mountain ranges, the Western Sierra Madres and the Eastern Sierra Madres, which meet in the South-Center of the country in a dense, neo-volcanic knot. The North, Center, and Northwest hydrological regions have 77% of the country's population, but only 32% of the available wáter, whereas the four hydrological regions in the Southeast account for 68% of the country's water availability, but only 23% of its population. In fact, the states of Chiapas, Tabasco, Veracruz, and parts of Oaxaca, Puebla, and Hidalgo—a mere 10% of the national territory—have a staggering 60% of the total national surface runoff. That is because the country's three largest rivers all flow down into the Gulf of Mexico in this area of the Isthmus of Tehuantepec: the Coatzacoalcos (32.8 km3 of runoff), the Papaloapan (44.7 km3),

---

53    https://larouchepub.com/eiw/public/2007/eirv34n47-48-20071207/64-73_747-48.pdf
54    https://knoema.es/atlas/M%c3%a9xico/Utilizaci%c3%b3n-del-agua

and the enormous Grijalva-Usumacinta, whose 115.5 km3 of run-off make it one of the major rivers in the world. So the great challenge in Mexico has always been to take the water from where it is abundant, and transfer it to where it is no.[55]

According to a proposal developed by Mexican engineer Manuel Frías Alcaraz, and which he has dubbed the TzenValle System,

> Neither the PLHINO nor the PLHIGON would carry water up to the Great American Desert, to the arid center-north of Mexico. They would have to be complemented by other projects that would bring water up from the coasts to the central highlands. From the western side, this is not very feasible in physical-economic terms, since the Western Sierra Madre is quite high—it reaches heights of 3,000 meters above sea level. But on the Gulf side, it is much more feasible, given that the Eastern Sierra Madre ranges between 2,000 and 2,500 meters above sea level.Frías Alcaraz's other idea,
>
> … is to divert about one-third of the water from the Pánuco River and its tributaries, where these originate in the Eastern Sierra Madre in the state of San Luis Potosia. By means of a series of dams, tunnels, and canals located at some 250-300 meters above sea level, water would be carried north, and then pumped up as far as Monterrey, which is at 540 meters above sea level. In other words, the cost of the pumping would be kept to a minimum, because the water would only need to be lifted an additional 250 meters or so. The TzenValle System would carry an additional 6.9 km3 of water per year to this arid zone.[56]

As the late Mexican President, José López Portillo, urged in his memorable October 1982 address to the United Nations General Assembly: "Let us make that which is reasonable, possible!"

But the economic integration doesn't end there. Germany's *Deutsche Welle* reports, "South America's new transcontinental railway is considered to be one of the biggest infrastructure projects of the century and is also known as the 'Panama Canal on railway tracks.'"[57] As the Status of implementation in South America of the Vienna Programme of Action for Landlocked Developing Countries for the Decade 2014-2024 report explains, a "Bi-oceanic Railway Corridor will connect the Pacific and At-

55      https://larouchepub.com/eiw/public/2007/eirv34n47-48-20071207/64-73_747-48.pdf

56      Sources: Parsons Company, North American Water and Power Alliance Conceptual Study, Dec. 7, 1964; Hal Cooper; "Building a Bridge to the Future" conference, Manuel Frías Alcaraz, Sonora, Mexico

57      Germany and Switzerland to help build coast-to-coast railway in South America, Victoria Dannemann, WD, December 17, 2017

lantic Oceans through 3,700km of railway networks that cross through Brazil, Bolivia, Peru and Paraguay."[58]

The transcontinental railway will connect three South American countries: Brazil, Bolivia and Peru. The trilateral megaproject is estimated to cost $10 billion USD and will stretch from the Atlantic port city of Porto do Açu, Brazil, to an undetermined Pacific port city in Peru.

Two other large-scale projects being negotiated are "the Motacucito-Mutún-Puerto Busch railway stretch to support strategic ventures, notably: the development of Bolivia's steel industry around the Mutún deposit; and the development of Puerto Busch to enhance inland water transport of Bolivian freight along the Paraguay-Paraná Waterway. The second project is the Montero-Bulo Bulorailway stretch, to establish connection with the Eastern Railway Network (Red Oriental) and establish a transport route to export urea and ammonia to the markets of Brazil, Argentina, and Santa Cruz."[59]

The proposed canals across Latin America make key linkups to form a continuous inland water route. "The Great Waterway" is the name given by Brazilian expert Vasco Azevedo Neto, for the north-south link-up of the Orinoco to the Amazon system, and the Amazon to the Rio de La Plata. Neto's 1996 work, *Transportation in South America: Continental Development and Integration,* spoke of how rivers unite. "Visualize from the mouth of the Orinoco, continuing the water route northward throughout the Caribbean Sea, and into North America via the Mississippi and Tombigbee Basins, or the East Coast – thus, an intercontinental "Great Waterway of the Americas."[60]

# Latin American Resource I: Raw materials

The economic history of Latin America is a treasure trove of looted raw materials: the gold and silver that attracted early explorers, platinum, sugar, coffee, copper, and the "black gold" in the 20th century, to name just a few.

Minerals and metals can be sorted into three groups:

1. *Precious metals:* largely gold, silver, and the platinum group, all of which have industrial uses, but are also held for their value as a monetary reserve.

58    Status of implementation in South America of the Vienna Programme of Action for Landlocked Developing Countries for the Decade 2014-2024, ECLAV United Nations report, Gabriel Pérez, Ricardo J. Sánchez, p.21 2019.
59    Status of implementation in South America of the Vienna Programme of Action for Landlocked Developing Countries for the Decade 2014-2024, ECLAV United Nations report, Gabriel Pérez, Ricardo J. Sánchez, p.22 2019.
60    Reflections on the South American Transcontinental Railway, Cesar Augusto Lambert Azevedo, Revista Brasileira de Politicas Publicas y Internacionais, September 17, 2017.

2. *Industrial/base metals:* Seven of these – bauxite, copper, iron, lead, nickel, tin, and zinc – account, by weight, for 70% of all the non-carbon, non-wood, non-stone-based finished manufactured products in the world. No industrial society can exist without the finished products that come from them.

3. *Strategic metals and minerals:* These are mainly used as alloys, because they are frequently lightweight, have high tensile strength, or resist heat well. They are often used in defense and high-technology production.

According to the annual publication from the British Geological Survey (BGS) World Mineral Production report, which contains mineral production statistics for the five-year period from 2013 to 2017, for more than 70 mineral commodities, by country worldwide,

... for the essential 26 minerals and metals, the world rank of each nation in Latin America that is among the top six world producers. Latin American countries are the top producers of five minerals or raw materials: Mexico, silver; Peru, bismuth; Chile, copper; Mexico, strontium; and Brazil, columbium (niobium). Three Latin American nations produce more than half of the world's output of three minerals: bismuth (Peru, 63%), strontium (Mexico, 53%), and columbium (Brazil, 86%). Latin America produces 15% of the world's output of two of the seven most important base/industrial metals; 20% of the world output for one of the metals; and at least 25% of the world output for three metals. It produces one-third of the world's output of copper.[61]

Furthermore, according to the World Bank,[62] much of Latin America's GDP is also generated in countries that rely heavily on fiscal revenues from commodity production. Of the seven economies (LA-7), which make up approximately 85 percent of regional GDP, six have a substantial commodity revenue-share in overall revenues, ranging from 10 to 49 percent on average. The six are Argentina (agricultural export commodities), Chile (copper), Colombia (oil), Mexico (hydrocarbons), Peru (mining), and República Bolivariana de Venezuela (hydrocarbons). Oil revenues in the remaining LA-7 economy, Brazil, are also growing with recent discoveries. In addition to the LA-7 countries, some smaller economies in

61      World Mineral Production 2013-2017, British Geological Survey 2013-2017, Brown, T.J., Idoine, N.E., Raycraft, E.R., Hobbs, S.F., Shaw, R.A., Everett, P., Kresse, C., Deady, E.A. and Bide, T., 2019.
62      Natural Resources in Latin America and the Caribbean: Beyond Booms and Busts?, Emily Sinnott John NashAugusto de la Torre, The World Bank, p.6-7, 2010.

the region are highly dependent on commodity revenues, particularly the hydrocarbon producers Bolivia (natural gas) and Ecuador (petroleum).

The problem is, in the 1990s,

> between 75% and 80% of all mining properties in Latin America were owned either by state-controlled mining companies, or by private concerns owned by that country's nationals. Today, as a result of liberalization of mining legislation, and privatization, between one-third and two-thirds of the mining properties in several Latin American nations, are owned by foreigners, both in their own names and through dummy corporations.[63]

This has been encouraged by the World Bank. "The critical factor of ownership is a key area of their drive for global control. In the development of natural resources, the requirement of significant up-front investments, among other things, creates pressure for government ownership. Cross-country studies have demonstrated that productivity generally improves significantly after privatization."[64] Of the foreigners, by far, the principal owners are companies of the British Commonwealth raw materials cartel, including the four most powerful: Anglo American, Rio Tinto, Barrick Gold (whose International Advisory Board includes former U.S. President George H. **W.** Bush[65]), and Newmont Mining.

# The Greatest Resources II: Food

As I write these lines, over a billion people around the world are going hungry or starving. There are roughly two billion people across the world who spend more than 50 percent of their income on food. The effects of the 2007 economic meltdown have been staggering: 250 million people joined the ranks of the hungry in 2008 – a number never seen in the records.

> In a sense it's a genuine paradox. Our planet has everything we need to produce nutritious natural food to feed the entire world population many times over. This is the case, despite the ravages of industrialized agriculture over the past half-century or more. Then, how can it be that our world faces, according to some predictions, the prospect of a decade or more of famine on a global scale? The

---

63      Ibero-America's Raw Materials Wealth, EIR, April 13, 2001, p.27
64      Natural Resources in Latin America and the Caribbean: Beyond Booms and Busts?, Emily Sinnott John NashAugusto de la Torre, The World Bank, p.32, 2010.
65      https://larouchepub.com/eiw/public/1997/eirv24n02-19970103/eir-v24n02-19970103_019-inside_story_the_bush_gang_and_b.pdf

answer lies in the forces and interest groups that have decided to create a scarcity of nutritious food artificially.[66]

# World Trade Organization

One of the organizations most responsible for this tremendous growth in world hunger is the World Trade Organization. Created in 1994 out of the GATT Uruguay Round, the WTO introduced a radical new international agreement, Trade-Related Aspects of Intellectual Property Rights" (TRIPS), which permitted multinationals to patent plant and other life forms for the first time.

The WTO was created after World War II by internationalists in Washington to serve "as a wedge to push free trade among major industrial nations, especially the European Community."[67] It was given birth out of wedlock on January 1, 1995, when the Marrakech Agreement replaced GATT, which had commenced in 1948.

According to their publicity machine, the World Trade Organization establishes a framework for creating non-discriminating, reciprocal trade policies. Reality appears quite different. The WTO's anti-nation-state intent can be readily seen in its 1988 slogan: "One World, One Market." That slogan came from the GATT Montreal summit of its predecessor, the Uruguay Round of Agriculture "Reform" (1986-94) – the process in which WTO was birthed.

A watershed moment came in 1993, when the European Union agreed to a major reduction of their national agriculture protection. This reduction was a multi-stage process. First step, according to the incoming WTO game rules, the member nations were to be forced to open their borders, to grant the right to operate freely within those borders to other nations, and to eliminate national grain reserves. Grain reserves were no longer to be the dominion of independent nation-states. They became property, to be managed by the "free market;" meaning, in other words, private, mostly American mega-corporations, running the world markets.

These companies were already dominant, but now, "they had a new unelected supranational body to advance its private agenda on a global scale. WTO became a policeman for global free trade and a (predatory) battering ram;"[68] with an annual budget worth trillions of dollar. "Its rules are written with teeth for punitive leverage to levy heavy financial and oth-

---

66      F. William Engdahl, "Getting used to Life without Food: Wall Street, BP, bio-ethanol and the death of millions," globalresearch.com.
67      Ibid
68      Stephen Lendman, Seeds Of Destruction; F. William Engdahl, Review, January 22, 2008.

er penalties on rule violators."[69] Under this regimen, agriculture control is a priority.

What's more, the rules, sold as the beacon of hope for underdeveloped countries, were written by the corporate giants who form the nucleus of 'World Company Inc'. The blueprint for "market-oriented" agricultural reform was written by D. Gale Johnson of the University of Chicago for David Rockefeller's Trilateral Commission, and former Cargill executive Dan Amstutz played a prominent role in drafting the agriculture rules of the GATT Uruguay Round. Cargill is the world's largest grain company.

# Genetically Modified Conspiracy

New draconian rules have been forced upon a free and integrated global market to control its products. The new agreements have also banned agricultural export controls, even in times of famine. Today, the cartels' domination over the world export grain trade has become even more expansive.

Further, this international pact forbids countries from restricting trade through food safety laws, calling them "trade barriers." This deception has also opened the world markets to unrestricted GMO food imports with no need to prove their safety; but more on that, later.

Agriculture is food, and food is what we eat. We too often take it for granted – especially in the first world – that we will always have an abundance of food. A trip to the supermarket and our needs are taken care of. What happens if one day soon, you wake up, and there is nothing to eat? The shelves are empty. Then what?

WTO propaganda tells us that the "world market" and so-called "free-trade" will somehow provide the favorable conditions necessary for growth. However, with the creation of multi-nation trading zones, citizen-responsive governments lose power and control at the expense of these supra-national agencies that supersede the authority of nation-states. These agencies do not, in any way, represent the people of any one nation. Instead, their loyalties lie with the corporations and financial organisms that elect them, fund them, and support them. These organizations form one of the nodes of elite rule, a top-down imperious structure that seeks to enslave populations through many guises, including subtle psychological warfare and other hybrid warfare techniques.

Agreements such as GATT and NAFTA have subtly destroyed national economies by putting them under the imperatives of world commerce

---

69      Ibid

and globalization without borders. Globalization is a top-down concept, which means that the farmers – the people who actually put the food on our table – are wiped out and replaced by giant multi-faceted corporations dedicated to the God of Profit, which strive to control the production and distribution of food.

During the last two decades, millions of farmers in the United States, Europe, Canada, Australia, and Argentina have been wiped out. Today, there are about 2 million farms in operation in the U.S., a steep decline from 1935, when the number of farms peaked at nearly 7 million.[70] Meanwhile, back in 1840, workers in the agriculture industry made up 70% of the American workforce; today, farmers make up just 1.3% of the employed U.S. population, totaling around 2.6 million people.

This is no accident – fewer independent farmers mean greater corporate control over what you eat. People can pretty much get used to anything in life, except not having enough to eat. Even death is easier. You only have to suffer it once.

GATT, North American Free Trade Agreement (NAFTA), Central America Free Trade Agreement (CAFTA) and every such binding agreement has helped spawn ghettos and shanty towns in cities throughout Latin America, Asia and Africa by creating conditions that force people off their land, while elites take over the means of production.

> Today in Central America, life-saving medicines are more expensive due to monopoly protections that CAFTA gave to pharmaceutical corporations. And the headlines from several CAFTA countries do not report economic prosperity, but economic instability, drug violence, and forced migration.[71]
>
> Now Donald Trump is scapegoating Latin American immigrants for the economic insecurity facing many Americans with his racist attacks and xenophobic obsession with building a wall along our southern border. But it is the same U.S. trade policies that harm working people in the United States that also have left many in Central America with no option but migration as they struggle to feed and care for their families.[72]

Shanty towns and ghost towns equal depopulation on the one hand. On the other, if you can force people off their land and into the cities,

70    https://www.ers.usda.gov/data-products/ag-and-food-statistics-charting-the-essentials/farming-and-farm-income/
71    https://citizen.typepad.com/eyesontrade/2014/08/central-america-crisis-belies-caftas-empty-promises.html
72    https://www.citizen.org/article/central-america-free-trade-agreement-cafta/

you are creating a perfect storm of over-crowding and discontent amongst the masses. Mass unrest requires armed forces control: Problem, reaction, solution.

This is precisely the prediction of the UK's Ministry of Defense *Strategic Trends* report. In its latest report, it states that over 50% of the world's population is living in urban rather than rural environments. The report says: "There will be a substantial growth in shanty towns and unplanned, random urban settlement, increasing the resource cost and environmental impact."[73]

With the destruction of nation-state republics and the creation of mega-economic blocks, which are linked to each other through a globalized marketplace, independent countries can be "replaced by Mega-Cities" with population bases of over 20 million people. Caused by massive population displacement, these cities will swell to unimaginable proportions, "which will already have experienced endemic lawlessness and high levels of violence."

One of the first experiments to bring about the depopulation of large cities was conducted in Cambodia by the Pol Pot regime. It is interesting to note that a model for Pol Pot's genocidal plan was drawn up in the United States by one of the Club of Rome's supported research foundations, and overseen by Thomas Enders, a high-ranking State Department official.

The Club of Rome, founded in 1968, is made up of some of the oldest members of Venetian Black Nobility. As I explain in my book, *TransEvolution: The Coming Age Of Human Deconstruction*, the Club is the most important institution in the world to push the Malthusian depopulation scheme. A report by the Club of Rome leaves little room for doubt as to their real agenda: In search for a new enemy to unite us, we came up with the idea that pollution, the threat of global warming, water shortages, famine and the like would fit the bill.

They concluded with the following: The real enemy, then, is humanity itself. Thus, leading international institutions are pushing policies of retrogression in technology, and reduction of the world's population by several billion people – that's a genocidal trick, in case you didn't notice.

And there is no better or cheaper way to reduce population than through starvation. British free trade starved[74] millions during Ireland's potato famine in the 1840s. And in order to starve a people to death, you

73    http://www.ssri-j.com/MediaReport/Document/GlobalStrategicTrendsOutTo2045.pdf
74    https://archive.schillerinstitute.com/economy/nbw/pot_famine95.html, Schiller Institute, Paul Gallagher, May 1995

must take control of their food production away from independent farmers and put it into the hands of giant corporations subservient to the interests of World Company Inc. – some refreshing food for thought the next time you have your breakfast cereal.

Within the WTO regulations, nations are prohibited from protecting local economy or taxing goods, even when these goods clearly were produced with slave labor. Furthermore, nations are not allowed to give preference to local economies that hire local people at decent wages to produce goods that then benefit local business and the real economy – people who paid taxes, played by the rules and reinvested their hard earned wealth into the local or national market.

The truth is: "free trade is rigged trade, and the 'fairness' question is diversionary propaganda for deluded lawmakers, farmers, and the public. It is run by an international financial cartel. The cartel interests control the playing field: who plays and the rules of the game."[75]

When you expand the cartel's control into strategic areas such as food, the situation gets serious in a hurry.

# Food as a Weapon

Since the imposition of WTO rules, internationally, over the past 15 years food processing and trade have come to be monopolized by a small, tight clique of cartel companies. These firms dominate international commodity flows, and even the domestic food supplies and distribution of most nations.

Today, food warfare is firmly under the control of just a few corporations. The largest food company in the world is Nestlé. It was founded in 1867, based in Switzerland. "It is the number-one world trader in whole milk powder and condensed milk; the number-one seller of chocolate, confectionery products, and mineral water (it owns Perrier); and the number-three U.S.-based coffee firm. It also owns 26% of the world's biggest cosmetic company, L'Oreal."[76]

Much of the rest of the milk-powder business is controlled by the Anglo-Dutch-owned Unilever, the result of a 1930 merger of a British and a Dutch firm. Unilever is the number-one world producer of ice cream and margarine, as well as a key player in fats and edible oils. Unilever owns vast plantations and runs Africa's largest trading company, United Africa Co.

75      Marcia Merry Baker, "Food cartels: Will there be bacon to bring home?" EIR Volume 26, Number 27, July 2, 1999.
76      "The True Story Behind the Fall of the House of Windsor," EIR Special Report, September 1997.

In Zimbabwe, Congo-Zaire, Mali, Chad and Sudan, the United Africa Co. is projected by British intelligence as ushering in a United States of Africa.

"The boundaries among states are to be dissolved, and their contents organized as a new business franchise with two purposes: first, the security of foreign investment and seizure of property titles on raw materials by primarily British Commonwealth mining and other companies;"[77] and second, of course, the lining of the pockets of the government enforcers of the policy.

These policy enforcers already primarily agree with the ideology of zero growth – the idyllic primitive life of "useless eaters," as Henry Kissinger has called anyone living below the Tropic of Cancer. "Not only in Africa, but Third World peasant populations will be organized to do what has come 'naturally' for years – apply their quaint picks and hoes to land wasted by centuries of labor-intensive farming to scrape together tribute (taxes) to the World Bank in the form of food. The result will be a net decline in food production and consumption worldwide."[78]

But, it gets worse; much worse. Minnesota-based Cargill Company is the world's largest grain company. Grain constitutes a dominant portion of most standard diets. Since the 1920s, the billionaire MacMillan family have run Cargill. John Hugh MacMillan, president and chairman of Cargill from 1936 through 1960, held the title of hereditary Knight Commander of Justice in the Sovereign Order of St. John (Knights of Malta), one of the Vatican's most important orders. Cargill's international trading arm, Tradax, Inc., is headquartered in Geneva, Switzerland. The Lombard, Odier Bank, as well as the Pictet Bank – old, private and very dirty Swiss banks – owns a chunk of Tradax. The principal financier for Tradax is the Geneva-based Crédit Suisse, which is one of the world's largest money-launderers. Archer Daniels Midland's purchase of Töpfer,[79] a Hamburg, Germany-based grain company vastly increased ADM's presence in the world grain trade.

Then, there are the seed companies. By far the biggest and the dirtiest of them all is Monsanto, with an international workforce of 21,035, in 404 facilities in 66 countries. Monsanto has power that supersedes the influence of most governments on the planet. An associate of Monsanto, Dr. Roger Beachey, was appointed by President Obama in 2010, as the Science Advisor to the Agriculture Department. This is a good example

---

77      Ibid
78      "The Food Crisis: Who Shall Rule?" – Editorial, Campaigner magazine, November 1973.
79      Richard Freeman, "The Windsors' Global Food Cartel: Instrument for Starvation," EIR, December 8, 1995.

of the interlocked financial, economic, political and business interests dominating the food industry. The following information comes from my book, *TransEvolution: the Coming age of Human Deconstruction*:

> The DuPont Chemical Co., owns Pioneer HiBred International Inc., an Iowa based largest seed-corn company in the world. It sells a range of crop and forage seeds in 70 countries. Syngenta is based in Switzerland and operates in 90 countries, with a workforce of 26,000. It was created in 2000 from the merger of Novartis Agribusiness and Zeneca Agrochemicals. Novartis was itself formed by the merger of the legendary Swiss chemical firms, Sandoz and CibaGeigy. Zeneca Agro came out of the British firms ICI (Imperial Chemical), and AstraZeneca.
>
> DowAgroSciences LLC is based in Indianapolis and is a subsidiary of The Dow Chemical Co. It was formed in 1997 as a joint venture between Dow's agriculture sciences division and the Eli Lilly Co. BASF Plant Science, based in Germany, was established in 1998 as centralization of all the agriculture biotechnology capacity of the longstanding BASF Chemical Co. BASF Plant Science has a 700-person research effort, focusing on plant genetics and patentable traits, in collaboration with the mega-seed companies. Bayer CropScience is also based in Germany, and is the second-largest pesticide firm in the world. It operates in 120 countries, with 20,700 employees, making and selling fungicides, insecticides, and other plant protection, while also working on new bio-engineered formulate.[80]

Richard Freeman, in *EIR*, wrote:

> In other words, ten to twelve pivotal companies, assisted by another three dozen, run the world's food supply. They are the key components of the Anglo-Dutch-Swiss food cartel, which is grouped around Britain's House of Windsor. Led by the six leading grain companies – Cargill, Continental, Louis Dreyfus, Bunge and Born, André, and Archer Daniels Midland/Töpfer – the Windsor-led food and raw materials cartel have complete domination over world cereals and grains supplies, from wheat to corn and oats, from barley to sorghum and rye. But it also controls meat, dairy, edible oils and fats, fruits and vegetables, sugar, and all forms of spices.
>
> The first five of the companies are privately owned and run by billionaire families. They issue no public stock, nor annual report.

80     Marcia Merry Baker, "Food cartels: Will there be bacon to bring home?" EIR Volume 26, Number 27, July 2, 1999.

They are more secretive than any oil company, bank, or government intelligence service. While these firms maintain the legal fiction of being different corporate organizations, in reality this is one interlocking syndicate, with a common purpose and multiple overlapping boards of directors. The Windsor-centered oligarchy owns these cartels, and they are the instruments of power of the oligarchy, accumulated over centuries, for breaking nations' sovereignty. To understand the reality as opposed to the rhetoric of their involvement in world economy, it is better to study what companies do rather than what they say.

Cartel's Big Six grain trading companies own and control 95% of America's wheat exports, 95% of its corn exports, 90% of its oat exports, and 80% of its sorghum exports. The grain companies' control over the American grain market is absolute. The Big Six also control 60-70% of France's grain exports. France is the biggest grain exporter in Europe (the world's second-largest grain exporting region), exporting more grain than the next three largest European grain-exporting nations combined.

In sum, the Anglo-Dutch-Swiss food cartel dominates 80-90% of the world grain trade. In fact, however, the control is far greater than the sum of its parts: The Big Six grain companies are organized as a cartel; they move grain back and forth from any one of the major, or minor, exporting nations. Cargill, Continental, Louis Dreyfus et al. own world shipping fleets, and have long-established sales relationships, financial markets, and commodity trading exchanges (such as the London-based Baltic Mercantile and Shipping Exchange) on which grain is traded, which completes their domination. No other forces in the world, including governments, are as well organized as the cartel.[81]

By the early 21$^{st}$ century, the four largest beef packers controlled 84% of steer and heifer slaughter – Tyson, Cargill, Swift, and National Beef Packing; four giants controlled 64% of hog production – Smithfield Foods, Tyson, Swift, and Hormel; three companies controlled 71% of soybean crushing – Cargill, ADM and Bunge; three giants controlled 63% of all flour milling, and five companies controlled 90% of global grain trade; four other companies controlled 89% of the breakfast cereal market – Kellogg, General Mills, Kraft Foods and Quaker Oats. In 1998, Cargill acquired Continental Grain to control 40% of national grain elevator capacity; four large agro-chemical/seed giants controlled over 75% of the

---

81    Richard Freeman, "The Windsors' Global Food Cartel: Instrument for Starvation," EIR, December 8, 1995.

nation's seed corn sales and 60% of it for soybeans, while also having the largest share of the agricultural chemical market – Monsanto, Novartis, Dow Chemical and DuPont; six companies controlled three-fourths of the global pesticides market; Monsanto and DuPont controlled 60% of the US corn and soybean seed market – all of its patented GMO seeds – and 10 large food retailers controlled $649 billion in global sales in 2002, and the top 30 food retailers account for one-third of global grocery sales.

Please understand, this interlocked self-perpetuating syndicate decides who eats and who doesn't, who lives and who dies. It is a virtual spider web of financial, political, economic, and industry interests with the Venetian ultramontane fondi model at the center. These people own and manage the affairs of an interlocking corporate apparatus that dominates choke points within the global economy, especially finance, insurance, raw materials, transportation, and consumer goods.

Cargill, the largest privately held agribusiness corporation, along with Archer Daniels Midland, have become the arbiters of death. The question is: Why are mega-corporations and a small socio-political elite allowed to own our food – to control the very basis of human survival?

# How it Works

The control works as follows:

> The oligarchy has developed four regions to be the principal export-ers of almost every type of food, in the process acquiring top-down control over the food chain in these regions. These four regions are, the United States; the European Union, particularly France and Germany; the British Commonwealth nations of Australia, Cana-da, the Republic of South Africa, and New Zealand; and Argentina and Brazil in Latin America. These four regions have a population of over a billion people, or 15% of the world's population. The rest of the world, with 85% of the population – 4.7 billion people – is dependent on the food exports from those regions.[82]
>
> Can the nations protect themselves? Not if they are mem-bers of World Trade Organization. If any country tries to protect its local markets, then the entire world community is entitled to rebel against the "protectionist policies." As economist William Engdahl writes in *The Seeds of Destruction*: The WTO rules assert that nations must eliminate food reserves, eliminate tariffs on food imports and exports, cease intervening to support their domestic

---

82      Richard Freeman, "The Windsors' Global Food Cartel: Instrument for Starvation," EIR, De-cember 8, 1995.

farm sector – all under the imperial rationalization that such na-
tion-serving measures would be 'trade-distorting' practices, which
would impede the free-market 'rights' of the globalist corporations.
Now one-seventh of the world's population lacks enough to eat.
Against this backdrop, the story of the WTO is one of the crimes
against humanity, and not an academic economics debate.

In the face of mass death, through starvation, through lack of
food, recall what the core WTO liturgy is: Nations must not keep
food reserves, because this would be trade-distorting. Nations
must not attempt to be food self-sufficient because this would deny
their citizens the right to access the world market. Nations must
not support their own farmers, because this harms farmers else-
where. Nations must not use tariffs, because this denies right-of-ac-
cess to your citizens by foreign producers. This fits like a glove with
the World Bank's explicit demands – privatize, privatize, and privatize again. According to them, "productivity generally improves
significantly after privatization. Hence, privatized firms are more
productive than nationalized enterprises in general."[83]

This policy serves to directly undercut the purpose of a government to
promote the general welfare of its citizens, and it furthers the intent of the
corporate imperial system, to drastically reduce world agro-industrial potential and create conditions for depopulation. Under the "markets" principle, the "global sourcing" of food by corporate monopolies, works to the
detriment of the populations in both the exporting and importing nations.

It may seem difficult to understand, but it is easy to explain. There
are currently approximately eight billion people unevenly distributed on
Planet Earth, a relatively small planet with limited natural resources and
an ever-expanding population base. Food and water are becoming ever
scarcer. For the elite to eat, you and I have to be culled, subjugated and
forced to die.

# The Greatest Resource III: Population

The last 75 years of a shift to free trade, cheap labor, and anti-infrastruc-
ture development have meant worsening poverty and dislocation for
tens of millions of people throughout the entire Western Hemisphere.

Across Latin America, mega-cities have grown with millions of dis-
placed people – Mexico City, Buenos Aires, Rio de Janeiro, Bogota, Caracas, and others – with no infrastructure base to serve the

83      Natural Resources in Latin America and the Caribbean: Beyond Booms and Busts?, Emily
Sinnott John NashAugusto de la Torre, The World Bank, p.33, 2010.

population. Millions have relocated to the slave-labor work camps, again with no infrastructure, by definition. Still, more from Central and South America have fled to the United States or Canada, driven there in an attempt to make a life. Remittances to the home country from migrants to the U.S., are now a significant source of local spending throughout Latin America.[84]

In 2005, 191 million people lived outside their country of origin. Today there are 232 million.[85]

According to the *Inter-American Dialogue* think-tank, "migrants from Latin America and the Caribbean are sending more money to their families back home than ever before. These annual remittances topped $69 billion in 2016,"[86] with about 40 percent of the money going to just one country – Mexico.

These findings are given greater geo-strategic contour in the British government's *"Global Strategic Trends – Out to 2045"*[87]; a 100-page report is a blueprint for UK's future strategic national requirements through the analysis of key risks and future shocks to the world's financial, economic, political, demographic and technological areas and markets. The focal point of the report focused on the cross-dimensional analysis of the future context for defense over the period of one generation.

> By 2045, more individuals are likely to define themselves less by their country of origin than they do today. In developing countries,[88] some people may continue to feel more closely bound by tribal allegiances or other loyalties than connected to the state. Globally, the state will probably be of less relevance to the individual due to the movement of people, information and ideas across national boundaries. As individuals feel less connected to the state, they are also likely to become less interested in supporting it.[89]

As expanding and aging populations grow more demanding of ever more personalized, technologically advanced medical, financial and oth-

84      Sovereign States of the Americas: Great Infrastructure Projects, Sept 26, 2003, EIR Chapter 5: Priority Projects For the Americas.
85      Figures from UN WPP, op. cit. show that the number of international migrants has already risen above 232 million (compared to GST 4's estimation that 230 million people would live outside their countries of origin by 2040).
86      https://www.thedialogue.org/events/remittances-to-latin-america-and-the-caribbean-in-2016/
87      https://espas.secure.europarl.europa.eu/orbis/sites/default/files/generated/document/en/MinofDef_Global%20Strategic%20Trends%20-%202045.pdf
88      Congressional Research Service (2013), 'Department of Defense's Use of Contractors to Support Military Operations: Background, Analysis, and Issues for Congress'
89      https://espas.secure.europarl.europa.eu/orbis/sites/default/files/generated/document/en/MinofDef_Global%20Strategic%20Trends%20-%202045.pdf

er services; and as supply chains become more complex, requiring more specialization and more sophisticated project management techniques, states may need to turn increasingly to the private and non-governmental sector to deliver essential services. While developed countries are likely to be able to have the resources to meet these demands – or at least are likely to be able to import or contract out the means to respond to them – this is less likely to be the case for some developing or underdeveloped countries. When countries are unable to provide vital services required by their growing populations, their citizens are likely to become increasingly agitated and discontent.

What's more, by 2036, nearly two-thirds of the world's population will be living in areas of water stress. The lack of food, water, medicine, proper hygiene, education, and basic human necessities could spell – collapse. Without mincing words, *"Global Strategic Trends – Out to 2045"* report states explicitly that the:

> ... growing gap between majority and a small number of highly visible super-rich is likely to pose an increasing threat to social order and stability. Faced by these challenges, the world's under-privileged might unite, using access to knowledge, resources, and skills to shape transnational processes in their own class interest.[90] The result of the growing desperation on the part of humanity will result in "civil war, intercommunal violence, insurgency, pervasive criminality and widespread disorder."[91]

The Pentagon is well aware of this. According to a shocking Pentagon promotional video,

> the future of global cities will be an amalgam of the settings of *Escape from New York* and *Robocop*. It will be a world of Robert Kaplanesque urban hellscapes — brutal and anarchic supercities filled with gangs of youth-gone-wild, a restive underclass, criminal syndicates, and bands of malicious hackers. At least that's the scenario outlined in *Megacities: Urban Future, the Emerging Complexity*, a five-minute video that has been used at the Pentagon's Joint Special Operations University.[92]

90    dcdc-global-strategic-trends-programme-2007-2036, DCDC Strategic Trends Report, p.80
91    dcdc-global-strategic-trends-programme-2007-2036, DCDC Strategic Trends Report, p.68
92    https://theintercept.com/2016/10/13/pentagon-video-warns-of-unavoidable-dystopian-future-for-worlds-biggest-cities/

The video was shown as part of an *Advanced Special Operations Combating Terrorism* course.[93] This is what it says:

> The future is urban. By 2030, urban areas are expected to grow by 1.4 billion, with that growth occurring almost entirely in the developing world. Cities will account for 60% of the world's population and 70% of the world's GDP. The urban environment will be the locus where drivers of instability will converge. It is the domain that by the year 2030, 60% of urban dwellers will be under the age of 18. The cities that grow the fastest will be the most challenged as resources become constrained and elicit networks fill the gap left by overextended and undercapitalized governments.
>
> The risk of natural disasters compounded by geography, climate changes, unregulated growth and substandard infrastructure intercept to frustrate humanitarian relief. Growth will magnify the increasing separation between rich and poor. Religious and ethnic tensions will be a defining element of social landscape. Stagnation will coexist with unprecedented development as impoverishment, slums, and shanty towns rapidly expand alongside modern highrises, technological advances and ever-increasing levels of prosperity.
>
> This is the world of our future. It is one we are not effectively prepared to operate within. And it is unavoidable. Mega-cities are complex systems where people and structures are compressed together in ways that defy both our understanding of city planning and military doctrine. It is an eco-system that demands a highly adaptive force to successfully operate within. Infrastructures will vary radically with concentrations of high-tech transportation, globally-connected air and seaports, contemporary water, utilities, and waste disposals intermixed with open landfills, overburdened sewers, polluted water, and makeshift power grids.
>
> Living habitat will extend from the highrise to the ground level cottage to the subterranean labyrinths, each defined by its own social codes and the rule of law. Social structures will be equally challenged, if not dysfunctional. As historic ways of life clash with modern living, ethnic and racial differences are forced to live together, and criminal networks offer an opportunity for the growing mass of unemployed.
>
> This becomes the nervous system of non-nation states, unaligned individuals and organizations that live and work in the shadows of national rule. Were physical domains can be seen, digital domains will have limitless potential to breed and expand with-

---

93    Advanced Special Operations Combating Terrorism Course—Alumni (ASOCbT-A) - SOC 3445, JOINT SPECIAL OPERATIONS UNIVERSITY, SOCOM.MIL/JSOU, 2019

out limit. Digital security and trade will be increasingly threatened by sophisticated, illicit economies and decentralized syndicates of crime to give adversaries global reach at an unprecedented level. This will add to the complexities of human targeting as a proportionally smaller number of adversaries intermingle with a larger and increasing number of citizens.

The scale and density of these domains is daunting. In a city of 10 million, where you hold the support of 99% of the population, the remaining 1% represents a threat of 100,000. It is an environment of convergence, hidden amongst the enormous scale and complexity of a megacity. These are the future breeding grounds, incubators and launching pads for adversaries and highbred threats. Linked globally, these are man-made labyrinths that provide refuge and movement across the vast sections of these cities for alternate forms of governments of taking control. The advice of doctrine from Sun Tze to current field manuals has provided two fundamental options: avoid the cities or establish a cordon to either wait out the adversary or drain the swamp of non-combatants and engage the remaining adversaries in a high-intensity conflict within.Current doctrines are inadequate to address the share scale of population reality because the eco-system of tomorrow's mega-cities are orders of magnitude greater in complexity. We are facing environments that the masters of war never foresaw. We are facing a threat that requires us to redefine doctrine and a force in radically new and different ways. The future army will confront a highly sophisticated urban-centric threat that will require that urban operations become the core requirement for the future land force.The alternative to this destruction? Launch the infrastructure projects. Begin the rebuilding of national economies and undertake mutual-interest trade. Outlaw slave-labor/free-trade practices. With the millions of new jobs, people of the Americas can look forward to building, not leaving, their homelands – old or new.

# Energy for Economic Development

The key to rebuilding the economy is the provision of plentiful, cheap energy.

This means the appropriate combination of high-tech use of fossil fuel deposits, hydropower potential where available, and everywhere, the resumption of nuclear power development. South America enjoys vast, untapped hydropower potential. The huge Itaipu Dam on the Paraná River illustrates the fact that throughout the continent, there are many favorable dam sites for power, as well as for water control and navigation.

It is nuclear power, today, the most advanced, energy-dense power source that must be resumed full-force. Soon after the 1953 announcement by President Eisenhower of the "Atoms for Peace" program, Argentina became the first nation to sign an agreement for cooperation on the peaceful uses of nuclear power. Its first reactor came online in 1974, the Atucha, and its second, the Embalse, came online in 1983. As of 1979, four new plants were planned to go operational between 1987 and 1997, but it never happened. The global economic downturn and IMF austerity dictates stopped all such programs. In Brazil, the same thing happened, although scientists were conducting experiments in nuclear fission there in the 1930s. Today, only two Brazilian nuclear power plants are operational, Angra I (1982) and Angra II (2000).

Currently, in Latin America, there are just seven[94] nuclear power reactors in operation, producing just 2.2%[95] of total energy consumption: three in Argentina, two in Brazil, and two in Mexico. Thus, oil and natural gas continue to be the two main energy staples of the planet.

Energy, as one of the most global sectors, playing a budget-forming role in many countries, has become the first hostage to the unilateral political agenda, and there are signs of this disease spreading to other sectors. The conditions in which oil and gas markets operate are constantly changing. This is due both to objective factors in the development of the world economy and energy and to subjective manifestations of a geopolitical nature. Today we are witnessing a growing influence on energy markets precisely from changes in geopolitics.

Today, the key challenge of the "global energy transformation," which implies the accelerated development of highly efficient energy-saving technologies, as well as their adaptation to the rapidly changing needs of the market (as a result of which, for example, the world's sulfur content in fuels will be reduced by 2020 in 2.6 times and sulfur dioxide emissions will be reduced by 5 million tons per year), geopolitical instability remains, which increases the risks of producing countries, primarily due to actions, policies and, even "tweets" of global Regulator in the face of the President of the United States.

Without a doubt, alternative energy (mainly solar and wind), while maintaining the current regime of regulatory and fiscal stimulation, will grow at the fastest pace – more than 2% annually. This will be facilitated by

94    Nuclear Power Reactors in the World, 2015 edition, International Atomic Energy Agency report, May 2015.
95    https://data.worldbank.org/indicator/EG.ELC.NUCL.ZS

a decrease in the cost of electricity of solar generation, which since 2010 has been reduced by two times and in some countries with unique climatic characteristics that allow solving the reserves problem, traditional energy has already "caught up" in efficiency, but the share of such countries in the overall energy balance is quite small. For comparison purposes, in absolute terms, the cost of the most efficient solar energy is still three to four times higher than the cost of electricity in the oil producers' domestic market, generated primarily from traditional fossil sources.

Nevertheless, despite the continuing decline in the cost of alternative generation and the apparent general availability of wind and sun, it still requires a solution to the problem of energy storage. As a result, the contribution of alternative energy to the global energy balance will remain relatively small, increasing from the current 12% to 16% by 2040. Unless, of course, by 2040 (and this, after all, is a long horizon), we will not see in any form the breakthrough progress of fundamental physical science in the matter of building a controlled thermonuclear fusion reactor, which can fundamentally change these estimates. However, the possibility of this for today remains rather low, given the next postponement of the launch of large pilot projects.

In the absence of such breakthrough solutions, gas, as the most environmentally friendly source of energy, will replace both coal and nuclear energy, as several countries consider this direction to be potentially dangerous. Generally speaking, nuclear energy, like the Internet, was and, I think, in the foreseeable future will remain part of the "dual-use" industry, which allows to compensate for the associated costs of the military-industrial complex.

Natural gas, unlike alternative sources of energy, can provide stable electricity production. Moreover, natural gas is a promising fuel for heavy vehicles and marine vessels. For example, Russian government reports forecast a 5-fold increase in gas demand from the transport sector by 2040. Therefore, demand for natural gas will continue to grow at the fastest rate among fossil fuels (at the level of about 2% per year), which will lead to an increase in its share in the energy balance from 22% to 25% by 2040.

Demand for oil will continue to increase at about 1% per year, which means an increase in consumption in absolute volumes. By the year 2040, oil consumption in the world will increase by about 20 million barrels per day. The demand for oil and petroleum products will be supported by an increase in living standards in developing countries and the mass distribution of cars in them, as well as steady demand from the petrochemical industry, which we see as one of the main growth points in the global energy industry. As a result, although the share of oil in the world energy balance will decrease from 32% now, to 28% in 2040, its consumption will grow in absolute terms, and its role as the basis of modern energy will remain central. The growth in oil demand is inevitable.

# Helium-3

However, as we speak, plans are also being drawn up to mine Helium-3 on the Moon. Helium-3 is a natural decay product of radioactive tritium and is the most effective, most efficient for the production of thermonuclear weapons. Therefore, it means we're making a leap in the amount of power available, per capita and per square kilometer, for the territory in the Earth, in the Moon, and so forth.

In April 1988, a meeting was held by NASA to understand the potential of using 3He (Helium-3) from the Moon for terrestrial fusion power production.[96] The fusion power session concluded (1) that 3He offers significant, possibly compelling, advantages over fusion of tritium, principally increased reactor life, reduced radioactive wastes, and high-efficiency conversion, (2) that detailed assessment of the potential of the D/3He fuel cycle requires more information, and (3) that although D/T fusion is most near term, D/3He fusion may be best for commercial purposes.

As a fusion fuel, helium-3 offers specific advantages beyond any fuel accessible on Earth. In a fusion reaction, two light nuclei combine to form a new element, and in doing so, release energy in the form of particles and electromagnetic radiation. While fusion, in general, is 100 times more energy-dense than fission, which is 100,000 times more energy-dense than fossil fuels, not all fusion fuels are created equal. A fusion reaction of deuterium and helium-3 releases 18.4 MeV, more than any other fusion reaction available to us, and its products are almost entirely in the form of charged particles, rather than neutrons.

Unlike neutrons, which don't respond to a magnetic field, the energy of charged particles can be directly converted to electricity through magnetohydrodynamics (rather than a steam cycle and turbine), making the energy conversion twice as efficient as that of prevalent methods. Because of these characteristics, is has been recognized that lunar helium-3 could power the Earth for 10,000

---

96      Lunar Helium-3 and fusion power, NASA Ofice of Exploration and the Department of Energy Ofice of Fusion Energy and held at the NASA Lewis Research Center Cleveland, Ohio April 25 and 26, 1988

years. But the promise of helium-3 can't be fulfilled on Earth. For this, man will have to develop the Moon.[97]

From a technical vantage point, "industrial materials processing on the Moon will be significantly different than conventional Earth technologies, which require vast amounts of water, chemicals, and other volatiles that do not exist in the lunar environment. Fusion has great advantages, even over nuclear fission, for materials processing and other industries: It requires a small amount of fuel, most of the fuel is already on the Moon, it produces no waste that requires recycling, it requires virtually no radiation protection, and it can make use of direct conversion technologies such as magnetohydro-dynamics (MHD) – getting rid of the steam turbine. Direct plasma processing, using the high-temperature charged-particle product of the fusion reaction itself, has the potential to increase productivity by orders of magnitude over today's chemical or even electrical processing technologies.

"From a very small amount of matter can thus come an inconceivably abundant and non-polluting source of energy. Numerous other applications can be conceived on the Moon, such as the utilization of the phenomenon of free superconductivity, available due to the cold conditions that reign on Earth's satellite.[98]

As Russian cosmonaut Alexander Volkov said in October 2014, "There is water on the Moon, and there is helium-3, which is better than any other energy source existing on the Earth.... One day, we will run out of oil and coal, and humankind will need energy. Then, we will start supplying it from the neighboring planet."

Where will the helium-3 come from for their fusion reactors?

The solar wind, which constantly spews high-energy particles and radiation from the Sun throughout the Solar System, has been found by spacecraft probes to contain about 20 parts per million particles of helium-3. However, these particles do not survive the Earth's atmosphere and are, therefore, not found deposited on the Earth's surface. Because the Moon has no atmosphere, the helium-3 bombarding it from the solar wind has collected there over billions of years. Samples of lunar soil returned by the Apollo astronauts and analyses from the Soviet unmanned Luna probes indicate that the lunar soil contains an estimated one million tons of helium-3.

The helium on the Moon will not be an unlimited energy supply in itself, but it could function as a one-century bridge to the

---

97      The Fuel of the Future: Helium-3, EIR, https://larouchepac.com/20160428/helium-3
98      Rudolph Biérent, "Exploring Space: The Optimism Of an Infinite Uni-verse," EIR, 23 March, 2012.

recovery of virtually limitless helium-3 from the outer planets. It will open the next millennia, providing humanity with the first biologically benign, non-polluting, efficient, and economical energy in human history. The abundance of this quality of energy will create the possibility. And is itself a prerequisite for the colonization of space and the necessary revolution of all economic activity on the Earth.[99] The Moon can open the fusion era.

From *EIR* in February 2010:

"Now, theoretically, with helium-3 as a fuel, you are approaching the possibility of a rate of acceleration – acceleration *of* acceleration – of an impulse toward Mars, which scientists have estimated at about three days, from Moon orbit to Mars. So, therefore, with access to a thermonuclear fusion approach to the power base of action in the universe, there is no visible limit to what humankind might be able to do.[100]"

*****

In closing, these types of projects would result in an explosion of economic development, technological and scientific progress, cultural optimism and greater purpose while unifying Latin America around a common idea of "Greater Good" in a post-crisis Latin America, now so mortally threatened by physical degradation, narco-terrorism, cultural pessimism and the advocates of one-world government.

We, as a society, need progress. We need technological progress, scientific progress, and cultural progress, not merely to become richer or more powerful, but because we need to be immortal, as no animal can be. We need to participate in the discovery and application of universal physical principles that no animal could do. And when we find our motivation and our morality, in that, we become morally and spiritually invincible.

Our mortal life has a beginning and an inevitable end. What, then, is our immortal interest in being a person? All of the leaders of society, especially in times of crisis, are leaders because they measure up to some approximation of that standard. And in good education, especially good *moral* education, we educate our children, and others, to understand this principle of immortality.

When we generate, and transmit, discoveries of principle, to our children, to those who come later, we live forever in the his-

99      "Mining Helium-3 on the Moon for unlimited energy," EIR Volume 14, Number 30, July 31, 1987
100      "The End of The Obama Administration," LaRouche webcast, EIR, Feb 5, 2010.

tory of humankind. Our mortal existence is no longer a matter of a beginning and an end: Our mortal existence is a place in eternity, from which we radiate the experience of generations before us, and radiate our existence into the future. We become the immortal children of the Creator of the universe.[101]

We become one with the universe.

101     How To Reconstruct A Bankrupt World, LaRouche speech, Decembe 27, 2002, Budapest, https://larouchepub.com/lar/2002/2950budapest_sch.html

# Chapter 2

# THE MONROE DOCTRINE

I t is a common belief that since the enactment of the Monroe Doctrine back in 1823, Latin America has become a sub-America; a sec-
ond-class America of nebulous identity, or as some disparagingly
prefer to call it, "America's backyard," with all the prerogatives and implications for the Big Brother of the continent; from legitimizing illegit-
imate pro-United States proxies on the continent, to monopolizing all
trade deals and excluding anyone who could legitimately be a competitor
with the United States' interests, and even deciding such issues as population planning through birth control in order to exterminate the "great
unwashed," as former Secretary of State, Henry Kissinger has called the
unprivileged strata of society.

However, the real story of the Monroe Doctrine still needs to be told.
We need to see the United States not as the enemy of Latin America, but,
rather, under the direction of a proper leader, as an ally, and a protector of
future common interests of all Americans, both North and South, in the
post-crisis world.

> With the declaration of the Monroe Doctrine on December 2,
> 1823, the United States pledged itself as the unique and sole de-
> fender of the republican independence of the nation-states of the
> Western Hemisphere, against the oligarchical adventures and in-
> trigues of the European nations of the Holy Alliance. Something
> must be said of the conditions existing in 1823 bearing upon the
> problem which the Monroe doctrine was to solve. Europe was un-
> der the control of the Holy Alliance. Originally formed by a com-
> bination of Austria, Prussia, Russia and Great Britain to administer
> upon the wreck of Napoleon's ambitions, the Alliance was contin-
> ued as a police body, to assure the peace of the civilized world.[1]

Most Americans believe that President James Monroe's declaration
was the "beginning of a new Anglo-American alliance for imperialist

---

1      John Quincy Adams and the Monroe Doctrine Author(s): Worthington Chauncey Ford
Source: The American Historical Review, Vol. 7, No. 4 (Jul., 1902), pp. 676-696 Published by: Oxford
University Press on behalf of the American Historical Association

domination of the emerging nations of Latin America."[2] But a review of American history shows that the primary target against which the Monroe Doctrine was established, and against which U.S. Presidents have invoked it, was the grasping British Empire, and that the Monroe Doctrine is a fundamental extension of U.S. constitutional law.

As historian Edward Spannaus writes,

> Great Britain had by no means given up hopes of expansion in the Western Hemisphere by the early 1820s, hardly a decade after the War of 1812. The United States had recognized the independence of Colombia, Peru, Chile, Buenos Aires (capital of what is now Argentina, then the United Provinces of the Rio de la Plata), and Mexico, but Great Britain had recognized none. Pleased that the empires of Spain and France had been curtailed in the New World, the British still had by no means reconciled themselves to the end of colonialism – as their control of colonial Canada today underlines.
>
> Yet in 1823 British Prime Minister George Canning made an offer to the United States which he believed it could not refuse. In discussions with U.S. Ambassador to London Richard Rush, Canning proposed a joint U.S.-British declaration to guarantee the emancipation of Spain's colonies in the Western Hemisphere. The fivepoint declaration stated that Spain's former colonies should not be recoverable by Spain, nor transferred to any other power, although it renounced claims by the authors to impede negotiations between Spain and the colonies or take possession themselves. Within this Wilsonesque rhetoric, however, there was one tell-tale omission: Rather than recognizing the former Spanish colonies as independent states, the Canning proposal said: "We conceive the question of the recognition of them, as Independent States, to be one of time and circumstance."[3]

John Quincy Adams, was the only principal in the Monroe administration not taken in by the Canning declaration. "While President Monroe was receiving advice from former Presidents Jefferson and Madison to the effect that such a de facto alliance with Great Britain would be the best protection for the militarily weak United States,"[4] Quincy Adams launched a campaign for a unilateral U.S. declaration against all the oligarchical powers of Europe.

2    The Monroe Doctrine was aimed at Britain by Nancy and Edward Spannaus, EIR, May 11, 1982, p.30
3    Ibid
4    http://www.americaslibrary.gov/aa/monroe/aa_monroe_doctrine_1.html

"Quincy Adams, who was to be elected to the presidency the next year, had, throughout his service as a statesman, worked to strengthen America's commitment to the spread of republicanism in Latin America."[5]

Even before the United States had recognized many of the continent's new nations, Quincy Adams wrote:

> The emancipation of the South American continent opens to the whole race of man prospects of futurity in which this Union will be called in the discharge of its duties to itself and to unnumbered ages of posterity to take a conspicuous and leading role .... That the fabric of our social connections with our southern neighbors may rise in the lapse of years with a grandeur and harmony of proportions corresponding with the magnificence of the means placed by Providence in our power and that of our descendants; its foundations must be laid in principles of politics and of morals, new and distasteful to the thrones and dominations of the elder world ..."[6]
> South America had for some time been in rebellion against Spain, and "the United States alone had recognized their independence and accorded to them the rights of independent nations.[7]

When Canning's proposal reached his desk later in 1823, world events made clear to Quincy Adams the necessity of defending the principles of non-colonization, and non-interference in the Western Hemisphere by all the powers of the Holy Alliance. "In 1821, Russia claimed control of the entire Pacific coast from Alaska to Oregon and closed the area to foreign shipping. This development coincided with rumors that Spain, with the help of European allies, was planning to reconquer its former Latin American colonies."[8]

France also had claims against Middle America. On the face of it, Britain was the only one of the Holy Alliance powers willing to renounce colonization and was the strongest of these powers in military terms. But John Quincy Adams argued that as long as Great Britain would not recognize the sovereign independence of the new nations in the Western Hemisphere, the United States could not even entertain the idea of signing a parallel declaration with the British, much less a joint declaration. He wrote:

---

5        https://ap.gilderlehrman.org/resource/monroe-doctrine-1823, The Gilder Lehrman Institute of American History
6        Letter to Richard Anderson, U.S. minister in Bogota, Colombia, May 27, 1823
7        https://www.jstor.org/stable/pdf/1834564.pdf
8        https://ap.gilderlehrman.org/resource/monroe-doctrine-1823, The Gilder Lehrman Institute of American History

So long as Great Britain withholds the recognition of that [in-dependence], we may, as we certainly do, concur with her in the aversion to the transfer to any other power of any of the Colonies in this Hemisphere, heretofore or yet, belonging to Spain; but the principles of that aversion, so far as they are common to both par-ties, resting only upon a casual coincidence of interests, in a na-tional point of view selfish on both sides, would be liable to disso-lution by every change of phase in the aspect of European politics ... Britain and America ... would not be bound by "any permanent community of principle."

Adams's concept of a "community of principle"[9] was well-known among the proponents of the American System at the time, including the Marquis de Lafayette:

It meant relations between states were to be based on mutual re-spect for national sovereignty, that sovereignty itself being defined not by the mere brute exercise of power, but by the commitment to the betterment of its population morally and materially. Such a commitment to the principle of sovereignty demanded peaceful relations among states and stood in total contrast to the maneu-verings for looting arrangements that characterized the relations among the European powers.[10]

Thus John Quincy Adams wrote in his diary of Nov. 7, 1823, that an independent American declaration of support for republics of Latin America against the European powers was necessary because: "It affords a very suitable and convenient opportunity for us to take our stand against the Holy Alliance and at the same time to decline the overture of Great Britain. It would be more candid, as well as more dignified, to avow our principles explicitly to Russia and France, than to come in as a cock-boat in the wake of the British man-of-war."

# Promulgation of the Monroe Doctrine

President Monroe was won to Quincy Adams's position.[11] On Decem-ber 2, 1823, the Monroe Doctrine was promulgated, echoing the pol-icy enunciated in the Federalist Papers and George Washington's great

---

9    Adams, *Works,* VI, 117. See also *ibid.,* VI, 469: letter to John Taylor of Caroline, April, 1814.
10    The Monroe Doctrine was aimed at Britain by Nancy and Edward Spannaus, EIR, May 11, 1982, p.30.
11    John Quincy Adams and the Monroe Doctrine Author(s): Worthington Chauncey Ford Source: The American Historical Review, Vol. 7, No. 4 (Jul., 1902), pp. 676-696 Published by: Oxford University Press on behalf of the American Historical Association.

Farewell Address, in which America's first President warned of entangle-
ments with the politics or controversies of Europe on the grounds that
the United States as a constitutional republic must not subordinate its interests to those of the European oligarchies.

The Monroe Doctrine extended this protection to all the nations of the
hemisphere:

> "as a principle in which the rights and interests of the United States
> are involved, ... the American continents, by the free and indepen-
> dent condition which they have assumed and maintain, are hence-
> forth not to be considered as subjects for future colonization by
> any European powers ... In the wars of the European powers in mat-
> ters relating to themselves we have never taken any part, nor does it
> comport with our policy to do so. It is only when our rights are in-
> vaded or seriously menaced that we resent injuries or make prepa-
> ration for our defense. With the movements in this hemisphere we
> are of necessity more immediately connected, and by causes which
> must be obvious to all enlightened and impartial observors. The
> political system of the allied powers is essentially different in this
> respect from that of America. This difference proceeds from that
> which exists in their respective Governments; and to the defense
> of our own, which has been achieved by the loss of so much blood
> and treasure, and matured by the wisdom of their most enlight-
> ened citizens, and under which we have enjoyed unexampled fe-
> licity, this whole nation is devoted. We owe it. Therefore, to candor
> and the amicable relations existing between the United States and
> those powers to declare that we should consider any attempt on
> their part to extend their system to any portion of this hemisphere
> as dangerous to our peace and safety.

Within a few years of Monroe's proclamation, it had become a guideline
for U.S. foreign policy. In 1825, President John Quincy Adams's Secretary
of State Henry Clay sent a set of instructions to Joel Poinsett, the U.S. minister in Mexico, directing Poinsett to bring the Mexicans' attention to Monroe's message "asserting certain important principles of intercontinental
law in the relations of Europe and America." The first principle was that the
Americas would no longer be considered subjects for colonization by European powers. The second principle, wrote Clay, is that "we should regard
as dangerous to our peace and safety" any effort on the part of Europe "to
extend their political system to any portion of this hemisphere. The political
systems of the two continents are essentially different."

In 1863, Mexican President Benito Juarez urged the United States to invoke the Monroe Doctrine against the attempts of the Swiss financial oligarchy to impose a monarchy on Mexico to guarantee the payment of that nation's foreign debt. Under the London Convention of October 1863, the navies of France, England, and Spain, and more than 20,000 troops, had combined to mount an invasion of Mexico to revoke the Mexican government's sovereign decision to impose a debt moratorium against those countries.

The weakness of the war-torn United States prevented Lincoln from going to the aid of his ally Juarez. There are numerous documents demonstrating that Lincoln's strategy was to fight his battles one at a time, with his basic concern at that time being to safeguard the Union, and to neutralize British agents of influence, who, like his Secretary of State Seward, were working against him from within.

## The Venezuela Dispute

In 1895, President Grover Cleveland invoked the Monroe Doctrine against Britain during the British-Venezuela boundary dispute concerning "British" Guiana.[12] The British raised the objection that the Monroe Doctrine was incomplete and not a part of international law. Cleveland responded that the doctrine "was intended to apply to every stage in our national life and cannot become obsolete while our republic endures." Cleveland added that the doctrine "has its place in the code of international law as certainly and securely as if it were specifically mentioned."

At Cleveland's instruction, his Secretary of State Richard Olney[13] delivered a long message to the U.S. ambassador in London for transmittal to Lord Salisbury. The Monroe Doctrine, wrote Olney, applied the logic of Washington's Farewell Address by declaring that American non-intervention in European affairs necessarily implied European non-intervention in American affairs. The rule is ... that no European power or combination of European powers shall forcibly deprive any American state of the right and power of self-government and of shaping for itself its own political fortunes and destinies. That the rule thus defined has been the accepted public law of this country ever since its promulgation cannot be fairly denied.

Olney continued:

12       Nelson M. Blake, "Background of Cleveland's Venezuelan Policy," American Historical Review, Vol. 47, No. 2 (Jan., 1942), pp. 259–277.
13       Thomas Paterson, J. Garry Clifford, Shane J. Maddock (2009), American foreign relations: A history, to 1920. Cengage Learning p. 205.

What is true of the material, is no less true of what may be termed the moral interests involved .... Europe as a whole is monarchical, and, with the single important exception of the Republic of France, is committed to the monarchical principle. America, on the other hand, is devoted to exactly the opposite principle.Although it is the case that British-influenced occupants of the White House and State Department in the 20th century, especially Theodore Roosevelt, have more often applied the Monroe Doctrine in service of the financial interests of the European oligarchy, the spirit of James Monroe and John Quincy Adams's original declaration was still alive in the April 19, 1939 speech of Franklin Delano Roosevelt to the Pan-American Congress:

The American family of nations pays honor to the oldest and most successful association of sovereign nations which exists in the world. What is it that has protected us from the tragic involvements which are today making the old world a new cockpit of old struggles? The answer is easily found. A new and powerful ideal – that of the community of nations – sprang up at the same time the Americas became free and independent. ... The American peace we celebrate today has no quality of weakness in it. We are prepared to maintain it and defend it to the fullest extent of our strength, matching force to force if any attempt is made to subvert our institutions, or impair the independence of anyone of our group.

# The Good Neighbor Policy

Starting in 1933, President Franklin Delano Roosevelt executed a revolutionary shift in U.S. strategic and economic policy in the Western Hemisphere. "In rejecting Hoover's approach, FDR essentially embraced a form of economic nationalism and committed the United States to solving the Depression on its own. He dismantled the London Economic Conference in the summer of 1933 and devalued the dollar by removing the United States from the international gold standard."[14]

Furthermore, Roosevelt uprooted the destructive policy of raw materials and financial looting of Latin America, which had been imposed by his cousin, President Teddy Roosevelt. "Under FDR's watch, the last American troops withdrew from the Caribbean, and the United States abrogated the Platt Amendment, wherein the government of Cuba had pledged to recognize the right of the United States to intervene in its country."[15] In

---

14      Franklin D. Roosevelt: Foreign Affairs, William E. Leuchtenburg, Miller Center, https://millercenter.org/president/fdroosevelt/foreign-affairs
15      Ibid

its place, he restored John Quincy Adams's foreign policy, as expressed in the 1823 Monroe Doctrine, premised on an overriding commitment to the establishment of a community of principle among perfectly sovereign nation-states, and large-scale industrialization.

In his March 4, 1933 inaugural address, FDR explained the principles of his New Deal, which would boldly transform the United States through an integrated package of Hamiltonian credit creation, magnificent infrastructure projects, public works, and protectionist regulation. Roosevelt stated, "In the field of world policy I would dedicate this nation to the policy of the good neighbor – the neighbor who resolutely respects himself and, because he does so, respects the rights of others – the neighbor who respects his obligations and respects the sanctity of his agreements in and with a world of neighbors." Roosevelt would start to implement in the Western Hemisphere, the same principles that would prove stunningly successful in the United States, through the New Deal of 1933-37, and the economic mobilization for World War II of 1939-45.

Already, in an article in the July 1928 issue of *Foreign Affairs* magazine, entitled, "Our Foreign Policy: A Democratic View," FDR tore apart the disastrous policy of his cousin, Teddy Roosevelt, specifically attacking the several decades old policy of looting, called "Dollar Diplomacy" backed up by Teddy's "Big Stick." Franklin Delano Roosevelt said,

> We must admit … that the outside world almost unanimously views us with less goodwill today than at any previous period. This is serious unless we take the deliberate position that the people of the United States owe nothing to the rest of humankind and care nothing for the opinion of others so long as our seacoasts are impregnable, and our pocketbooks are filled. The time has come when we must accept … many new principles of a higher law.

That higher principle meant getting rid of British-French-Portuguese imperialism.

As President, Roosevelt went to work on this immediately. At the Seventh International Conference of American States, meeting in Montevideo, Uruguay in December 1933, the U.S. delegation, acting for Roosevelt, voted for a resolution that stated, "No state has the right to intervene in the internal or external affairs of another." As the full impact dawned on the delegates, that this vote reversed 30 years of U.S. foreign policy, Puig Casauranc, the Mexican delegate, stated, "I wish to submit my profound conviction that there is in the White House an admirable, noble, and good man – a courageous man."

Among the many initiatives Roosevelt undertook, two stand out as exemplifying the Good Neighbor policy: the ground-breaking U.S. Mission to Brazil of 1942-43, which developed detailed plans to transform the leading nation of Brazil into a modern industrial powerhouse; and Roosevelt's deft handling of Mexican President Cárdenas' nationalization of foreign oil companies operating in Mexico in 1938.

In 1942, Roosevelt appointed a Mission to Brazil. To head it, he named Morris Llewellyn Cooke. Cooke, who had been head of Philadelphia's Public Works in the 1910s, played a key role in developing the plans for taming the Mississippi River in the 1930s and 1940s; and in 1935, headed the Rural Electrification Administration, which lit up rural America. Now, in his 70th year, Cooke headed a U.S. team of 12, consisting of geologists, metallurgists, engineers, etc., which worked with a similar team of Brazilians. They developed plans to transform Brazil from top to bottom.

# Mission to Brazil

Cooke expressed the anti-imperialist, pro-development thinking that characterized the mission. He stated that "The whole history of industrial civilization [ie, American System methods] demonstrates that international trade develops best between nations that are prosperous, not between rich nations and poor nations, nor between nations trying to gain prosperity by retarding their neighbors." He counterposed this to the model of 19th-Century British imperialism, which he described as the theory "based on the right of one nation to dominate the lives of other peoples because of an alleged superiority of race."

Imperialism will be overturned by science and technology: "Latter-day technological developments, especially in the large-scale production and long-distance transmission of electrical power, have sealed the doom of typical 19th-Century [free trade] ... Brazil should plan to do as much of her own manufacturing as is economically feasible." The Mission had several objectives, of which three are most note-worthy:

1. Manufacturing – Recognizing that manufacturing was crucial to Brazil's development, Cooke's team examined every major manufacturing process, inclusive of textiles; pulp, paper, and cellulose fiber making; chemicals; alcohol and fuel; ammonia; rubber; and so forth. For each industry, it made recommendations for methods of manufacture that would increase productivity from 30-300%.

2. Sao Francisco Valley – Cooke's Mission enthusiastically examined the Sao Francisco River as a "multi-purpose river" basin. The Sao Francisco River is 1,802 miles long, with its headwaters at Cabrobo; it crosses five Brazilian states in the eastern part of the country, with a watershed of many thousands of square miles. At places such as Itaparica Falls along the river, Cooke's team saw huge possibilities for the generation of hydroelectric power. He also saw "the possibilities for … designed industrial developments, extensive irrigation works, controlled sedimentation, improved balanced agriculture, flood control, recreation, and vastly improved transportation facilities – all on a coordinated basis." Cooke's team did a detailed study of the Sao Francisco Valley and concluded that it could replicate many of the breakthrough features of the Tennessee Valley Authority in the United States.

3. Volta Redonda Steel plant – The President of Brazil, who represented the best of that country's nationalist tradition, was Getulio Vargas. In 1941, Vargas and the Brazilian Congress created the National Steel Company (CSN), which would erect an integrated steel mill in the village of Volta Redonda, located 90 miles south of Rio de Janeiro. This was to be the first modern steel plant of its type in Brazilian history. The plant project would cost approximately $70 million to construct (approximately $1 billion in today's dollars). The largest component of the project's financing, $45 million, representing two-thirds of the cost, was provided by the United States. Jesse Jones' Reconstruction Finance Corporation lent this money through its Export-Import Bank division. It had an initial annual capacity of 50,000 tons of pig iron and 295,000 tons of steel, with Brazil's intent to raise its steel output to 1 million tons. At the plant's site, an entire new city was constructed to build the plant, complete with machine shops, repair shops, homes, etc. Volta Redonda was the seed crystal for Brazil' s industrialization."[16]

> On May 7, 1943, President Vargas summed up the vision of the Volta Redonda plant: "In the presence of an undertaking of the magnitude of the one we are carrying out here, I cannot conceal my patriotic enthusiasm and my confidence in the capacity of Brazilians…. The [once] semi-colonial agrarian country, importer of manufactures and exporter of raw materials, will meet the exigencies of an autonomous industrial life, providing its own most urgent defense and equipment needs…. The plant will set the ground to institute a new standard of living and a new mentality in our country.

16    https://larouchepub.com/eiw/public/2003/eirv30n38-20031003/eirv30n38-20031003_046-the_american_republics_fight_for.pdf

Vargas and Roosevelt became close friends; Roosevelt said that Vargas and Brazil would play a major role in a post-World War II world.

## Roosevelt and Mexico

Roosevelt worked with Josephus Daniels, whom he appointed as U.S. Ambassador to Mexico, to fundamentally change U.S. relations to Mexico, and beyond that to all of the Americas.[17]

On March 18, 1938, Mexican President Lázaro Cárdenas signed an order that expropriated the assets of nearly all of the foreign oil companies operating in Mexico. "Prior to expropriation in 1938, the oil industry in Mexico had been dominated by the Mexican Eagle Company (a subsidiary of the Royal Dutch/Shell Company), which accounted for over 60% of Mexican oil production, and by American-owned oil firms including Jersey Standard and Standard Oil Company of California (SOCAL – now Chevron), which accounted for approximately 30% of total production."[18]

The oil companies screamed, and Standard Oil of New Jersey's President William S. Farish, who would soon play a leading role in providing fuel to the Nazi war machine during World War II, demanded that Mexico pay $450 million for the expropriated properties. Meanwhile, Standard Oil, Royal Dutch Shell, and others ran a vicious campaign against Mexico, declaring it a lawless nation influenced by Bolshevism.

Josephus Daniels took an opposite view, writing to Roosevelt:

> Having made big money on absurdly low wages from the time [of] the oil gushers, all oil producers oppose any change in taxes and wages, and resent it if their government do not take their point of view. Mexico can never prosper on low wages and we must be in sympathy with every just demand.... I need not tell you that as a rule the oilmen will be satisfied with nothing less than that the United States government attempt to direct the Mexican policy for their financial benefit.... They would like to have an Ambassador who would be a messenger boy for their companies, and a Government at Washington whose policy is guided by Dollar Diplomacy.

American oil experts investigated the worth of the expropriated oil properties, and according to one historian, "were shocked at the discrepancy between [oil] company claims and what they found in Mexico – ob-

17    https://finding-aids.lib.unc.edu/00203/ Collection Number: 00203 Collection Title: Josephus Daniels Papers, 1863-1947
18    Mexican Expropriation of Foreign Oil, 1938, Department of State https://history.state.gov/milestones/1937-1945/mexican-oil

solete equipment 25 years old and badly in need of repair, miles of pipeline corroded almost beyond use." The oil companies had just extracted oil – and done nothing else. One team of U.S. experts stated that they thought the Standard Oil holdings were worth only $10-20 million.

In 1940, Mexican President Cárdenas wrote to FDR, "I want to express my thanks for the understanding and patience you have shown in solving the numerous and inescapable difficulties that always arise between neighbors." Cárdenas added, "Only with your administration have we Mexicans felt able to discuss problems freely, disregarding our differences as far as power is concerned, and thus pursuing the common decisions solely dictated by our search for justice."

Roosevelt, aided by the work of Daniels and others, worked out a universal agreement in November, 1941, by which Mexico started the payment of compensation to the oil companies at greatly reduced, but fair prices, while the U.S. government injected money into Mexico, through buying Mexican silver, a $30 million U.S. Export-Import bank loan for road construction, and so forth. An explosion was avoided, and Mexico's sovereignty was respected and strengthened. "Finally, on April 18, 1942, the U.S. and Mexican Governments signed the Cooke-Zevada agreement, whereby the Mexicans agreed to pay roughly $29 million in compensation to several American firms, including Jersey Standard and Socal. The British, however, held out until 1947, when they received $130 million."[19]

## The Postwar Future

Meanwhile, Roosevelt was working with Latin American patriots to develop other countries. In Chile, the United States Eximbank extended a $60 million credit to the Chilean Development Corporation, an entity involved in construction of a modern steel mill, building hydro-electric plants, cement factories, a tire factory, and a copper wire factory; importing agricultural machinery, and planning modernization of the Santiago and Valparaiso transportation systems. "FDR was eager to build goodwill at a time when the administration wanted to lessen German influence in South America."[20]

In Peru, the Corporación Peruana de la Santa was set up to be the counterpart to the TVA. "In Colombia, a Development Corporation was set up, and after the conclusion of World War II, David Lilienthal, the

19      Mexican Expropriation of Foreign Oil, 1938, Department of State https://history.state.gov/milestones/1937-1945/mexican-oil
20      Encyclopedia of U.S. - Latin American Relations, by Thomas Leonard, Jurgen Buchenau, Kyle Longley, SAGE Publications, 2012, p.180, ISBN: 978-087289-762-5

former head of the TVA, traveled to Colombia, to collaborate with Colombian patriots on the idea of constructing a TVA in Colombia. There were plans, that would have involved Venezuela and Brazil, to dredge and connect the upper Orinoco River and the Negro River."[21]

All the above plans formed part of a pattern of intensive work for the development of Latin America. Morris Cooke wanted to extend his plans to the hemisphere; after his work in Brazil, Cooke wrote a 50-page memorandum, entitled "Promotion of the Development of the Brazilian Economy as a Pattern for Hemispheric Economic Relations – the Long View."

President Roosevelt oversaw this process, which during World War II carried out some important work in infrastructure, improvement of health standards, etc.; and moreover, made major plans for Roosevelt to activate as soon as the war would end. Had he lived past the conclusion of World War II, there would have been a Good Neighbor Policy hemispheric economic explosion on an unprecedented scale.

John F. Kennedy's early-1960s Alliance for Progress was an attempt to revive aspects of the Good Neighbor Policy, but his 1963 assassination aborted any possibility of achieving that goal. This leaves the revival of America's mission of justice entirely in the hands of the present generation.

---

21    https://larouchepub.com/eiw/public/2003/eirv30n38-20031003/eirv30n38-20031003_046-the_american_republics_fight_for.pdf

# Epilogue

# THE WORLD IS CHANGING

*The world* is changing and changing fast. There is no denying it. This inevitable change has created fear and anxiety. No age has been more fraught with insecurity than our own present time. There *were*, of course, substantial political and social upheavals *that* roiled *our world* in the past decade but none like today. Paraphrasing historian Andrei Fursov, the familiar world is in the process of disappearing; sociologists, politicial scientists, economists, social engineers are analyzing not so much today's world as – by inertia – yesterday's world; humanitarian and social studies provide the student with a larger picture of the world that has already left and is never coming back.

Science, in its current state, can't catch up to the profound global changes around us. This gap, between what used to be our reality and the world of the near future, is growing, for three reasons. First of all, the changes in the world are accelerating. Secondly, in the modern world, there are many influential and powerful forces interested in hiding the essence and direction of the processes occurring in it and successfully camouflaging our reality. Thirdly, although the current era is almost over, we still, to this day, have a poor idea of its essence.

The years teach much, which the days never knew. Our understanding of the lessons of history, as a rule, comes to us as collective humanity only in the twilight of old age, when it's too late to change our destiny. To understand the essence of the new era, or at least get closer to understanding what is coming in the near future, we must first determine what is leaving and why? In our context, this means defining the essential components of Modernity, the era of its "farewell bow," and at the same time the "farewell bow" of capitalism that we are seeing all around us.

We, collectively as humanity, have already left the old world, but have not yet entered the new one – *ceteris paribus* – today we live between worlds, on the chronological divide. Such a situation provides fantastic opportunities for an attentive observer of history and of social systems: the past, not entirely gone, its shadows and smells still lingering in the distance. Memory, in this sense, is not a quest for truth but a refusal of death. The refusal is vain in the literal sense, since nothing will bring the past back. Beyond all easy spiritualism, the past does speak, it counsels us through memory, through our late but often luminous understanding of what once was and shall never be again. My thematic design stands as a pattern of redemption of loss, and perhaps the only redemption of loss there is. Loss is irredeemable; it goes on and on, an endlessly discomposing face in the mirror.

Modern society and the capitalist system, and much in the post-capitalist, post-modern order can be understood from the logic of the development of their predecessor. Through the prism of the tendencies of development of the capitalist system of the Modern era, converging at one point, the point of bifurcation (1975-2025), this is the moment-eternity, the world between the past and future, the "in between-world"; we will try to look into the future that comes as a nesting doll crisis and reflect on the nature of this crisis.

To some, the proposed analysis may seem to be what science fiction author and futurist Stanislaw Lem called "black-sightedness." For this reason, I have a question: what is better – to prepare for the worst or to exist in accordance with the "Sidonia Apollinaria Syndrome?" He was a Roman who lived on the eve of the destruction of Rome by barbarians and nevertheless short-sightedly painted in his letters to friends a glorious and peaceful picture of life on the eve of the death of his civilization. I think that the rule should be the Roman dictum – *praemonitus praemunitus* (forewarned is forearmed). I will be glad to make mistakes in my predictions and have someone point out the errors of my way. At the same time, precisely the clear vision of the world, without illusions – the courage to know – is a necessary condition for the courage to *be*. Time and space, the tricks of the damage-strewn world, the pile of debris we call history, also represent our successes. They are our successes. Like Time, they sustain the magic that made our world what it was.

Contrary to Marx, who believed that a system dies when its underlying contradictions are aggravated (for him it was a contradiction between productive forces and production relations), the system dies when it fades; its fundamental, system-forming contradiction is developed, when it decides in its development, removes this contradiction and thus implements its sociogenetic program. Aggravation of systemic contradictions leads to intrasystemic, i.e. structural crisis when a new structure takes the place of another in a revolutionary-military way. A systemic crisis is caused by the attenuation of a basic contradiction, which, as a rule, is accompanied not so much by an explosion as by a giant sob – *vixerunt* in Latin.

# Three Explosions, Three Problems of the 21st Century

The first explosion, according to Fursov, is connected with the population: Stanislaw Lem noted that the destructive possibilities of humanity are growing along with the creative ones, and sometimes overtake them. The Upper Paleolithic crisis destroyed 75-85% of the population. Today, the results of the reduction in numbers with the types of weapons of mass destruction that are available can leave such an imprint on the population, inflict such a blow on the gene pool that causes it psycho-physical degeneration, i.e., degeneration of man as a species.

The second explosion is universal (global) criminalization. Social crises, especially systemic ones, are always accompanied by the breaking of social rules – criminalization is growing globally. At a minimum, this means that the old society begins to die off – its control mechanisms no longer work; at the maximum, a new society begins to emerge, moreover, in a criminal, asocial form. So, blurring the boundaries of normal life, the socialization of post-crisis society, this is another potential explosion (crisis factor) of the 21st century.

Then, there is a third crisis factor to be considered. In periods of acute social crisis, the social element is stifled, and the role of what is called the "biological component" in human behavior increases dramatically. Strictly speaking, it should be not so much about the biologization of social processes (although outwardly the case often looks like this), but rather about bringing to the forefront of subhuman forms of sociality ("non-social animals do not exist"), zoosociality[1]. Crisis epochs are epochs of increased zoosociality when, within a human being, in a society, it is as if a prehuman past is pushing to the fore.

In different epochs, a person in different ways correlates social and biological, zoosocial[2] (prehuman sociality) and human sociality proper. In a period of great crisis, revolutionary eras, predatory, asocial individuals may take center stage. The social revolution is organized not so much by the social lower classes, but by "the biological excrement of mankind," wrote Ivan Solonevich one hundred years ago, a Russian, anti-Soviet philosopher. Of course, the revolution is a more complex process than the ejection of zoosociality, but on the whole, Solonevich has fixed a critical feature that can be seen in all catastrophic revolutions – from the French to the Russian communist in 1917, and anti-communist in 1991.

1    Biology Bulletin of the Academy of Sciences of the USSR, L.V. Osadchuk, January-February 1991, Volume 18, Number I, p.65.
2    Osadchuk, L. V.; Biology Bulletin of the Academy of Sciences of the USSR, Volumen 18, Número I, p. 65, 1991.

263

Of course, the ejection of "biology," zoosociality in crisis periods itself occurs according to social laws; It's another matter that these laws are implemented differently in normal and crisis eras and their individuals with different ratios of anthroposocial and zoosocial ("biological") are implemented. The time of crises is a time mainly of reptile people, homosaurs. I am not talking about little green men from Space. This is not a metaphor, but a fixation of reality associated with the historical structure of the human brain.

According to American neuroscientist Paul D. MacLean, who formulated this model back in the 1960s, morphologically, the oldest part of the brain is the reptilian, inherited from the reptiles, the first creatures in which the amount of information in the brain exceeds the amount of information in the genes. The next evolutionary system, superimposed on the reptilian brain and enclosing it according to the nesting doll principle, is the limbic brain, which is the achievement of mammals. And finally, the neocortex, which is a human contribution. Between the three brain structures, there is a certain division of labor.

The neocortex is responsible for specific Human efforts (sensory perception, cognition, generation of motor commands, spatial reasoning, and language), including the use of signs, anticipating events, empathy, and a number of other functions. The limbic system, in the depths of which the pituitary gland is located, generates vivid emotions associated with the joy of discovery, with the aesthetic perception of the world, with altruistic behavior, perception of taste, creativity. Finally, the reptilian brain plays a vital role in aggressive, ritual, and territorial behavior, in establishing a group hierarchy, including through sexual behavior (control of females, control of access to them) and control over the territory. There are no feedbacks; most often there is an impassive implementation of any behavior dictated either by one of the hemispheres or by genes, instincts.

Predators of different caliber, a bastard in the strict sense of the word – this is the brute force of any revolution, any crisis. In the post-crisis epochs, a significant part of the homosaurs (alpha males) is shot, replaced by smaller predators – thieves (vivid examples are today's thief nomenclature/bureaucracy in Russia), social life becomes less dangerous and more systemic and limits reptile behavior.

The global systemic crisis will cause a global release of homosaurs with their biology and zoosociality at all levels, from top to bottom. It will dramatically increase their role, and therefore, the role of biosociality in social processes. Many features of this process are already visible on the changed exterior of movie heroes (greetings from the Stone Age), advertising of demonstratively antisocial behavior on TV, aggressive forms of homosexuality and feminism, homophobia and misogyny.Thus, the global crisis may well put on the agenda the issue of the survival of *Homo Sapiens*. Since the crisis will take place in the context of the growing population's struggle for decreasing resources (including food and water), in its conditions, the question will arise of reducing the population – an issue if not biosocial, then socio-biological. *Homo* already went through this during the Upper Paleolithic crisis and "survived" (with huge losses) in 15-20 thousand years. Back then, however, the crisis was of a local rather than global nature; there was no single planetary humanity; Earth was not crammed with nuclear power plants, enterprises with harmful production, nuclear, biological, chemical and other weapons of Mass Destruction.

The finale of the global crisis of capitalism (especially in the context of the increase in geological activity predicted by geologists in the second half of this century, the probability of a change in the inclination of the Earth's axis, the onset of a new ice age, etc.) may turn out to be a battle between Homo sapiens and the biosphere, and inside Homo itself – Homo sapiens and Homo robustus – on the principle of "winner take all."

To overcome the crisis, we need a fundamentally new philosophy of relations with nature; we must rethink, and not just rethink, but unthink, not only the geoculture of the Enlightenment but also Christianity, with medieval theology, coupled with ancient philosophy, starting from its fathers/founders in another intellectual way – taking into account all, or almost all, of the intellectual and political mistakes made in the subject stream of historical development over the past 25 centuries. We need the Promethean-Faustian spirit of burning – we stand on it and cannot do otherwise. Fire was the first real piece of technology. The Titan of myth, Prometheus, gave humankind fire, a gift he stole from the Gods. Prometheus represents the ability of humankind to discover new forms of technology, new universal physical principles, and to incorporate them into the life and lives of the human species to change the relationship of human beings with the universe as a whole.

The world is living through the last relatively calm decades before the "matryoshka crisis," which has no analogs and which, it seems, will sweep away not only capitalism with its supporters and opponents but also the entire post-Neolithic civilization. And if humanity succeeds in surviving it, even if it has decreased in number to 0.5-1.0 billion, then the new society will most likely be different from "Civilization of the Pyramids" – (in the sense that the Egyptian pyramids are the main symbol of the whole post-Neolithic era) no less than it differed from the Paleolithic.

The current late capitalist crisis (which began with the collapse of Soviet anti-capitalism) is objective. The real task is to overcome it with minimal losses and as quickly as possible, not allowing it to stretch for millennia, but reducing it to a half or a maximum of two centuries. It reminds me of Isaac Asimov's Foundation series, where, according to his fictional mathematician Hari Seldon, the collapse of the galactic empire due to its objective nature could not be avoided, but the crisis "dark centuries" could be reduced from thirty thousand years to one. Of course, science fiction is science fiction, and reality is reality. Still, in our life they are closely intertwined – and the further we progress or, in this case, digress as humanity, the more apparent this becomes.

Overcoming the crisis involves the creation of new knowledge, fundamentally new disciplines (or epistemological programs), with new methodologies and new research subjects. We must in a short period of time (time waits for no one) develop an adequate theory of post-capitalism as a special case of the theory of social systems, methodologically built on the denial of, above all, the heritage of the bourgeoise 19th century triads, "economics - sociology - political science"; this is the path of criticism of political economy that Marx took in his work on Capital and which he never went through to the end, and the Marxists, with the rarest and most rare exceptions, turned away from him altogether.

On the basis of this theory, we have to rethink a lot on the question of the relationship between the subject and the system, "project-conscious" and "natural" in history, first of all, in its crucial periods, when the project and decisions of a small group "weigh" no less than the mass rush. We have to revise the entire geoculture of the Enlightenment and many Christian ideas, especially all that relates to biology, the "natural nature" of man in its various dimensions. And for this, it will be necessary to delve deeply into ancient philosophy.

Of course, this is easier said than done, but there is no other way. It is the creation of new knowledge, in the center of which is the Great Turn of the 21st century, the formation of "sinister intellectual superiority" over the enemy, that is the front line in the struggle to overcome the crisis of the maximum number of people in the shortest possible time, for a more egalitarian and a just world, rather than a capitalist or some new edition of pseudo-slavery in the form of a global fascist caste system, sanctified by neo-Judaism (a synthesis, or even just a mixture of Protestantism, Judaism and Masonic ideas) or occultism. May we live in interesting times.

Toronto, Canada, January 1, 2020

# Index

Venetian Black Nobility  11, 229
Venice  10, 11, 67, 68, 161
Volcker, Paul A.  143, 144, 150
Volkov, Alexander  243
Volotsky, Joseph  99

# W

Warburgs (family)  11
Washington Consensus  78, 93, 159,
    160
Washington, George  205, 250
Wen-wang  117
Wittelsbachs (family)  11
World Bank  28, 36, 134, 140, 159, 209,
    224, 225, 231, 235
Wriston, Walter  150
WTO  28, 140, 145, 160, 226, 227, 230,
    234, 235

# X

Xi Jinping  101, 102, 106, 109, 111, 112,
    113, 115, 118, 122, 153, 154,
    167-171

# Y

Yeltsin, Boris  79, 155, 156

# Z

Zhou Enlai  94, 110
Zhu De  110